THE 'NICE' COMPANY

The 'Nice' Company

Tom Lloyd

BLOOMSBURY

First published 1990 by Bloomsbury Publishing Limited, 2 Soho Square, London W1V 5DE

Copyright © 1990 by Tom Lloyd

British Library Cataloguing in Publication Data

A CIP record for this book is available from the British Library

ISBN 0 7475 0346 X

10 9 8 7 6 5 4 3 2 1

Typeset by Hewer Text Composition Services, Edinburgh
Printed by Butler & Tanner Limited, Frome and London

To Sheila Bradshaw

Contents

Preface

This book has evolved over several years from two fascinations – with business and finance on the one hand, which has been the focus of my professional life for the past 20 years, and on the other with the theory of evolution.

It seems to me that an individual's intellectual development is generally driven by a relatively small number of big ideas or 'tools for thought' as C. H. Waddington called them. Several of mine have been associated with books: *A Theory of Justice* by John Rawls, most of Stephen Jay Gould's volumes of essays, *The Selfish Gene* and *The Blind Watchmaker* by Richard Dawkins, *The Evolution of Cooperation* by Robert Axelrod and *The Share Economy* by Martin Weitzman.

This book has also been shaped by a few fundamental beliefs – in Darwinian evolution, in the allocative power of the free market, in the Popperian model of scientific progress, in the idea of cooperation as a model for business, in the principles of game theory and in the fact (and not merely the hope) of progress.

But the most important origin of my ideas has been conversations with interesting people. Because of constraints associated with space and memory I cannot name all those whose ideas have helped me to make sense of mine. They include Maurice Anslow, Ronald Fagerfjall, Jane and Mike Hainsworth, Peter Johnson, Judy Lloyd, Jon May, Wolfgang Munchau, the New Information Paradigms group, Wally Olins, Geoff Smith, Norman Strauss, Karl Erik Sveiby, Chris Valle and Jane Wynn.

I am also indebted to my agent, Anne Dewe and my editor, Kathy Rooney, both of whom have contributed to the encouragement all writers need to commit idle and ephemeral thought to paper.

Introduction

The company has had a bad press. In its many incarnations it has been condemned for its gluttony and ruthlessness, castigated for its irresponsibility and universally execrated for being immoral and corrupt.

The general view persists, witness the various opinion surveys mentioned in Chapter one, that companies are nasty, brutal and thoroughly untrustworthy creatures. They symbolise all that is base and inhuman. Their insatiable lust for profit represents the dark, atavistic side of human nature – the bestial past of our species which, with art and altruism, we have struggled constantly to overcome.

By human standards the company has an excessively feral energy. It seethes with suppressed violence. As a vehicle for enterprise and production we accept it as a necessary evil but the company, unfettered and rampant, is a familiar villain in the dystopian visions of the future depicted in our literature.

We are ashamed of this monster capitalism has invoked because we acknowledge its parentage. It is both our punishment and our reproach. How could we, civilised and caring, have given birth to such a thing? If it represents and reflects us, as it surely must since we are its creators, why is it not more like us? Why do we have to muzzle it with laws, to chain it with regulations and to watch it vigilantly for signs of incipient malice?

When Union Carbide seems to behave after the Bhopal disaster in a way that only a human being lacking all scruples and all generosity of spirit would behave, we are disgusted and disturbed. We feel tainted by such callousness because Union Carbide is the creature of, and so should be both a servant and an ethical analogue of, people.

We have tried diligently to contain the excesses of our *enfant terrible*. Company law and institutions like anti-trust agencies, standards organisations, food- and drug-licensing authorities, regulatory bodies and pollution control – agencies are all evidence of our failure to imbue the company with our ethical principles. Their existence reflects our conviction that if left to their own devices companies will behave badly.

It is the central contention of this book that the distaste we feel for companies is the result of a mistaken view of what they are. The error stems from two beliefs: that the company is a human artefact and that all social artefacts, by virtue of their provenance, must incorporate the values of their creators. The former belief is true but trivial. The second is false.

We are the company's creators but we are not and can never be its keepers. It cannot help being what it is although, as we shall see, it can and does appear to be what it is not.

The first of the three major propositions of this book is that **companies collectively constitute a sentient, intelligent, non-human species at a relatively early stage in its evolution.**

If it is reasonable to view the company as an alien life form, and obviously I shall have to persuade the reader of this, it follows that it is quite wrong to judge its behaviour by human standards. Though human beings create companies, run them and are a very important part of the corporate environment, they are not of their essence.

The corporate species has evolved and will continue to evolve in response to environmental pressures that are very different from those that characterise our habitat. The chapters that follow explore this 'corporate ecology' in some detail. I will try to demonstrate the non-humanity of the corporate species, and, with the help of recent developments in evolutionary biology and game theory, I shall endeavour to shed some light on the nature of the forces that are driving corporate evolution.

My second major proposition follows from the first: if companies constitute an intelligent, alien species (the first we have encountered – the second will probably be the intelligent computer) **the theory of evolution represents a powerful, ready-made model for a dynamic theory of business economics.**

It is hard to overestimate the implications of this proposition. If it is valid, i.e. if it can be shown that Darwinian theories are sufficiently general to explain *all* kinds of evolution, not just the biological, then business economics (and perhaps economics as whole) will become sub-disciplines of the wider discipline of evolutionary biology.

It is clear to me, though sociobiologists would disagree, that companies are **not** biological systems and so their development and evolution **cannot be driven by genetics**. I shall therefore have to propose a non-genetic mechanism that has the power to explain corporate evolution.

The effort is worthwhile because the companies, despite their rather equivocal reputation, constitute an extremely important species. Companies and their precursors have been much the most powerful agents of economic development since man emerged from the caves and they are certain to continue to be the driving force behind wealth creation throughout the world for the foreseeable future.

And if one can escape, for a moment, the thrall of the popular prejudices about companies; if one can forget, for instance, their lack of humanity and of an intrinsic morality, companies can appear to be a noble species. They have created order out of chaos, wealth out of rubble and work out of idleness. By and large, where companies have had the nourishment they need to prosper, our lives have been the better for theirs.

The corporate species has been a stalwart champion of progress. It has been cruel, predatory and, on occasions, vicious but it has never been cowardly or indolent. On the contrary, its boldness and vigour have inspired us to great achievements. With the help of companies, people have tamed the elements and moulded our habitat.

The Spaceship Earth has been equipped, if not built, by companies and, if one subscribes to Jim Lovelock's 'Gaia' hypothesis, which casts man in the role of Earth's creature and the means by which she can defend herself against a cosmic threat, then the corporate species has been Gaia's armourer.

Or if one adheres to Richard Dawkins' 'Selfish Gene' hypothesis which gives the initiative to DNA and casts man in the role of a mere carrier, then it is the company that has been the carrier's vehicle. Without the company the carrier would have remained earthbound and DNA would have been imprisoned on a small planet of a minor sun on the outskirts of a medium-sized galaxy.

I make no apologies for the hyperbole. I overstate the case for the corporate species because it is so seldom put. We humans rarely dignify companies with the status of a separate species, subject to its own peculiar version of natural selection and driven by its own will to survive and grow.

In this book the corporate species is cast in the role of a symbiote of man which, once created, has acquired, like Frankenstein's monster, its own hungers, its own desires and its own will to live. Like us it evolves, but in a very different way and in response to forces we are only just beginning to understand.

Over the past few decades the corporate world has been turned upside down by two changes of catastrophic proportions which I believe mark a turning point in corporate evolution.

The first is the advent of the era of rapid and accelerating technological change. I have compared this event (*Dinosaur & Co.*) to the catastrophe that overwhelmed the dinosaurs 65 million years ago. I have suggested it is leading to the emergence of a new evolutionary paradigm that selects for agility and flexibility rather than for strength and size, particularly in technology-driven industries.

The argument goes as follows:

- Rapid change leads to shorter product life cycles.

- Size ceases to be an advantage when product life cycles are short because there is no time to achieve cost leadership through high-volume production.

- Short product life cycles shift the focus of competitive advantage from the production process to the speed of new product development.

- Small companies are better (ie quicker) at new product development because it is easier for them to recruit and keep the people they need to establish and maintain a technological lead.

In *Managing Knowhow* I and my co-author Karl Erik Sveiby generalised the argument. Instead of focusing only on technology-driven companies, we argued that the advent of the Information Society was leading to the emergence of a new kind of corporate creature we called the 'knowhow company'.

In addition to technology-driven companies, examples of the new breed include law and accountancy firms, advertising and design agencies, consultancy firms, financial services groups, banks, hospitals, universities and government departments.

We described the features that distinguish the knowhow company from conventional companies and provided a detailed agenda for knowhow company management. We also suggested that knowhow management problems are common to all companies where there are pockets of knowhow working (which we called 'pro-teams'), like research and development laboratories and top management teams.

The speed of change is contributing to this development but its main stimulus is the second major change in the corporate environment, namely a decisive shift in the balance of power from money to people.

One of the most conspicuous features of the modern corporate environment is the rapid accumulation in recent years of huge financial surpluses in capital markets and the banking system, despite periodic orgies of unsound lending. This heralds the end of the tyranny of capital.

The glut of money swilling around the corporate world is precipitating a democratic revolution. It has led to a desperate shortage of viable business ideas, and of the skills needed to make them work. Power is devolving to those who possess those skills and ideas.

A symptom of this change is the intense interest that has grown up in recent years in the subject of 'people management'. The current idea that the competitive advantage of a company resides in the skills and experience of its employees is central to my argument. That the new secret of business success is an ability to recruit and keep good people is the internal imperative that is driving the evolutionary change I shall be describing in the pages that follow.

The third of my major propositions is that **recent changes in the chemistry of the corporate medium favour the emergence of strategies, internal as well as external, that are 'nicer'** (i.e. more sensitive to the ethical, moral and social features of the corporate environment) **than traditional strategies.**

I shall argue that the pressures that are driving the emergence of the nice company have nothing to do with the influence on corporate behaviour of ethical human beings (not directly at any rate) and everything to do with what constitutes, in this day and age, effective and successful business strategy. The nice company will become dominant not because it is more ethical but because it is, in the long run, more profitable.

Business is becoming more complicated and more competitive; the pace of change is rapid and continues to accelerate; there is more information around about customers, competitors, suppliers and local communities. In short, there are, these days, fewer places for corporate delinquents to hide.

Though evolutionists generally proscribe value judgements, it is reasonable in this case to think in terms of a kind of progress. Corporate society is emerging from a feudal era (characterised by ignorance and poor communications) in which strength and aggression were the key survival qualities, into a democratic era (characterised by widely disseminated knowledge) in which such qualities as friendliness, neighbourliness and a propensity to cooperate are the keys to long-term success.

One result of this change is that the attitude of the company's symbiotes, human beings, will alter. As companies become nicer popular attitudes towards them, and towards business in general, will become more positive. Companies, some of them at any rate, will cease to be seen as necessary evils and come to be seen as agents of good.

In case all this seems a little too philosophical, let me reassure the reader that this is designed first and foremost to be a practical book for managers. Its purposes are to introduce the idea of the nice company; to describe the basic elements of the nice strategy (as we shall see in Chapter two, nice is by no means 'weak'); to show how such a strategy can be developed and implemented in particular cases and to explain how and why the nice strategy works in practice.

I hope the attendant philosophising does not interefere too much with this essentially pragmatic aim. Its purpose is to convince the heart as well as the head because it is my belief that for the nice strategy to work well its merits have to be felt as well as understood.

Business is in dire need of a positive philosophy. The 'caring professions', those enaged in social work, health, teaching and the like, have so styled themselves to distinguish them from the 'uncaring' profession of wealth creation. The pejoration is the product of the widespread anti-business attitude inspired by the brutish corporate behaviour of the past.

When companies, for good business reasons, begin to behave in a nicer way the corporate life should become attractive to a wider range of people. This will improve the quality of business men and women, and therefore of business itself.

For these reasons the emergence of the nice company is to be welcomed. By removing the rationale for the anti-business prejudice, the rise to dominance of the nice company will expose the basic nobility of the wealth-creating process. Being in business will become more respectable and the long-maligned corporate species will get a better press.

But the theory of the nice company is one of those ideas many people would like to believe and it is healthy to treat such wishful thinking with some scepticism. Just because the world would be a nicer place if companies were nicer creatures does not guarantee they will become so.

I admit to a liking for a world where companies behave better than they do at present but I would not have written this book if I did not believe this was more than a dream wish. The world and the corporate habitat are changing. The impossibilities of yesterday become the probabilities of today and the orthodoxies of tomorrow. What begin as the hopes of idealists have a habit of becoming prosaic facts of life.

Who had heard of the word *perestroika* five years ago and who, knowing what it meant then, could have imagined what it would come to mean? And who would have thought 10 years ago, when the Conservative election victory ushered in a new materialist age, that we would now be in the grip of an environmental obsession?

The hero of this book is the corporate life form. It is still at a relatively early stage in its history, but is evolving fast. It resembles the 'meme', conjectured by Richard Dawkins in *The Selfish Gene* as culture's equivalent of the gene.

I share with Dawkins the conviction that if life has emerged, as I hope it has, elsewhere in the universe, it will have done so according to one fundamental principle. Dawkins put it this way:

All life evolves by the differential survival of replicating entities . . . just as genes propagate themselves in the gene pool by leaping from body to body via sperms or eggs, so memes propagate themselves by leaping from brain to brain via a process which, in the broad sense, can be called imitation.

I would put it this way: 'all life (including corporate life) evolves by the differential survival of strategic themes. Just as genes propagate themselves in the gene pool, so strategic themes (or 'stremes') are propagated in the streme pool by the propensity to emulate winning strategies.'

The complexity of the evolutionary process means that only very simple, fundamental stremes can be selected. My thesis is that in the corporate world the ruthless streme is doomed and that henceforth the nice streme will become the blueprint of the vast majority of successful strategies.

It is not as if the nice strategy has to be invented. It has been lurking in the streme pool for centuries, waiting for the right concatenation of ecological circumstances to become dominant. Early signs of it were evident in the ideas of men like Robert Owen, Charles Fourier and the other evangelists of the cooperative movement of the early nineteenth century. Corporate vestiges still survive of the nice Quaker economics, derived from the teachings of the seventeenth-century mystic George Knox, and the nice streme's influence can be detected too in the mutual tradition that still retains a strong presence in the insurance industry and the building society movement.

And it would not be stretching the point too far to suppose that the partnership model that still dominates many of the knowhow professions, is also a carrier of the nice streme.

I embark on this attempt to inject the adrenalin of evolutionary theory into business economics with great trepidation. Earlier drafts of the book have attracted much scorn from evolutionists. Their subject is so rich, so complex and so utterly fascinating that the professionals tend to treat encroachments by amateurs like myself with deep suspicion. If we even appear to flout the most trivial of rules, we are instantly branded barbarians and are denied the opportunity for debate and discussion.

It is quite all right for professionals like Stephen Jay Gould to personify a species by talking about it as if it were one of its individual members – such as 'the Panda's thumb' and 'the Flamingo's smile' – but amateurs have no such licence. I cannot say 'the company' evolves; I must say 'the corporate species' evolves.

This insistence that only the professionals can break the rules obliges me to make a unilateral declaration of independence. I am not bound by the profession's rules. So long as I understand them, I am free to express evolutionary ideas in ways I think will be understandable to business people. And I am free to use whichever parts of evolutionary theory I like, as long as I specify and justify the partiality of my plunder.

The main problem for the theory of corporate evolution is that Darwinian evolution seems to be exclusive to biological systems which reproduce and are mortal. Companies do not reproduce, at least not in ways comparable to biological reproduction, and they do not always die.

I gave some talks about corporate evolution after my first book, *Dinosaur & Co*, appeared in 1984. There was one question from the audience I feared above all others because I thought it would expose a central flaw in the idea. I felt sure some bright spark in the audience would stand up and ask: 'At precisely what point do companies become sexually mature?' Now I know the answer to the question that was never put. Sexual maturity and biological reproduction have no equivalents in corporate evolution because companies are not biological systems.

Modern evolutionary theory consists of two theories – Darwin's theory of natural selection, which is a very general theory, and Mendel's theory of genetics, which is exclusively biological. To acknowledge that genetics cannot apply to companies, other than in a metaphorical way, does not oblige the business economist to reject natural selection too.

But corporate evolutionists are obliged to provide a substitute for genetics and the criteria of reproductive success. Companies must have qualities which the environment selects or rejects, even if the process does not apply to the company as a whole. There must be things about companies that sometimes fail and die and sometimes succeed and spread.

For reasons I shall explain later, I think natural selection in the corporate world works on strategies and on the management teams that conceive of and deploy them. Successful strategies survive by winning and are propagated because of the tendency of managers to imitate winning strategies.

I shall conclude this introduction with a plea on behalf of the method. I am convinced the evolutionary approach to business economics has enormous potential. I have tried to show some of the ways in which it can be applied. I hope others will explore the correspondences in more depth.

SUMMARY

- Companies constitute a discrete species evolving in response to the pressures of its own peculiar environment.

- Evolutionary biology is a rich source of ideas and theories about how creatures evolve and develop which can be adapted and applied to business economics.

- There are reasons to suppose changes in the corporate environment are encouraging the emergence of a new strategic paradigm which can be characterised as nice.

- A proper understanding of why niceness is good for business, and of how it can be incorporated in strategy, are essential ingredients for success in the modern business world.

CHAPTER 1

Business Ethics

The question of where and in what manner business in general and companies in particular fit in to human society has yet to be resolved. The company, for all its apparent antiquity, is young in an evolutionary sense. It is humanity's *enfant terrible* – a precocious problem child whose true nature has yet to emerge but whose development to date is, frankly, not very encouraging.

The provisional nature of the company's status in the human scheme of things has led to a kind of armed truce between man and company, similar to the relationship between a father and his adolescent son. Society feels unable to trust the company to behave properly and the company, for its part, seems unable to trust society not to interefere with it. Because power in the West rests largely in the democratic institutions of the human species, the fear of government interference is very real for the corporate species. That is why the latter has become, if not *ethical*, at least more or less law-abiding.

And since the ultimate creative potential in the Western world lies with the institution of the company, man has been obliged to reach an accommodation with business. He has become, if not benevolent towards his awkwardly unbiddable monster, at least more or less indulgent.

This chapter explores the differences between the behavioural characteristics of man and company, paying special attention to behaviour that would be likely to be judged by reasonable people to have *moral* or *ethical* content.

My purpose in this is two-fold. In the first place I believe an investigation into the meaning of the term 'business ethics' is a

1

worthwhile exercise in its own right because much confusion has been generated in recent years by good, well-meaning people who have been urging business to become more ethical. 'Ethical' is an adjective most commonly used with its negative prefix because ethical behaviour is less remarkable than its opposite. For this reason the term 'business ethics' is usually to be found in statements regretting the lack of them. I shall try to show why I believe the correct answer to the question 'what do such statements mean?' is 'not a lot'.

Secondly, it is my hope that a discussion of business ethics, or what passes for them, will aid me in the task which I set myself in the introduction, namely to persuade the reader of the merits of my assertion that companies should be regarded as an alien species. Since variations in *mores* and codes of ethics are amongst the most striking manifestations of human cultural difference, something of the nature of the alienness of the company should be illuminated by a better understanding of the ethical distinctions that separate it from humanity.

THE GODLY COMPANY
A survey by the Market Research Society in early 1988, asked a random sample of UK adults how they rated the standards of honesty among various groups.

The results were as follows:

		High %	Low %	No View %
1.	Doctors	83	2	15
2.	Police	62	7	31
3.	TV & Radio	47	10	43
4.	The City	22	24	54
5.	MPs	18	23	59
6.	Top Businessmen	17	29	54
7.	National Newspapers	12	41	47

As a journalist I am inclined to attribute the bottom score to sampling error but as a business economist I regard the fact that almost two-thirds of those who expressed a view thought our top businessmen were a dishonest lot, as very significant if not very surprising. Businessmen would score better in some other countries such as West Germany, Japan and Sweden, but it is clear there remains in the British culture a deeply-rooted anti-business pre-judice.

The same sort of prejudice persists in the US too. A *Business Week* Harris Poll of 1,247 American adults conducted in May, 1989 asked: 'If you had to say, which of the following things do you think business would do in order to obtain greater profits?'. The questions elicited the following answers:

Harm the environment 47%
Endanger public health 38%
Sell unsafe products 37%
Knowingly sell inferior products 44%
Deliberately charge inflated prices 62%
Put its workers' health safety at risk 42%
None 8%
Not sure 4%

All but the last two include the 25% of respondents who said business would do all of the above.

In the same month a Gallup survey of the confidence Americans feel in their institutions ranked business last and, in a ranking of the ethical standards of 25 professions, business executives came 16th, behind funeral directors and journalists.

Alex Beam, columnist in *The Boston Globe*, linked the Gallup results with what was for him an even more striking symptom of the low esteem into which business and businessmen had fallen; namely the emergence in the March 1989 issue of *The Adventures of Superman* of arch-villain Lex Luthor as the chief executive of LexCorp, a huge multinational with interests in the media and avionics. These days, evidently, no seriously villainous super-villain can get by without a villainous corporation at his beck and call.

Survey results and pop-cultural symbols like these are grist to the mill of the Institute of Business Ethics (IBE), formed in Britain in 1986 to 'provide a forum for responsible study, research and opinion formation in the field of business ethics'. They validate the IBE's purpose and make excellent marketing copy for such propaganda pamphlets as *Company Philosophies and Codes of Business Ethics* published by the IBE in June 1988.

3

The IBE is an august and enormously reputable organisation. Its patrons include The Archbishop of Canterbury, The Cardinal Archbishop of Westminster, The Moderator of the Free Church Federal Council, The Chief Rabbi and The Imam of the London Central Mosque. Its council consists of a number of senior businessmen, a cleric and a handful of business philosophers.

Embedded within the idea of the IBE is the presumption that God and Mammon are reconcilable and that the ecumenical Church is both qualified and has a duty to officiate at and sanctify the reconciliation. The IBE's patrons reflect a belief that the ethical authority of humanity's clerics is as legitimate in the business world as it is in the human. The clergy, the IBE implicitly asserts, are the ethical authority. They need no knowledge of business to judge the behaviour of companies.

The IBE's philosophy is that, contrary to the public perceptions revealed in various surveys, 'industry and commerce are highly ethical undertakings' (IBE chairman Neville Cooper) and 'there is no real difference between business ethics and individual ethics. It is a matter of personal behaviour and individual moral responsibility' (the otherwise enlightened and sagacious Sir John Hoskyns, an IBE council member and the then director general of the Institute of Directors).

But despite its clerical pedigree and the passion with which it prosecutes its crusade, the IBE's exhortations seem empty to the corporate evolutionist. Despite their greatness and goodness, its associates and patrons have lacked the wisdom to see that companies and people are different species.

Recruiting clerics to lend moral authority to the crusade for business ethics is like asking a nun to referee a boxing match. To whom is all this sermonising directed? If it is to people, they can hear it in church; if it is to companies, they cannot hear it at all.

But notwithstanding the futility of its litany, the Institute's formation in 1986 was a significant event. We shall return to the IBE later because it epitomises an important feature of the new corporate ecology. For the present it is enough to note that Neville Cooper is mistaken if he believes 'industry and commerce are highly ethical undertakings' and Sir John Hoskyns is quite wrong to suppose there is no difference between business and individual ethics.

THE GUILTY COMPANY

To understand why these statements are false let us look first at the worst kinds of corporate behaviour. Catastrophes, like the disasters at Seveso, Bhopal and Zeebrugge, are the most striking examples of corporate wrongdoing. They do not, as do some kinds of corporate crime like fraud, routinely give rise to criminal charges, but they can be classified loosely as such egregious breaches of the duty of care as to constitute cases of criminal negligence.

The execration heaped on the corporate perpetrators of such catastrophes is inspired more by the way the company responds to the consequences of the disaster than by the disaster itself which is usually acknowledged to be accidental. Companies seem incapable of doing the 'right thing' after disasters. They invariably come across as callous and unfeeling. In situations which demand expressions of deep and instantaneous regret, swift and fulsome recompense and a prompt admission of guilt, companies too often reach for their lawyers and do all they can to minimise their compensation liabilities.

Why should this be? The guilty company is, after all, run by human beings who are, on average (though some would question this), no more or less moral than other human beings. Why do they not make the right decisions?

Let us consider the two cases of an ethical individual and a company, both of whom have caused, through negligence, a major disaster each of which has led to great loss of life.

Human beings can respond in a variety of ways. They can, in an agony of remorse, take their own lives as partial recompense for the lives of those who have died. They can acknowledge their guilt and give all they have to the victims and their families. They can devote the rest of their lives to good works in an effort to atone for their crime. They can remain forever afterwards haunted by the ghosts of those who died, a reminder to all who know them of the crippling weight of remorse that carelessness can bring down on an individual's head.

In short, individuals have the ability, if not always the inclination, to do all that is 'humanly' possible to make their punishments fit their crimes. They can feel the full weight of their guilt and can be seen by others to be doing so.

But put one of them in the position of chief executive of a company responsible for a similar disaster and he or she (let's assume the latter) will behave very differently. As a human being

5

she may react in much the same way although the feelings of regret and guilt will be vicarious (because of where the buck stops) rather than personal. She may quit – a form of suicide – or may seek out those immediately responsible and fire them.

But if she decides to stay at the helm she cannot force the company to commit suicide and neither can she permit it to make swift and fulsome recompense. The nature of the company prevents her. As chief executive she is the senior agent of the company's owners, the shareholders. She has a responsibility to them to maintain the company's value and a responsibility to the company's employees to preserve jobs. She is not her own mistress. Her fiduciary duties deny her the right to be human.

The company is nothing without humans but is anything but human. The interests of its various human constituencies are so bound up with its instinct to survive and prosper that humanity is squeezed out. A company cannot proffer recompense and regret spontaneously, if, in so doing, it compromises its own survival.

But though companies are disarmed ethically by their nature, there *is* a corporate *ethos*; a set of guiding principles and standards that governs the behaviour of the corporate community. Although these rules and conventions could not be construed by any stretch of the imagination as comparable to human ethics they are, within the limited domain of corporate life, the counterpart of a moral code.

A variant of the third major proposition of this book is that, for reasons to do with the action of natural selection on corporate evolution, **the ethos of business is changing in ways that make it increasingly less at odds with human ethics.** Companies are being forced by environmental pressures to become nicer. This does *not* mean they are becoming more ethical, but merely that apparently ethical behaviour is becoming better for business.

It is a slow process but, as we shall see when we discuss the mechanics of corporate evolution in the next chapter, it is both inexorable and irreversible.

First, we shall take a closer look at the two basic elements of the contemporary business ethos – company–human relationships on the one hand and company–company relationships on the other – and at the attitudes and prejudices on which they are based.

The significance of the dualism becomes clear when one considers the widely differing ethical criteria we apply to our treatment of each other on the one hand, and to our treatment of animals and our planet on the other.

6

It would be surprising if this ethical relativism did not also exclude companies from the highest domain of human ethics.

In view of the company's provenance, it would be just as surprising if the mirror image of this ethical relativism were not reflected in the corporate ethos too. Just as human beings apply different standards to companies and other human beings, it is to be expected that companies will apply different standards to human beings and other companies.

Companies are thus obliged to adapt to two kinds of ethical constraint: those that concern the conduct of a company in its relationships with its human customers, neighbours and their social institutions, and those that concern a company's conduct in its relationships with other companies. These two 'ethical domains' are depicted in Figure 1.1.

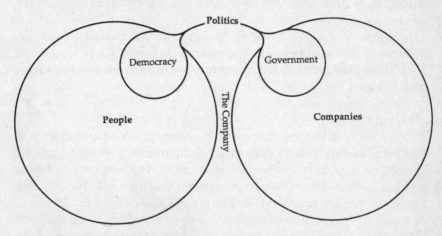

Fig 1.1: The Two Ethical Domains
The corporate species inhabits two ethical domains. Later chapters will consider how the democratic process, via politics and government, 'extrudes' domain one into domain two.

A company's relationships with people are intimately bound up with the human moral code and, though the contemporary business ethos is in more or less constant conflict with human ethics, it is adaptable. It must and does comply with new law and it responds to the commercial exigencies of new human attitudes.

Most companies appear to behave in an ethically acceptable way most of the time because it would be bad for business to do otherwise.

Given adequate policing, compliance with the law is forced on companies and so is of limited ethical significance. Of much more interest, from our point of view, are those other, less obligatory and so more genuinely ethical, decisions such as whether or not to supply the military establishment with goods and services; whether or not to persist with a project in the face of the passionate opposition of the local community; whether or not to maintain trading links with repugnant regimes (such as South Africa); whether and to what extent to engage in charitable work; whether it is sufficient merely to meet minimum standards for product safety or whether a company is morally if not legally obliged to exceed them.

A company's personality and reputation will be determined to some extent by the answers it give to such questions. Some answers will be dictated by clear commercial considerations but there will always be a grey area where leaders will be required to exercise judgement.

In this way changes in the judgement of business leaders about the proper trade-off between short-term expediency and long-term reputation determine how tomorrow's business ethos will differ from today's.

CORPORATE ETHICS
The second kind of evolution in the corporate world concerns a company's relationships with other companies – with its suppliers, its competitors and its corporate customers. This is a very different and less overtly ethical set of influences, but it reveals much more about the nature of the corporate species.

We shall begin our discussion of corporate ethics of this second kind (ethical domain two) with a variation of our definition of the company as an alien species: **the company is a primitive, non-moral species, motivated in the first place by a will to survive and, in the second place, by greed.**

In stark contrast to the apparently ethical behaviour evident in company–human relationships, there seems to prevail within the community of companies a state of total war. All is fair. No holds are barred. Theft is habitual, conspiracy commonplace, grievous bodily harm an everyday occurrence and wanton murder hardly worth a mention.

There is nothing right or wrong in this; it is simply the way things are in a market economy. Free market economies are superior to centrally-planned economies because they create more wealth. That is all that matters. Questions about the ways in which the wealth is, or should be, distributed do not arise. They are political, not economic questions.

Society has not deemed it fit to impose on company–company dealings standards similar to those it has imposed on dealings between companies and humans. In the former arena self-interest is the only arbiter of behaviour and *force majeure* is its most common expression. This uncaring official attitude to intercorporate viciousness reflects not callousness but a belief held more strongly now than at any time this century that this very viciousness lies at the root of the company's fecundity and creativity. It is an axiom of contemporary supply-side economics that private sector vices are public virtues.

And it is certainly true that just as excessive interference by humans in company–company relationships inevitably undermines the allocative power of the market, so young companies infused with the humanity of their founding entrepreneurs are weakened by adherence to codes of behaviour appropriate to human intercourse.

Most of the older and larger companies that still dominate the corporate world and which constitute a young company's suppliers, customers and competitors have long outgrown such scruples. A few examples will help to illustrate the point.

Within any population of businesses consisting of companies that are customers, suppliers and competitors of each other, there is a sum of money called 'trade credit' that floats between the three principals – the company's suppliers, the company itself and the company's customers. True title to trade credit is never entirely clear. Part is owed by the company to its suppliers and part is owed to the company by its customers. In an ideal world these sums should be in balance leaving the company cash-neutral as far as trade credit is concerned.

But in the real world the exercise of *force majeure* always frustrates this balance. Because trade credit is an important component of working capital it is in the interests of each protagonist to appropriate as large a slice of this cash 'float' as circumstances permit. Hence the emergence of the management principle that creditors should be put off as long as possible while debtors should be pressed to pay as quickly as possible.

To the extent that a particular company's market strength enables it to establish a cash-positive position in trade credit, implying cash-negative positions elsewhere, *injustice* is done. There

9

is a *theft* of working capital; an *unfair* diversion of cash-flow. I have emphasised these value-laden words to suggest how this kind of behaviour, quite routine in business, would appear to the ethical human being.

The usual means by which trade credit is *stolen* by the strong from the weak is the habitual late payment by large companies of the sums they owe to small companies. (There is some evidence to suggest the prevalance of such *sharp* practice is linked to the local business culture. Habitual late payment is less common in the US and Japan than in the UK, which may mean the business cultures of the former are more evolved than that of the latter).

The British conglomerate GEC is an infamously slow payer and its cash-positive position in trade credit is an important component of its equally famous cash mountain. GEC's 1987 accounts show debtors (the money owed to GEC) of £1,348m and creditors (the money owed by GEC) of £1,951m, indicating a cash surplus position in trade credit of £603m. To put it another way, over half GEC's £1.1bn cash mountain consisted, at the 1987 balance sheet date, of the proceeds of a *systematic plundering* of trade credit from suppliers.

Another less common but more *vicious* practice is the simple refusal by large companies to pay the full amount they owe to small suppliers. The *extortion* goes something like this: small company is owed £40,000 by large company. Payment is late. Small company complains. Large company, perhaps in the process of preparing its end-of-year accounts, says it will pay £30,000. Small company insists on the full amount. Large company sends cheque for £30,000 and invites small company to sue for the rest.

The large company assumes the costs of litigation will deter its victim from suing and that anyway the small company will not want to alienate utterly a large customer, however unprincipled.

A solution to this dilemma that has proved effective is for the small company to take out insurance against bad debts with a credit insurance and scoring agency. This is an example of how the constant improvement of monitoring systems within a population of companies can exert pressure on general standards of behaviour.

In this case the enlistment of the services of another company unconnected with the imediate area of activity provides protection against the insolvency or aggression of trading partners. It is not so much that insurance limits the loss but that it exposes the *bully* company to an external sanction. If the *victim* company reports the *bully* company to the credit scoring agency, this leads to a damaging reduction of the *bully's* credit score.

The unequal struggle over trade credit is not the only kind of bullying a small company has to contend with. Large companies will occasionally employ the weapon of malicious rumour against troublesome competitors. They will put it about that their rival is in financial difficulties or that its products are of poor quality or perhaps that its after-sales service is sub-standard.

If the whispering campaign is conducted with some subtlety there may be no legal recourse available even if the victim is, in principle, prepared to sue.

Market confidence in a company is crucial, but fragile. It is extremely vulnerable to malicious gossip because what may be completely without foundation when first alleged will often become true as a result of the allegation. The self-fulfilling calumny is what makes corporate slander so effective.

Thus, the victims of corporate bullying can sometimes take steps to defend themselves. My purpose here, however, is to show how conspicuous by their absence in ethical domain two are humanly recognisable codes of ethics. That there is such a thing as an ethical code of business conduct is a fiction put about by the more cynical members of the corporate establishment. It reassures the public, pacifies politicians and serves to make naive competitors less aggressive than they might otherwise be and thus more easily disposed of.

Quite often it is the most *iniquitous* of companies that, like bullies, squeal the loudest when given a taste of their own medicine. Such occasions bring to mind a grafitto spotted by a friend of mine on a London hoarding a few years back: 'Hell hath no fury like a vested interest masquerading as a moral principle.'

CORPORATE CRIMINOLOGY

Why it is that no vestige of a general ethical sense survives in the business world is a puzzle. Businesses are run, after all, by people as personally ethical as everyone else.

One reason may be that the divorce of ownership from control – the result of the emergence of the financial institutions as the main owners of business – has displaced the human leadership associated with the family company. At the same time business has become more competitive over the past few decades.

Better communications have destroyed the integrity of local

monopolies and cartels; a more volatile marketplace has caused a contraction in the average product life-cycle and a more efficient labour market has caused business talent to become more mobile.

The result is that it is now more difficult for a company to maintain its position in the marketplace, let alone to improve it. The erosion of ethical standards is a sign of desperation. Ethics are a luxury the efficient company can no longer afford. That greed and fear are the two inspirations of business is truer now than it ever was.

The process has been encouraged by an increase in the scale of business organisations. Unethical behaviour tends to become institutionalised in large organisations; it becomes known as something else, something altogether more admirable like toughness, hard-headedness, opportunism, or shrewdness. In this way behaviour that would be regarded as reprehensible in an individual is, in a company, transmuted by euphemism into a desirable efficiency.

As it is with young animals, so it is with young businesses. They weaken themselves when they, or rather the entrepreneurs who run them, cling to an inappropriate altruism. The extent to which they cheat and lie, indulge in underhand forms of competition, join conspiracies and generally make pests of themselves, should be determined not by their sense of right and wrong but by pure, commercial expendiency.

The aim of entrepreneurs should be to win. If the game is dirty then they will have to play dirty or at any rate play better. Scruples are liabilities; unnecessary impediments that can only slow them down.

But the predicament of the moral individual running the non-moral company is more easily described than resolved. The tension is often palpable. Entrepreneurs of goodwill often feel deep dismay when confronted by the need to corrupt the purity of their dreams with venal pragmatism.

Their dilemma is comparable to the problem of evil with which mystics and divines have been wrestling for centuries: how could an omnipotent and benevolent God have created an animal world so red in tooth and claw?

The life-style of the ichneumons, a group of wasps that appeared to many natural theologians to be the very incarnation of evil, was a particular difficulty. They live their adult lives freely but during their larval stage they are parasites, feeding on the bodies of other

12

insects, usually caterpillars. Sometimes the mother wasp injects her eggs inside the doomed host. For a while the caterpillar is unaffected. Then the larvae hatch and begin to feed.

Other kinds of *ichneumonida* lay their eggs on the back of the host and then, to prevent the eggs from being dislodged by the caterpillar's movements, they inject the unfortunate creature with a chemical that paralyses it.

Ichneumon larvae thrive on fresh caterpillars so it is in their interests to keep their hosts, whether active or paralysed, alive for as long as possible. Displaying an impressive instinctive knowledge of caterpillar physiology the larvae begin with body fat, move on to the digestive organs and leave the vital organs like the heart and the central nervous system for their last, pre-metamorphosis supper.

It is all too ghastly; such an apparent violation of 'natural' morality that one is tempted to dismiss the ichneumons as grotesque aberrations until one discovers there are thousands of different types, all with equally gruesome life-styles.

So how can such obscene horror be reconciled with the idea of a benevolent God? 'The answer,' according to the eminent evolutionary scientist Stephan Jay Gould, 'to the ancient dilemma of why such cruelty (in our terms) exists in nature can only be that there isn't an answer – and that framing the question "in our terms" is thoroughly inappropriate in a natural world neither made by us nor ruled by us.'

But is such a question inappropriate in a business world made by us and, in theory anyway, ruled by us? Should not each player in the game assume, as the Institute of Business Ethics insists, an individual responsibility to use his or her best endeavours to ensure that, so far as possible, business behaviour adheres to society's ethical norms?

The simple answers to these two questions are: 'yes, it is inappropriate to judge companies in our terms because the company, though our creature, is not human' and 'no, individuals can have no responsibility to run businesses according to society's ethical norms because if they did and others did not their businesses would fail'.

ETHICS BY DEFAULT

Although capitalism, like nature, is a nonmoral system which works best (is most productive in the long-term) when left well alone, companies operate within human societies and therefore must accept some of the strictures imposed by ethical norms.

We have seen how rules, regulations and laws administer some of this ethical discipline when they elicit compliant behaviour, but ethical pressure is also exerted in less formal ways by, for example, public opinion (sometimes expressed by boycott) and the company's internal culture.

Companies, therefore, cannot ignore social *mores*. The corporate environment is ethically saturated. The interactions between the nonmoral company and the moral human being are often complicated and are frequently unexpected, but company leaders must take them into account and must always seek the right balance between the costs of ethics and the costs of moral turpitude. If they get it more right than their rivals their companies will do well, and if a community of companies, constituting an economy, get it more right than other economies, the country will do well.

Somewhere within this complex web of inter-species relationships there is an optimum behavioural balance that will maximise production and welfare. How competition steers the corporate ethos towards this balance will be described in the next chapter, but we need first to get a flavour of the ecological aspects of the corporate environment that derive from a society's ethical norms.

Companies need to take ethical norms into account for two main reasons. First, their employees and their ultimate customers are ethical beings and may therefore extend or withdraw their labour and custom on ethical grounds. Secondly, companies trade under political systems in which they have no representation. They can and do lobby like mad, but when all is said and done, they have no vote. They remain ultimately vulnerable to the scruples as well as the appetites of their customers, whether expressed individually or collectively.

This is not to say the political process cannot be and is not, from time to time, suborned by corporate pressure, licit or otherwise, or that political institutions may not, on occasions, feel that their best interests lie in defending corporations against accusations of immoral conduct. It is a regrettable fact of modern life that some very large corporations are such significant parts of their host economies that they can sometimes get away with anything.

Such lapses cannot, however, be regarded as signs of any failure of business ethics because, as we have already seen, there are no business ethics. They are more properly regarded as evidence of a

14

failure of the political and judicial institutions whose task it is to impose on the nonmoral company the standards of a moral society.

A striking example of a failure of this kind was the case of Stanley Adams versus the Swiss pharmaceuticals group Hoffmann-La Roche (the full story is recounted by Adams in his book *Roche versus Adams*.

Hoffmann-La Roche, in a chillingly cynical exercise of political pressure, caused Adams to be arrested by the Swiss police in 1975, interrogated, imprisoned, tried and convicted for espionage and, in the process, to be rendered a widower by his wife's suicide.

His 'crime' was that he reported Hoffmann-La Roche, his employer, to the European Commission's competition agency DG4 for commercial practices that contravened clauses in Switzerland's Free Trade agreement with the European Economic Community. Hoffmann-La Roche was later found guilty of the violations and was fined.

The story demonstrates how direct the conflict between the moral individual and the nonmoral company can be. It is not just a matter of a difference in emphasis; it is, or it can be, a collision between two almost diametrically opposed outlooks on life. In order for an individual to begin to comprehend Roche's extraordinary behaviour, it is necessary to resort to the schoolboy analogy. Roche behaved like an unprincipled bully caught stealing by a younger boy and reported to the headmaster. The 'sneak' had to be punished severely otherwise the whole bullying system on which Roche depended for its prosperity would be put in jeopardy. That in this case political institutions (the headmaster and his staff) failed to mete out more than a token punishment to the bully for the theft, and no punishment at all for his persecution of the sneak, merely indicates that standards of discipline in this school were abysmally low.

But perhaps the most important lesson to be learned from the affair is more positive. Roche's behaviour can only have been inspired by fear. The company would not have chosen to expose itself in this way because it is bad for business to be seen to be behaving unethically. Had the Adams affair not already caused Hoffmann-La Roche to reek of the sewer, it is doubtful whether the company's involvement in the Seveso disaster in northern Italy in July 1976 would have received so much attention. Roche owned the company that owned the factory that omitted the ghastly cloud of dioxin into the atmosphere.

Roche clearly regarded Adams as an extremely dangerous man. He threatened the company in a fundamental way. Though a tiny adversary, he was armed with a profound knowledge of his opponent's physiology, particularly its weak spots. Roche will never be quite the same again.

Could, or should, Roche have behaved differently? Would it have been better from a business point of view for the company to have adopted a softer line in its dealings with Adams? My answer is an emphatic yes. It is possible that the time will come when Hoffmann-La Roche stockholders will regret their failure to dismiss those responsible for the persecution of Adams, not for their lack of ethics, but for their lack of competence.

The relationship between the moral human and the nonmoral company is not a stable one. Just as business has become more competitive as it has become more international, so society has become better organised and more vocal. It is more important now for a business to be seen to be behaving well.

The days of the robber barons are gone. They cannot be brought back in a new corporate guise, or at any rate the window in the mid-twentieth century when such a reincarnation seemed possible is closing.

Companies which trade with South Africa or peddle powdered milk to the third world; which, through negligence, sell dangerous drugs like Thalidomide and Opren or emit toxic wastes; which defy the law or attempt to subvert political institutions; which use oil from sperm whales; or which have lead in their products – are not now, and have not been for some time, long-run profit maximisers.

They and those who run them are deluding themselves if they believe the 'do-gooders', the 'epidemic of consumerism', the cry-baby element in the customer base, are minor irritants that will pass away given patience and a little judicious scratching.

Corporate behaviour that invokes public execration is bad for business for the simple reason that the public these days have the power to express their opprobrium with increasing force and conviction. They have recognised business, and particularly big business, as an alien species and are bent on taming it. And in the end the public hold the only ace that matters – their custom.

Those who acknowledge the theoretical power of a consumer revolt, but insist that the public lacks the collective will to inflict significant damage on companies, should consider how consumerism has developed over the past few decades.

Ralph Nader's victory over the Corvair – he described the rear-engined Chevrolet car as 'unsafe at any speed' and caused it to be withdrawn from production – was just the first of a long and continuing series of consumer victories over the world's largest corporations. Chemical companies have been dissuaded from making napalm, tobacco firms have seen their markets contract, British brewers have been forced to re-introduce 'traditional' ales, oil giants are having to abandon toxic additives in petrol and companies all over the world have been persuaded to withdraw from South Africa.

The new Institute of Business Ethics is another agent of change in the corporate environment. It exerts pressure by articulating a view of how companies should behave. Though the IBE's exhortations make no sense to the company their effects are palpable. Corporate reputations wax when approbation is given and wane when it is withheld, and companies care deeply about their reputations. The IBE, for all its flaws, plays a part in the dialectics of corporate evolution. It is helping both to mould and express public opinion.

Another kind of pressure examined more fully in Chapter Six was exerted by the British Medical Association in 1985 when it reported that 350 or more health organisations and charities had investments in tobacco. Tobacco shares tumbled in the City as the named organisations hurriedly unloaded their carcinogenic holdings.

That was hitting companies where it hurts – in their equity base. For the moment it remains fashionable for the 'tough' company executive to express contempt and indifference for consumerism. It will be interesting to see how long this attitude survives when the despised consumerism begins to infect financial markets and the company's cost of capital.

MORE THAN A NICE IDEA

We have seen how fruitless it is to expect companies to behave in what we would consider ethical ways as a matter of course, but we have also seen how hard it is for some entrepreneurs to come to terms with the nonmoral nature of their corporate vehicles.

Though the idea of the ethical company is a chimera, it has power. As we shall see, it is desired not just by principled entrepreneurs but also by consumers, neighbours, investors and employees. Apart from anything else, it would be a nicer place in which to work.

The so-called ethical business has quite a bit going for it,

17

particularly these days when the ability to recruit and keep able people is the key management skill. The business does not have to be ethical, it just has to seem to be ethical.

There is nothing to be gained from unethical behaviour for its own sake. No one will join a company or buy its products or shares because it behaves unethically – though some will do the opposite.

So other things being equal one would expect companies that are seen to be ethical to do better. They will be less exposed to the threat of scandal, they will enjoy greater customer loyalty, they will be more responsive to changes in consumer tastes and attitudes and should benefit from more loyal, high-quality personnel.

The ethical style is a promising strategy, but how can it establish itself? Though it would be better in the long-run for all concerned, how can the nice strategy overcome the aggression and hostility endemic to modern business life? This is the question we shall address in the next chapter.

SUMMARY

- The term business ethics is misleading, if not meaningless.

- Managers' fiduciary duties deny them the right to be human.

- There are two kinds of business ethics – those relating to people and those relating to other companies.

- There is nothing right or wrong about brutish corporate behaviour.

- A human ethical code is a liability for the entrepreneur.

- The apparently ethical company has some business advantages.

CHAPTER 2

The Sociable Company

The last chapter showed how companies can be regarded as nonmoral creatures inhabiting a business jungle in which survival depends on brawn and, increasingly these days, on brain. In such an environment *a priori* adherence to a code comparable to the rules of behaviour that have evolved in human societies, is a recipe for extinction. Companies that appear to be ethical are merely enlightened, long-term profit-maximisers. Niceness is a strategy, not a quality. But it is a very interesting strategy.

This chapter takes a closer look at niceness in the business world. I shall try to show that the significance of the nice strategy extends far beyond its ability to generate a semblance of morality; that niceness is, in fact, the basis of a thoroughly modern and extremely powerful strategic approach to business, strong enough to overwhelm utterly the 'nasty' style still dominant today.

The first and most important part of this exercise is to answer the question with which I ended the previous chapter: granted that niceness confers advantages on all businesses, how can the nice style establish itself in a nasty world?

This is a particular form of a general and important question, variations of which are to be found in areas ranging from evolutionary biology to international relations.

THE NOT-SO-NASTY JUNGLE
Since the question we need to answer is an evolutionary one it is natural to begin our search for enlightenment in the jungle.

The conventional wisdom would conclude that if the analogy of the jungle is valid in the business world, the nice company is doomed. It shouldn't get past first base. When the game is hardball, nice guys finish last. How could a nice company be expected to survive in the business jungle where the life of the weak must be as Thomas Hobbes described the life of man: 'solitary, poor, nasty, brutish, and short'?

But a closer look reveals that contrary to popular belief ferocity is by no means the only behavioural style evident in the jungle. The jungle is neither always nor everywhere 'red in tooth and claw'. Alongside the brutal violence of the predator and the parasitical horror of the ichneumons there have evolved more pacific, sociable behaviour patterns.

Animals cooperate with each other in a myriad of ways. They look after their young with a tenderness that seems like altruism but which is, in reality, genetically programmed, and members of different species, like the lion and the hyena or the pilot fish and the shark, form symbiotic attachments.

The rationales of these two kinds of collaborative behaviour are obvious. The first is an evolutionary necessity because it helps to ensure the propagation of the species. The second is a special, opportunist form of adaptation to an environment that includes other species.

Equally logical are the collective behaviour patterns of insects like ants, termites and a wide variety of mammals and birds. *En masse* locusts, ants and bees are formidable adversaries even for the largest mammals. Swarms, armies and colonies are logical strategies – examples of zoological unionism. By subordinating survival of the individual to survival of the group, they improve their chances. They discovered long ago the motto paraded on the banners of humanity's trade union movement – 'unity is strength'.

Biologists have found it hard to explain how such behavioural styles could have evolved. Just because a particular behaviour pattern is logical and effective does not guarantee its emergence. A mechanism derived from 'chance and necessity' (Jacques Monod's twin engines of evolution) is needed to explain how theoretically successful strategies actually evolve.

Little credence is given these days to the obvious explanation of social behaviour patterns, namely that Darwinian natural selection works on big numbers as well as on individuals and can therefore choose, at the species or population level, those behaviour patterns that are fittest.

It is now thought that natural selection is an extremely weak force at the population and species levels and that any plausible

20

explanation of cooperative behaviour must be consistent with the original Darwinian insight which asserts that natural selection works almost exclusively at the level of the individual.

Robbed of the big numbers explanation, evolutionary theorists have recently developed two special sub-theories to account for the extraordinary variety of cooperative behaviour in the natural world.

Kinship theory, exemplified in the 'Selfish Gene' hypothesis proposed by Richard Dawkins in his book of the same name, is the more fully developed. Cooperative and apparently altruistic behaviour should be understood in terms of the benefits it brings to reproduction within the kinship group.

Kinship theory provides great insight into the conundrum of cooperation in the jungle but it has a weakness. It relies on close family relationships between the cooperators. Though it is a necessary explanation of cooperative behaviour it is not sufficient because there are many examples of cooperative behaviour where relatedness is either low or non-existent.

The second evolutionary sub-theory that has emerged to explain cooperative behaviour is known as *reciprocity theory* and it brings us to the central theoretical part of this book. The argument becomes a little technical in places but these parts can be skipped if the reader can accept the conclusion: that the application of the theory of games to corporate evolution suggests that a particular strategic theme or 'streme' will become dominant.

Robert Axelrod, in chapter five of his book *The Evolution of Cooperation*, considers various kinds of cooperative behaviour with no relatedness that have inspired the development of reciprocity theory.

His examples, compiled with the help of the British evolutionist William Hamilton, include the relationships between the fungus and algae which compose lichen; between the ants and ant-acacias where the trees house and nourish the ants which reciprocate by protecting the trees; between the fig wasps and the fig tree where the wasps eat the fig flower but then redeem their parasitism by acting as the tree's only means of pollination and propagation; and between hermaphrodite pairs of sea bass who take turn-and-turn-about with egg production and fertilisation.

Before looking more closely at Axelrod's work the reader should be clear about the *kind* of argument being put forward and what *kind* of organism the company is.

SOCIOBIOLOGY VERSUS STRATEGY SELECTION

Corporate evolution must be distinguished at the outset from so-called sociobiology which tries to explain social behaviour in terms of the action of Darwinian natural selection on genes. The sociobiologist will argue, for example, that change in corporate behaviour occurs because of the reproductive success of managers carrying a specific genetic variation.

The trouble with this approach however is that the time scales involved are far too long. The speed of adaptive change in the business world cannot be explained by the natural selection of genetic variation. Apart from the obvious problem of the selection itself (is it likely that bad businessmen will be routinely lynched by shareholders before they achieve sexual maturity?), it is clear that to gain enough speed to explain the rate of corporate evolution, one would need to invoke a *Lamarckian* view of business change which would allow managers to inherit learned (as well as genetic) characteristics from their predecessors.

Since managers do learn from other managers, from consultants and from business theorists, this is by no means as absurd a notion applied to business as was the Lamarckian model of evolutionary biology, which was first challenged by Darwin and then finally discredited with the understanding of genetics.

The American Stephen Jay Gould, for one, is a convinced cultural Lamarckian. He argues that: 'The useful discoveries of one generation are passed directly to offspring by writing, teaching, and so forth . . . Five minutes with a wheel, a snowshoe, a bobbin, or a bow and arrow may allow an artisan of one culture to capture a major achievement of another.'

And Gould warns against pushing the 'cultural evolution' analogy too far. He says that, whereas *biological* evolution is divergent, in the sense that lineages are constantly separating, *cultural* evolution is convergent. Learning and shared knowledge fuse the various strands of cultural change together, both strengthening and narrowing them. The cultural past casts a long shadow on the future, making culture's walk through time far less random than that of genes. Gould concludes: ' "Cultural evolution" needs laws of its own.'

I believe these laws are to be found in the second way in which we can learn, from evolutionary biology, something about evolution in the social world – a way that involves forgetting about genes altogether and concentrating instead on the idea of natural selection.

We can admit the truth of Gould's belief that culture evolves within a closed system and with the help of Lamarckian imitation (remember the Dawkins idea of the 'meme' encountered in the introduction), while remaining free to conjecture that the basic mechanism of cultural evolution is that of Darwinian natural selection.

Biological evolution employs a scatter gun approach. It fires bundles of randomly varying genetic material at the world leaving natural selection to judge their fitness. How natural selection selects has nothing to do with how genetic variation varies. The genes don't care. They just like to randomise.

In the theory of corporate evolution, natural selection can be seen as a quality of the marketplace that rewards and punishes strategy and so acts as the template for strategy-making.

THE OPTIMISING COMPANY

It is only necessary to make two assumptions about companies to demonstrate their interest in developing good strategies. They must have something equivalent to a survival instinct and they must be motivated to do well.

Economists have identified three kinds of corporate motivation. Companies can 'satisfice' – attempt to achieve a satisfactory level of performance; they can 'maximise' a single performance parameter such as sales, profits, shareholder value or earnings per share; or they can 'optimise' – try to achieve an optimal blend of performance between a number of target parameters.

There are occasions, in an agreed takeover bid, for example, or a voluntary winding-up, when the survival instinct seems to be absent and it is not uncommon to find companies that appear to be satisficing rather than optimising. In normal competitive conditions, however, most companies behave as if they wish both to survive and optimise.

Companies are therefore *strategic beings*. They are compelled by their natures to seek and adopt good strategies. In the business world, natural selection works not on the genetic endowments of managers and other human change-agents but on strategies. In business, strategies are not the expression of genes but are the counterparts of the genes themselves.

All that is needed is a mechanism, derived from ideas of natural selection, that has the power to explain how strategic variation might arise in the business world.

Before we consider this mechanism we must be clear on one point. Natural selection operates in the business world but not in the same way as it does in the natural world. There is no equivalent of the biological inevitabilty of death for members of the corporate species.

They are not locked, by their genetic endowment, into a strictly circumscribed behaviour pattern. This means the term 'corporate evolution' is actually a misnomer. Companies cannot be directly involved in the evolutionary process because they lack essential mortality. They bear the same relationship to the selectable strategies as chromosomes bear to the selectable genes. They are carriers. Natural selection works on strategies, not companies.

But strategies, though crucially important in the long run, are not the only manifestations of corporate behaviour. A good strategy can be killed by bad tactics. A company's adaptability – its willingness to change a strategy in response to a change in its environment – is also a crucial survival characteristic.

For this reason it is appropriate to regard management teams as 'selectable' too. Just as strategies appear and die, so do the creators and the implementers of strategy. They may not 'die' (be fired) if one strategy 'dies' (fails) but their chances of retaining control of the company are slim if they fail repeatedly.

THE PRISONER'S DILEMMA

Having armed the company and its leaders with their survival instinct and their propensity to optimise, let us consider how they should respond to an instruction from an anti-monopoly agency to withdraw from a price-fixing cartel they have formed with their competitors.

The answer is simple. They should comply (cease to fix prices). As soon as one member withdraws from the cartel because it perceives the benefits of staying in will no longer exceed the costs (of court action, possible conviction and punishment), the value of the cartel to the remaining members will fall and this may well precipitate a similar change in strategy on the part of a second member . . . and so on. In this way the price-fixing strategy becomes extinct not because the price-fixers have become extinct but because the price-fixing strategy has become bad for business.

To understand how the cartel and the anti-monopoly agency could have evolved through the action of natural selection on strategic variation we shall look at 'the prisoner's dilemma' – a

24

conundrum that has played an important role in game theory in recent years. Specifically we shall consider the iterated (repeated) version of the game featured in Robert Axelrod's *The Evolution of Cooperation*.

Two accomplices are arrested and interrogated separately. Each can either confess to the crime or protest his or her innocence. If the first confesses, so implicating the second, he or she may get a lighter sentence but only if the second pleads innocence. If both confess, both are convicted and sentenced as charged. If, on the other hand, both plead innocence, the case cannot be proved and both receive a light sentence for a less serious offence. The dilemma is that innocence is the worst plea if the other confesses but confession is a bad plea if the other confesses too.

The game can be represented as a matrix of possible outcomes. In Axelrod's version there are two point-maximising players and two available strategies: cooperation (pleading innocence) and defection (confession).

Each player knows if he or she chooses defection (*D*) and the other chooses cooperation (*C*) he or she will win the maximum five points (temptation to defect = $T = 5$) and the opponent will score nothing (sucker's pay-off = $S = 0$).

Each also knows that if both choose *C* both will score three points (reward for mutual cooperation = $R = 3$) and that if both choose *D* both will score one point (punishment for mutual defection = $P = 1$). Axelrod's matrix of possible outcomes is shown in Figure 2.1.

Notice how the scoring system adds up. Mutual defection – nasty meets nasty – generates a total of two points; nasty meets nice generates a total of five points; nice meets nice generates a total of six points. There is a presumption about the nature of the game embedded in this arrangement, namely that cooperation is the best strategy insofar as it maximises the combined scores of the two players.

Any arrangement that involves positive but no negative scores is a **positive-sum game**. Axelrod's scoring defines a further feature of the proto-strategy: there is a premium on cooperation. Many scoring arrangements will do this. Some would force cooperation by giving it an absolute premium over defection, so removing the dilemma, but in our case there is a conditional premium of 67% on defection, the condition being that the other player is a sucker (cooperates).

The 'expected' return for each play – the average of the two possible outcomes – is twice as high for defection ($[5 + 1]/2 = 3$) as

25

Player A

		Cooperate	Defect
Player B	Cooperate	Both get $R = 3$ Reward for mutual cooperation	$A=T=5, B=S=0$ Temptation to defect & sucker's payoff
	Defect	$A=S=0, B=T=5$ Sucker's payoff & temptation to defect	Both get $P=1$ Punishment for mutual defection

Fig 2.1: The Prisoner's Dilemma
Axelrod's version of the game is 'iterated' and has a particular scoring system.

it is for cooperation ($[3 + 0]/2 = 1.5$). This means the best strategy, for one play, is to defect. This is true even though each player knows the other will see the game in the same way and so the chances of winning are slim. Game theory requires the assumption that one's opponent will make the best possible move – defect. The player has to go for five knowing that in all likelihood he or she will end up with one.

But suppose the game is iterated as Axelrod proposes. Suppose each player knows there will be many plays but not how many. In this situation the mutual cooperation result becomes, in theory, very attractive. A string of threes in an indefinite number of plays is three times as good as a string of mutual-defection scores.

The difficulty is that, given the sucker's pay-off, it is risky to initiate cooperation. You are virtually certain to be taken to the cleaners. What you need is some way of communicating to the other player your cooperative intent. Since the rules forbid off-game diplomacy the only way to signal to the other player is through the moves themselves.

The forced defection of the single-play game is a signal of sorts – it says 'I'm no pushover' – but the language is limited. Signalling only becomes truly communicative when the cooperative move is introduced, but as we have seen it is dangerous to be the first to cooperate.

26

The task in Axelrod's iterated version of the game is to develop a strategy that, in a finite series of moves in a game of indefinite length, will communicate to the other player your willingness to cooperate if he or she will. In business each player is engaged in many games at once – with employees, shareholders, customers, suppliers, competitors, neighbours and government. Therefore the company whose strategy communicates cooperative intent soonest, and so elicits cooperation, has a good chance of emerging the overall winner.

THE BEST STRATEGY

Axelrod invited professional game theorists to submit programmes for a series of iterated prisoner's dilemma games, to a round-robin computer tournament. Each strategy was to play one 200-move game with every other strategy. The tournament winner would be the strategy that achieved the highest overall points score.

'Surprisingly,' Axelrod wrote, 'there is a single property which distinguishes the relatively high-scoring entries from the relatively low-scoring entries. This is the property of being nice, which is to say never being the first to defect.' The distinction was quite marked. The top eight of the 15 entries were nice and none of the others were. The average scores of nice strategies ranged from 472 to 504 points, while the best the nasties could do was 401.

One of these nice strategies had the humiliating experience of never winning a game. It was the simplest of all the strategies entered and was christened 'tit for tat' (TFT). TFT always cooperates on the first move and then always repeats what the other player did on the previous move. Despite never winning a game, TFT won the tournament by achieving the highest overall score. It also, of course, had the highest average score – 504 points a game.

Axelrod was not content. The tournament had too few players for his liking and the 200-move limit had inspired some tricky end-game tactics in which he was not particularly interested (but they *are* interesting for business economists – see below). In addition there were two strategies that would have beaten TFT in that tournament had they been submitted. One of these was the even nicer 'tit for two tats' – always cooperate unless your opponent defects twice running.

The beauty of the computer tournament is that you can play it as many times as you like and it will always give the same result. You can introduce another strategy and see how it would have done against the original contestants and, by taking out weaker strategies (playing the natural selector, death), you can see how individual strategies perform in different competitive environments.

But Axelrod wanted more data and he also wanted to see how the lessons learned in the first tournament would be digested by game theorists. He convened another, larger tournament which attracted 63 entries.

All entrants were given the full report of the first tournament complete with Axelrod's analysis, including the strategies that would have won had they been entered. This time, to inhibit messy endgame tactics, the duels were made of indeterminate length.

Axelrod's report on the second tournament reads as follows (one can sense how he relishes the significance):

TIT FOR TAT was the simplest program submitted in the first round and it won the first round. It was the simplest submission in the second round, and it won the second round. Even though all the entrants to the second round knew that TIT FOR TAT had won the first round, no one was able to design an entry that did any better.

This time there were no strategies Axelrod could think of that would have beaten TFT in this larger and more complex game. 'Tit for two tats' and the other strategy that would have won the first tournament had they been entered were crucified by the tougher competition.

But Axelrod, though impressed by TFT's performance, wondered if it might have had something to do with the high proportion of nice strategies in the second tournament. Perhaps TFT would have fared less well in a more hostile environment. Axelrod tested TFT's robustness by entering it in a series of hypothetical tournaments, each with a very different distribution of strategy types.

TFT emerged from this examination with flying colours. It won five of the six major variations and was second in the sixth. TFT is therefore very robust. It does well in many different environments.

Axelrod then subjected TFT to a further test. He conducted another series of hypothetical tournaments after each of which he played the grim reaper by weeding out the poor performers. This meant that as the series progressed each surviving program was playing against opposition that was increasing in average quality each round.

28

Axelrod's selector works like this: a winner in round one earns the right to propagate itself in round two. The system does not mimic evolution because no mutant strategies are introduced during the series. This was a test not of how strategies evolve but of how fit they are to survive over several generations. As Axelrod put it, the system 'provides an ecological perspective because there are no new rules of behaviour introduced. It differs from an evolutionary perspective, which would allow mutations to introduce new strategies into the environment.'

The results of the simulation provided TFT with yet another resounding success. TFT achieved a slight lead in the original tournament and never lost it. By the one-thousandth generation it was the most successful strategy and was still growing at a faster rate than any other.

THE SOUL OF TFT

What is it about TFT that makes it so strong? It is crude in its simplicity, it never wins games and yet at the end of the day it invariably achieves the highest overall score.

Axelrod attributes TFT's success to four basic qualities:

- It is **nice**. By never being the first to defect it maximises its chances of hitting a long run of mutual-cooperation scores.
- It is **retaliatory**. Though never the first to defect it retaliates immediately its opponent defects. It will often lose against nasty rules but it will make damn sure the price of its opponent's victory is a low score.
- It is **forgiving**. TFT does not bear grudges. It immediately retaliates if its opponent defects but will cooperate again if its opponent does. It does not overpunish and so reduces the chances of a series of mutal-defection scores.
- It is **clear**. TFT's simplicity makes it easily recognisable and since it tends to acquire a considerable reputation it should quickly elicit cooperation.

BUSINESS AS A POSITIVE-SUM GAME

But what has all this to do with business? It is a real world out there, not some obscure parlour game.

The first point to establish is whether or not the positive-sum game, of which the iterated prisoner's dilemma is an example, is a good strategic model of business. This, oddly enough, is a matter of some debate among business economists. I know of at least one strategic management consultancy where it is axiomatic that business is a zero-sum game in which every success must be at the expense of another's failure.

I shall try to show why this is wrong but I recognise that for those I fail to convince, little of what follows will make much sense. Die-hard zero-summers should stop here. For them the business game is irredeemably characterised by the naive, 'red in tooth and claw' version of Darwinian natural selection. In such a world the nice strategy cannot win. Ruthlessness and brutality are the only winning qualities in a world characterised by the philosophical negativism of writers like Gore Vidal: 'It is not enough to succeed. Others must fail', and Allen Ginsberg: 'You can't win. You can't break even. You can't even quit the game'.

It seemed to me self-evident that business is a positive-sum game. I could not see how wealth could be created in the first place, and accumulated, if each accretion of wealth had to be paid for, elsewhere in the economy, by an equal destruction of wealth. I still regard this argument as conclusive but the zero-summers are not so perverse as to deny the very possibility of economic growth.

However, they base their view on a notion I find almost equally bizarre – that success in business should be measured not in terms of a company's profitability but in terms of the share of its market it manages to wrest from its competitors.

This *is* a zero-sum game. An accretion of market share by one company must be paid for by a corresponding loss of market share elsewhere. But this leads to the absurd result that it is better for a company to have a high market share than to be profitable. I cannot accept this. I do not believe Ford's shareholders were dismayed to learn in 1988 that their European subsidiary had achieved sharply increased profits but had lost a few points of market share.

If maximising market share is good for business, and I know of no evidence that it is, then it must be as a means to an end and not as an end in itself. It is hard to see what that end might be other than profit. Market leadership is an example of what the late Fred Hirsch called, in his book *Social Limits to Growth*, a 'positional good'. It can only be possessed by one player at a time. The fight for it is of the 'beggar my neighbour' kind and must lead to the impoverishment and ultimate failure of all players.

Only in the special case of a monopoly protected by infinitely high barriers to entry can maximising market share be reconciled with maximising profits. The zero-summers must be wrong because their position leads to absurdity – to an inconceivable business world, entirely populated by chronically loss-making monopolies. Axelrod's 'prisoner's dilemma' models this game too, weird as it is. All one has to do is to define victory in terms of the number of encounters won, rather than in terms of the number of points scored.

THE RATCHET OF CORPORATE EVOLUTION

So, bidding farewell to the incorrigible zero-summers we shall proceed on the assumption that business is a positive-sum game and that therefore Axelrod's positive scores are appropriate.

It also seems reasonable to suppose that in a game between two companies, the one that cheats will do well in that transaction if the other business plays fair and so loses money. Equally, it is reasonable to suppose that if both companies cheat neither will profit much but neither will lose.

It follows logically from these two suppositions that if both companies play fair the positive sum game will normally ensure that both do reasonably well. If this were not the case there would be no business.

Axelrod's ranking of outcomes, if not their actual values, seems reasonable and it does not matter what the actual values are. His results hold so long as unilateral defection earns more than mutual cooperation, mutual cooperation earns more than mutual defection, and mutual defection earns more than unilateral cooperation.

But TFT is a weak strategy in a single play. It only starts to show its paces when there is a series of plays and only then if the results of subsequent plays are important. If business A wants to win a first encounter with business B so badly that it doesn't give a damn what happens in future encounters with B, then it will always pay A to cheat. If, on the other hand, A cares what B might do in future encounters then A will do better if it cooperates.

This is the case in business. It is an iterated game, in that the same players meet each other at irregular but relatively frequent intervals, and the shadow the future casts over the present is relatively long. It can be expressed as the inverse of the discount rate on money (the interest rate) which has, historically, been in excess of 90%. In the game this would mean that earnings from the play a year hence are valued by both players at 90% of the nominal value of earnings from the current play. We shall return in Chapter Six to an interesting consequence of this, namely that high interest rates have a tendency to lead to a reduction in the general standards of business behaviour.

Now suppose cheating is rife despite a low discount rate. Is there a way TFT could prevail in such an environment? If all other businesses cheat then a single business employing TFT will lose. It won't lose much because on the second play with each cheater it will become a permanent cheater itself, but it will never recoup the original loss. But what if there is more than one business using TFT?

Suppose, for example, that out of a population of 100 businesses, 10 pursue TFT strategies. In that case single players of each type will amass the following scores after 10 encounters with every other business:

TFT
Encounters with the 90 cheaters (90 × 1 × 9) · · · · · · · · · · · · · 810 points
Encounters with the 9 TFTs (9 × 3×10) · · · · · · · · · · · · · · · · · · · 270 points
$$\text{TOTAL} = 1080$$

Cheater
Encounters with the 89 cheaters (89 × 1 × 10) · · · · · · · · · · · · 890 points
Encounters with the 10 TFTs (10 × 5 + 10 × 1×9) · · · · · · · · 140 points
$$\text{TOTAL} = 1030$$

It does not take many TFTs in a population dominated by cheaters for them to begin to out-perform the majority. No discount rate is used here but it is easy to see that with a reasonable discount rate, and provided businesses encounter each other frequently if not regularly, quite a small cluster of TFT businesses can invade, and ultimately dominate, a population of cheaters.

The larger the cluster the faster it will happen and if, as is probable, TFT businesses achieve a higher average number of encounters with each other than with cheaters (as it is clearly in their interests to try to do), it will happen faster still.

Moreover, the cheaters cannot re-invade. If a small cluster of TFT businesses can invade and dispossess a population of cheaters it is clear that even a very large cluster of cheaters will do badly in a population of TFT businesses. In game theory terminology a population of TFT businesses is 'collectively stable' which is to say it cannot be invaded by cheaters or by any other kind of strategy.

This means that businesses employing TFT will eventually come to dominate the corporate population and there will be no way back. As Axelrod puts it: 'the gear wheels of social evolution' [for 'social', read 'corporate'] 'have a ratchet.'

ENDGAME
Axelrod was not interested in endgame play because it tended to interfere with the pure strategic play, but the evidence of endgame tactics he found in his first tournament is an interesting validation of the prisoner's dilemma as a model for business.

Endgame variations indicate that players perceive a difference in the nature of the risk–reward mix if they know their relationship with their opponent will soon cease. Though content to notch up mutual-cooperation scores (3) for the most of the game, they may be tempted to sneak in a surprise defection (5) just before the end so that they can pip their opponent at the post.

Now suppose the word gets out that a particular company is in financial difficulties. Suddenly its suppliers and customers perceive their relationships with that company in a different way. The supplier, although it may have been cooperating with the troubled company in a mutually beneficial trading relationship over many years, will begin to question the wisdom of continuing to extend credit in case the company goes bust before payment.

It may therefore insist on cash-on-the-nail payment and, in so doing, increase the cash-flow pressure on the troubled company. This would be bad business if the company subsequently recovered and punished the 'defecting' supplier by taking its custom elsewhere, but there is clearly a probability of failure above which the supplier's best move is defection.

Similarly a customer of the troubled company, which has been in the habit of placing regular orders over many years, may deem it wise to take its business elsewhere (and so increase the cash-flow pressure on the troubled company) in case its supplier fails before it can deliver.

As we saw in the last chapter a company's reputation and credit worthiness are fragile qualities, very vulnerable to rumour and speculation. What I called the 'self-fulfilling calumny' is a powerful weapon in the hands of a 'nasty' company. It goes without saying that it is a weapon that would never be used by a nice company unless it was provoked by an opponent's or trading partner's previous defection.

THE RECOGNITION FACULTY

The elegance of Axelrod's conclusion is suspiciously seductive. The real world cannot be that simple, surely? Business, though not as complex as biology, is infinitely more subtle and varied than the crude formality of the prisoner's dilemma, even in its iterated form.

But those who know business and who run companies find the game disturbingly evocative. They recognise it. It seems to fit their view of the world even though they often find it hard to explain why.

Some have been struggling with the problem of how to create an attractive corporate culture that makes it easier to recruit and keep good people, and have been confronted by conclusions that are so 'nice' as to be counter-intuitive. They wonder how the exigencies of internal people management could lead them to styles which are so much nicer than the ones they feel obliged to deploy externally.

Karl Erik Sveiby has suggested another reason why the prisoner's dilemma may be becoming a more appropriate model of business. He points out that the growth of the 'Information Society' makes it more likely that the two requirements of Axelrod's game, that players encounter each other often and recognise each other, will be met.

Recognition requires data and data both extend and strengthen corporate networks. They make it easier for a company, and more profitable, to widen its range of contacts with other companies. A group of friendly companies, linked by networks both personal and electronic, is an Axelrod 'cluster'.

In the information society companies have acquired innumerable recognition systems. The City and the financial press subject listed companies to constant, and more or less public, scrutiny. The advertising industry peppers the financial pages with corporate image copy. The Companies Registry, open to all, includes extensive details of all companies, their structures, shareholders and performance.

It is far easier to recognise, investigate and analyse companies than it is to do the same to people. The corporate species – companies collectively – is a more public species than the human being. Its privacy is not only not respected, it is actually suspected. It would be very rare, and very foolish, for a company to enter into a commercial relationship with another company it knows nothing about or about which it is unable to discover anything.

This also is corroboration of the idea that Axelrod's work on reciprocity theory is relevant to business. Companies recognise each other very readily. They have what amounts to perfect memories (in the sense of there being routinely accessible sources of information) of other companies even before they encounter them.

Such faculties may not be necessary or even sufficient for the evolution of reciprocity but they cannot help but encourage it.

SUMMARY

- In business, niceness is a strategy, not a quality.

- Nice strategies with no relatedness are evident in the natural world. Reciprocity theory appears to shed light on the question of how they evolved.

- Corporate evolution selects for strategies and management teams, not companies.

- In the iterated prisoner's dilemma game the nice 'tit for tat' (TFT) strategy has so far proved unbeatable.

- Since the iterated prisoner's dilemma game is a good model for business, TFT should also prove to be a good business strategy.

- Clusters of TFT can invade and destroy communities of nasty strategies, endowing corporate evolution with a ratchet quality.

- Recognition is important in the iterated prisoner's dilemma which may explain why the recognition faculty has been selected for in the biological world.

- The faculty of recognition improves survival chances. Companies are more easily recognised than people.

CHAPTER 3

The Strategic Environment

An important theme of this book is the idea that companies form a discrete species, the corporate species, subject to the winnowing process of natural selection, and that therefore its evolution can be illuminated by an understanding of evolutionary processes and mechanisms that have been at work over much longer periods in the natural world.

This chapter reviews critically contemporary work in business economics and management theory in order to define, for the evolutionary approach in general and for the theory of the nice company in particular, the citadel of orthodoxy they must tear down.

The theory of evolution, and the similar trial-and-error model of scientific progress proposed by such philosophers as Sir Karl Popper and Thomas Kuhn, both tell us that the orthodoxy will not and should not be easily displaced by new ideas. If it is not strongly defended its successors will lack staying power. The harsher the environment both for new ideas and new species, the tougher they must be to prevail.

In the world of ideas 'speciation' (the emergence of what Kuhn calls new 'paradigms') can take place in three ways. It can be an internal development, stemming from ideas already existing within the discipline; it can be brand new, owing nothing to what has gone before, or it can be external – the application in one area of themes and theories already established in another.

The theory of the nice company is an example of the latter type. It applies to business economics, themes and theories already well established in evolutionary biology. It is a theory of correspondence and as such it has a great weakness and a great strength.

36

The weakness is that analogies can be pushed too far. There may be fundamental differences between the source and destination disciplines that are overlooked in the enthusiasm of the search for correspondences.

The strength of correspondence theories is that importing ideas from another discipline can represent a major injection into the destination discipline of tried and tested principles and theories which, if applied with care and discrimination, can make a great deal of ground relatively quickly.

It is hard to exaggerate the potential wealth of the source of new business economics ideas represented by the rich and rapidly developing field of evolutionary biology. If the correspondences exist then the risks attendant on extravagant analogising are far outweighed by the potential rewards.

THE INCOMPARABLE BAT
To illustrate the sophistication of the survival strategies and supporting technologies that have evolved in the natural world, and so to get a glimpse of the potential power of Darwin's ideas applied to business economics, we shall begin with a description of the echo-location of bats based on an account by Richard Dawkins in his book *The Blind Watchmaker*.

An animal's supporting technologies (its strength, perception, agility and intelligence, for example) are genetic endowments that shape its implied strategy. Its existing endowment is the product of past natural selection and its freedom to develop its strategy is the grist for future selection.

The bat's ultrasound systems, developed millions of years before their human equivalents of sonar and radar, are capable of what Dawkins describes as 'feats of detection and navigation that would strike an engineer dumb with admiration.'

When cruising, the bat contents itself with a stroboscopic impression of its environment, updating its picture of the night world with 10 pulses a second. When this sampling transmission detects nearby prey the pulse rate soars to 200 a second (mains electricity pulses 100 times a second and is just detectable in fluorescent lights by acute human peripheral vision).

It is believed the lower frequency cruising rate is used for reasons to do with energy and signal-processing economy and the problem of pulse/echo interference at long distances.

A difficulty in echo systems is the relative weakness of the return signal. This requires very sensitive receivers (ears) and very powerful transmitters if the system is to work over any distance. The dilemma is that powerful transmitters can damage sensitive ears. The solution is to switch off the ears during transmission. Some bats have developed send/receive switching that can turn their ears off and on 50 times a second.

Another problem is that sounds have to be brief if they are not to interfere with the returning echo but it is hard to achieve volume, and so range, with brief pulses. Human engineers have developed so-called 'chirp' radar to solve this problem. Instead of transmitting the pulse at the same pitch, they mark each part by modulation – making the frequency decline so that if the echo of the early part returns while the latter part is still being transmitted they will not be confused. Bats use frequency modulation for the same purpose.

And to measure the relative speed of their prey bats exploit the phenomenon known as the Doppler Shift – the way the apparent frequency of a wave changes depending on whether its source is approaching or moving away from the listener or observer. Some bats use a subtle variation on conventional Doppler computation. Instead of measuring the shift, they vary the pitch of their pulses so the echo returns at the same pitch (the pitch at which their ears are most sensitive). Relative speed is deduced by the adjustment needed to keep the echo's pitch stable.

With such awesome technology (and that is probably not the half of it) available to the bat it is a wonder any moths and other nocturnal insects survive.

After reading the Dawkins account of the bat's virtuoso echo-location skills I talked to a defence technology expert. He told me of moth 'counter-measures'. Some nocturnal lepidoptera have 'learned' to detect bat sonar and to confuse it by using the hairs on their bodies as 'chaff'. Others have perfected an evasion tactic.

They track the approach of the predator by monitoring the Doppler Shift of the incoming pulses and just before the bat arrives they fold their wings. The intercepting bat eats air as its intended victim plummets from its computed flight path.

A theory that can explain the bat and the rest of the myriad of highly sophisticated niche strategies of the natural world's flora and fauna, is clearly very powerful. Though the flora and fauna of the business world have been evolving for a tiny fraction of the time bats and moths have been competing, it is clear that as far as explanatory power goes, business economics is not in the same league as the theory of evolution.

As business economists seeking enlightenment we should be mindful of the power of evolutionary theory to explain the bat, and be humble.

THE IMPORTANCE OF HISTORY

One of the first insights into business provided by Darwin's ideas concerns the role of the past. Bat strategy is intimately connected with, and in a sense is equivalent to, the bat's evolutionary history. Modern business theorists pay far too little attention to the histories of the corporate creatures they are endeavouring to understand.

The common presumption is that a company's past, which has made it what it is, imposes a negligible constraint on what it can or will become.

The business strategist, it is proposed, should act as an eye in the skull, taking only the features of the external environment, like the structure of industries and the nature of competitors, into account. The implicit assumption is that a company's internal environment, the subject of Chapter Five, is as mutable as strategy itself.

But evolutionary theory tells us adaptive change is a rough and ready process. Perfect adaptation is not to be expected. Our ancestors adopted an upright stance five million years ago and yet we are still plagued by backaches and hernias associated with the simple fact that large, four-footed animals were not designed to walk on the toes of their hind feet.

The American evolutionist Stephen Jay Gould has made the point time and again in his wonderful columns in *Natural History Magazine*. 'Our world is not an optimal place, fine tuned by omnipotent forces of selection,' he wrote in an essay about the alleged sexual cannibalism of the preying mantis. 'It is a quirky mass of imperfections, working well enough (often admirably); a jury-rigged set of adaptations built of curious parts made available by past histories in different contexts.'

The same applies to the business world. The company itself is a jury-rig, imperfectly adapted to modern business life. As we shall see, the historical division of power between owners and employees causes serious problems in modern conditions and, as we have already seen, the tensions between the moral human being and the non-moral company remain unresolved.

Practical strategy must take into account not only the generic

39

nature of the company but also the peculiarities of individuals. Each company is the product of its history. It can be changed and improved only to a limited extent. Just as bats, for all their technology, cannot become birds, so companies are constrained in what they can do by what they already are.

Corporate strategy cannot be divorced from corporate physiology. The question must be not what a company should do, but, given what it is, what is the best it can become?

This Darwinian insight into business leads to a conclusion that is both important and unorthodox: **corporate phenomenology** (what a company is) **takes precedence over corporate strategy** (what a company does). There are things a company cannot do because of what it is and things it should not do. A company must be understood before it can be advised. Corporate phenomenology has priority over corporate strategy because it defines a company's strategic opportunity set. We will return to this point later, in Chapter Five.

THE INCOMPARABLE PORTER

The most important figure in contemporary management theory is Michael E. Porter, Professor of General Management at Harvard Business School. His *Competitive Strategy: Techniques for Analyzing Industries and Competitors* was published in 1980. It remains the definitive work on corporate strategy.

Porter is the high priest of what he calls 'explicit' strategy. He acknowledges in his introduction to *Competitive Strategy* that companies always have at least an implicit strategy dictated by the 'professional orientation' of their departments and by the 'incentives of those in charge' but he insists that the sum of departmental approaches 'rarely equals the best strategy'.

Formal strategic planning is necessary, he argues, to ensure the policies of functional departments are 'coordinated and directed at some common set of goals'.

Porter provides a set of techniques to help firms analyse their industries, understand their competitors and their own positions and so derive their own competitive strategies.

He identifies five factors driving competition:

- existing rivalry between firms
- the threat of new entrants
- the threat of substitute products and services
- the bargaining power of suppliers
- the bargaining power of buyers;

describes five generic industry environments:

- fragmented
- emerging
- mature
- declining
- global;

and proposes three generic strategies:

- vertical integration
- horizontal integration
- diversification.

(All three can be implemented by merger and acquisition.)

Competitive Strategy, probably because it is based on classical microeconomics, is full of good sense. It provides managers with a formidable collection of tools for thought about the competitive position of their firms and the structural qualities of their industries. It is, however, both too ambitious and too modest in its aims.

According to Porter, strategy formation is a formal, analytical process. Describing competitive and environmental features and classifying strategic options into a few basic types reduces the question of what to do next to a check list. Tick the boxes, hit the return key and hey presto, the ideal strategy will emerge.

Porter's world is static. Industries and competitors are as they are, and once they are understood strategic options become clear. There is no room for artistry and ingenuity and no danger of sudden upheavals.

Apparently mature industries are not transformed into emerging industries overnight; barriers to entry, though they can change, do so only rarely and never abruptly. By and large the structures are stable. Change is the exception, not the rule.

And in Porter's world the company itself has little significance apart from acting as the vehicle for strategy. The corporate mind exists independently of its body. It sees its competitors and its environment more clearly than it sees itself. It is like the thirsty prisoner who tries to lick raindrops outside his cell only to find his head will not fit through the bars.

Porter's neglect, and that of other business theorists, of the strategist's own company is typically human. The buddhist D. E. Harding described in his book *On Having No Head* a moment of

41

self-forgetfulness while walking in the Himalayas. In an effort to rebuild his sense of self he looked at 'khaki trouserlegs terminating downwards in a pair of brown shoes, khaki sleeves terminating sideways in a pair of pink hands, and a khaki shirtfront terminating upwards in – absolutely nothing whatever! Certainly not in a head.'

Porter and other headless strategists will doubtless argue that corporate self-awareness is not the business of the manager as strategist but of the manager as manager. Their mistake is to suppose these two roles can be separated. They cannot. They are inextricably linked. Appropriate and effective strategy cannot be formulated without a profound understanding and an acute awareness of the essential nature of the company implementing the strategy.

Porter aficionados will point out Porter's second major book, *Competitive Advantage*, was entirely to do with those qualities of companies that affect competitiveness. It is true *Competitive Advantage* discusses, at greater length than did *Competitive Strategy*, the company itself. However, it also shares two other qualities with its predecessor – it is concerned with the shape rather than the soul of things and employs an analytical approach that is fundamentally static.

According to Porter, competitive advantage is a function of both industry structure and of strategy. A company wishing to employ a particular strategy must first establish an appropriate organisational structure. The company is in the control of the strategist and the strategist is in thrall to the structure and maturity of the industry. Each company is located within the industry structure by its position in the 'value chain'. This is a datum which limits the scope of strategic variation. The role of the business leader is to develop a strategy that, given the industry structure and the company's position in the value chain, confers on the company a competitive advantage.

So although Porter appears to be focusing inwards in *Competitive Advantage,* the actual vantage point is little different from that of *Competitive Strategy. Competitive Advantage* is concerned with the role of strategy in developing competitiveness within a stable industrial structure. Porter has next to nothing to say about how the company, with its history, its culture and its personality, constrains strategy and adapts to change.*

* Michael Porter's new book *The Competitive Advantage of Nations* is much more 'dynamic' in this sense.

THE PROPHET OF EXCELLENCE AND CHAOS
In Search of Excellence by Tom Peters and Robert Waterman is
arguably the most successful management book ever written. It was
on the New York bestseller list for 40 weeks. The sequel, *A Passion
for Excellence*, by Peters and Nancy Austin, did almost as well and
at the time of writing *Thriving on Chaos*, written by Peters alone,
was doing pretty nicely too.

The approach of all three books is very different from that of
Porter – less academic, more passionate and more readable. Peters,
particularly in *Thriving on Chaos* rants and raves, belabouring the
managers of his domestic US companies with abusive epithets and
belittling comparisons.

Peters is much more interested than Porter in the exceptional
members of the corporate species; those that challenge the accepted
norms and flout the conventional wisdoms. For him successful
strategy is not the derivative of painstaking analysis but the product
of inspiration and creativity.

In biological terms, Peters takes a mutagenic view of corporate
evolution. The process is driven by new ideas and new approaches
rather than by Porteresque models deduced from analysis and
applied in a disciplined way within more or less static environments.

The environments Peters describes are uncertain and changing.
Surprises (and the Japanese) lurk around every corner. The
successful companies are those that make a virtue of agility and
that see opportunities where others see only dangers. Fred Buggie is
of the same view. He pointed out in his book *New Product
Development Strategies* that the Chinese word for crisis consists of
two characters, one standing for danger and the other for opportunity.

But though the strategist's company is much more important to
Peters than it is to Porter, its significance remains, for the most part,
implicit.

Good strategy means good management. The former is not the
product of the latter, not explicitly at any rate. Strategic innovation,
such as the bat's development of 'chirp' sonar, is seen as a rare
inspiration rather than the creative resolution of environmental
pressures on the one hand and the company's history on the other.

Both Porter and Peters have made important contributions to
strategic management and therefore to the process of corporate
strategy formation. Porter has highlighted the importance of

analysis and Peters has stressed the roles of agility and inspiration. These are necessary elements in good strategy formulation but they are not sufficient. To play Hamlet well one must pay much more attention to the Prince.

THE CORPORATE PERSONALITY

Wally Olins, a pioneer of the modern corporate design industry and one of its most illustrious practitioners, regards himself as a strategic management consultant but he has yet to convince the strategic consultants and their academic fellow-travellers.

The business of his company Wolff Olins is generally regarded as a branch of corporate cosmetics – an application to the company itself of artistic, design-based techniques that had previously been applied only to the company's products.

Corporate design is regarded by most theorists and consultants as a relatively superficial addition to the tool-box that has grown out of the advertising and communications industry.

It is a good business which has demonstrated strong growth over the past decade or so but even those who have 'got religion' about corporate design like Olins and Walter Landor, founder of Landor Associates, have been reluctant to claim too much for it.

They have characterised corporate design as a form of 'permanent communications' for the company in its marketplace. They use typography and colour to standardise the liveries and paperwork of corporate systems so that the company presents a consistent image or corporate identity to the outside world.

But the idea behind corporate design – that the company itself should play a role (sometimes starring, sometimes supporting) in the general corporate communications net – is fundamental. It breaks decisively with the 'eye in the skull' tradition of strategy. Its full significance has yet to be appreciated.

Olins hinted at the central role of corporate identity in his first book *The Corporate Personality: An inquiry into the nature of corporate identity*:

> In the first or heroic period of a company's development the personality of its founder gives it its identity. In the second or technocratic phase the carefully cultivated and developed corporate identity is the major element that provides this link. It becomes the substitute for the personality of the entrepreneur.

44

It is not such a huge step from here to the notion that the personality of the founding entrepreneur acts as the protopersonality of the company itself as it weans itself from total dependence on the energy and vision of its founder(s).

The second Olins book, *Corporate Identity* is a magnificent *trompe l'oeil*, so beautifully illustrated and designed that it comes close to obscuring the development of the author's ideas in the intervening decade. Everyone knew by then that Olins was a consummate corporate designer. Only a few recognised he was also a considerable corporate philosopher.

Olins expects corporate identity to become 'the most significant factor in making a choice between one company and its products and another' and he believes it will also come to be seen as a crucial factor in the recruitment and retention of staff. 'People need to belong,' he argues. 'They need to know where they stand, they need their loyalties underlined and emphasised, and they desperately need – we all desperately need – the magic of symbolism.'

In the absence of 'carefully cultivated and developed' corporate identities, companies have default personalities, just as they have default or, as Porter calls them, 'implicit' strategies. Both are more than mere appearance. They need to be understood in the context of the histories of the companies concerned and their contemporary environments before companies can make sound strategic moves.

OUCHI'S A–Z
The concluding chapter of William Ouchi's fine book *Theory Z: How American Business can meet the Japanese Challenge* has the intriguing title 'The Survival of Business Americanus'. It is one of the first hints in modern management literature of the idea that companies can be regarded as life forms engaged in a struggle for survival in a hostile environment. But Ouchi does not explore the idea in any depth.

He uses it as a rhetorical device in a four-page summary of the main argument in *Theory Z* which is that American companies will need to emulate certain aspects of the Japanese corporate culture if they are to compete successfully in world markets.

Ouchi points to the emphasis the Japanese place on generalism rather than specialisation; the importance they attach to clear and powerful corporate philosophies; their participative decision-making style and the very different perceptions the Japanese have of scale economies and the need for adaptability.

45

But Ouchi gets closer to the evolutionary approach and the idea of the nice company than most other theorists. He shares with Tom Peters the belief that corporate evolution is driven by mutagens – he calls his new Theory Z companies 'deviants' – and the way he describes the dialectical development process is classically Darwinian:

> Fortunately deviants exist in every age . . . (they are) the source of variation that makes possible the continued adaptation and survival of the population . . . As in any other competitive natural environment, what will follow will be a process of natural selection. If the Type Z indeed has superior competitive characteristics, then it will get the best people, produce the best goods and services at competitive prices, and survive. The others will be selected against by nature and will fail.

Ouchi is the opposite of an 'eye in the skull' theorist. He is fascinated by the insides of companies and he implies throughout his book, though he never states it, that competitive advantage consists, first and foremost, of managerial excellence at the business unit level, rather than of strategic skill.

Ouchi fails however to take the next logical step of regarding companies as a separate species. His evolutionary speculations are metaphorical, not literal. He says that 'only through generational change can a population of organisms change its dominant properties'. This identifies him, to the extent that he is evolutionist, as a sociobiologist.

He fails to recognise that relatively short-lived strategies and management teams are the selectable features of a company and that therefore significant *corporate* evolution can take place within a single *human* generation.

But in *Theory Z* Ouchi makes an important contribution to the debate. He reaches some of the same conclusions as the present book, though by a different route, and is enormously refreshing in that he is one of the few management authors of recent years who makes no mention of takeovers, mergers or acquisitions.

THE COLLECTOR AS STRATEGIST
Two decades ago something rather odd happened to management theory. Until then it was developing along a more or less coherent path, with the very reasonable purpose of improving the general

methodology of running companies. The idea that market share was important had evolved out of the more general notion of economies of scale, and in response to a growing awareness that, for the purposes of normal planning, market size was effectively finite.

Then Bruce Henderson, founder of the Boston Consulting Group (BCG), now one of the world's leading management consultancies, threw a mutagen into strategic theory. He made management teams aware of themselves as discrete organisms existing independently of companies. Management became a resource. If it could run one company, it could run several, thus raising the question of which it should run. The idea of 'portfolio strategy', plotted on the 'Boston matrix' as it came to be known, had been born.

Instead of one business unit generating a single figure at the bottom line, managers began to think in terms of a portfolio of businesses, each with its own peculiar qualities. The four types identified in BCG's original matrix were 'cash cows', 'stars', 'wild cats' and 'dogs.'

BCG's prescription, and that of many emulators of the portfolio approach, was to seek to achieve a proper balance between the basic types. Cash-generating 'cash cows' should be used to finance cash-consuming 'stars' and 'wild cats', and the 'dogs' (poor cash generators with slow growth) should be sold.

This reductionist approach to business gained a powerful grip on the imaginations of business leaders. The question 'how good is my business and how can I improve it?' was replaced by the question 'do I have the right mix of businesses and, if not, what should I sell and what should I buy?'

The matrix itself did not lead inevitably to the idea of the acquisition-led strategy because it can accommodate, in theory at any rate, the idea of mutable types (cash cows can be transmuted into stars, and dogs into cash cows).

But that was not the way it was interpreted or sold. In practice businesses were deemed to be typecast which left the buying and selling of businesses as the only practicable way of achieving the right mix. Big business leaders, particularly in the English-speaking world, copped out.

They repudiated the tradition of seeking profit improvement through good operational management and embraced instead the role of the portfolio manager. They became company traders, more interested in financial than in industrial matters.

As Porter pointed out in a 1987 *Harvard Business Review*

article, a large part of the management baby had thereby been thrown out with the bathwater. 'Competition occurs at the business unit level' Porter insisted. 'Diversified companies do not compete; only their business units do. Unless a corporate strategy places *primary* attention [my emphasis] on nurturing the success of each unit, the strategy will fail, no matter how elegantly constructed.'

Notwithstanding Porter's admonition, the diversified, acquisition-led corporation has become a prime focus of attention in the management literature. The disappearance of much of the management baby has gone largely unnoticed. Theorists have become increasingly preoccupied with the intricacies of acquisition pricing, financial engineering, and control systems. Business units have been neglected.

Michael Goold and Andrew Campbell, in their book *Strategies and Styles: The Role of the Centre in Managing Diversified Corporations*, exemplify the trend. The authors focus their attention entirely on the central management methodologies of 16 of the UK's largest holding companies.

They describe how the leaders of such organisations address the managerial problems associated with the fact of diversification, omitting to note the obvious solution to such problems which is to avoid them by not diversifying in the first place.

Even so, the contrast in styles is striking. At oil giant BP, for example, strategy is the prerogative of the centre while operating issues are the responsibility of divisional managers. At BTR, the holding company put together by Sir Owen Green with the acquisition of companies like Thomas Tilling and Dunlop, the system is the opposite. 'We delegate the decisions on business strategy down to the managers in touch with their markets,' said Lionel Stammers, BTR's joint chief executive, 'but we keep control of operating issues and ratios at the centre.' (*Strategies and Styles*.)

Goold and Campbell identified three generic styles in Britain's large diversified holding companies: Strategic Planning at one end of the spectrum, Strategic Control in the middle and Financial Control at the other end.

With the Strategic Planning system, employed by the industrial gases group BOC for example, the centre is very much hands-on. It can and does get involved in quite detailed issues within individual business units. It takes a long-term view of performance and is unlikely to fire managers because of poor short-term results.

The Financial Control system, employed by Hanson, the largest of Britain's acquisition-led conglomerates, and by BTR, GEC, Tarmac and Ferranti, is more hands-off and much tougher on short-term failure. In these companies the budget is all important. If it is met, well and good, but if it is missed there's hell to pay. As one senior manager interviewed by Goold and Campbell put it, 'If you succeed, you are rewarded. If you don't, you are out.'

All three systems are based on a form of corporate patronage which diverts the focus of management away from the marketplace in which each business unit operates and towards the centre from which the patronage is distributed. In this kind of environment, where the discipline of the patron is substituted for the discipline of the marketplace, it becomes more important to meet budgets than to maximise profits.

Although, as Goold and Campbell have shown, the emphasis on short- and long-term maximisation varies according to the control style of the centre, generally speaking holding companies and conglomerates depend for their success on the vision of the centre, sometimes acting as strategist and sometimes as banker. Since the centre has, by definition, less industry-specific knowhow than the business unit managers, it is very hard for the business units to sell long-term strategic ideas to the centre. Strategy at the business unit level becomes little more than a series of tactical plans. The full potential of the business unit is rarely considered and never exploited.

For these reasons, the acquisition-led strategy is not so much a strategy as a disciplinary procedure. It is appropriate only in 'mature' industries in which bad habits have evolved and where there is a consequent need for restructuring.

Once this restructuring has been completed and what Porter calls the 'added value of review' has been fully exploited, the rationale of holding company membership, from the business unit's point of view, disappears. As we shall see in the next chapter the once-and-for-all nature of the benefits that can be derived from conglomerations of business units is not recognised by conglomerate builders. The portfolios stay together long after the disciplinary procedures have completed their work. Moreover, acquisitive activity continues long after industries have been picked clean of inefficiencies.

TFT IN CONTEXT
The TFT strategy introduced in the previous chapter has very little in common with most of the ideas so far discussed in this one. Apart

49

from Ouchi, the popular business theorists of modern times have been almost wholly preoccupied with competition. The literature on cooperative strategies like TFT is sparse.

Richard P. Nielsen, of the Boston College School of Management, noted in the *Strategic Management Journal* (*SMJ*, *Vol. 9, 1988*), that since the launch of the *SMJ* only two articles had been about cooperative strategy (his was the third).

Nielsen is an intellectual Quaker. He acknowledges his debt to the Quaker economist Kenneth Boulding and to the principle of Quaker business philosophy which holds that harmony is desirable as an end as well as merely a means. He points to the Lloyds and Barclays banking groups, the Price Waterhouse accountancy firm, Lever Bros and the J. Walter Thompson advertising agency (bought in 1988 by the British marketing company, WPP) as examples of successful, modern organisations founded on Quaker principles.

Nielsen knows about Axelrod's work too. He is particularly interested in the game theory approach to strategy formation. He identifies four basic cooperative strategies (pool, exchange, de-escalate and contingency) and, echoing the BCG classification of companies, he proposes four generic market types: declining (negative sum), mature (zero sum), growing (positive sum) and transitional (changing from mature to growing).

Nielsen's fourth type – in transition from mature to growing – is of particular interest. In asserting that a zero-sum game can be transformed into a positive-sum game by the introduction of cooperative strategies, Nielsen denies the BCG assumption of immutable types. But he stops short of proposing the existence of evolutionary pressure driving strategic change towards the cooperative model. His is a pluralist view. He contents himself with the conclusion that 'Inter-organisation cooperation *can* improve efficiency and *can* make a great deal of short-, medium- and long-term strategic sense in a wide range of environments (and) circumstances' (my emphasis).

He also observes with some glee that none other than Bruce Henderson, the high priest of portfolio strategy, acknowledged at a 1985 symposium in Barcelona, that there are cooperative alternatives to a crude 'survival of the fittest' model.

The more thoroughgoing theory of corporate evolution proposed in this book asserts not that cooperative strategies can be better than competitive ones but that they are *better in all situations and at every stage* of an industry's life cycle. The point put formally goes as follows: the sum of the game will be maximised when cooperation is maximised. (Because the game involves people as well as companies, it automatically penalises price-fixing and other kinds of behaviour disadvantageous to the consumer.)

We are also more emphatic than Nielsen about the nature of the business game. He equates declining and mature industries with negative- and zero-sum games whereas my position is that the whole business game is positive-sum. It is the inherent ability of business to create wealth that drives corporate evolution.

But TFT is not just a good (and possibly the best) strategy for positive-sum games. It is also an effective agent of Nielsen-like transitions from lower- to higher-sum games or, as I would put it, TFT is the means by which the sub-optimal competitive style is replaced (through the operation of Axelrod clusters) by the optimal cooperative style.

If it is the case that switching from competition to cooperation invariably improves the creativity of the game (increases its sum), then a wholly new element of strategy is introduced. The goal of strategy formation extends from merely devising winning strategies within the game as it is presently played, to include the devising of strategies likely to change the game in ways which increase its sum.

THE MAXIMUM-SUM GAME

I have argued elsewhere that powerful disintegrative forces are at work within a corporate world apparently locked in a spasm of integration. They go by names like 'unbundling' and 'divestment' and are manifested by management buy-outs and buy-ins, de-mergers and the increased use of sub-contractors (for example computer maker Amstrad's use of Far Eastern manufacturers, and the so-called 'food brokers' which give small food manufacturers access to large retailers).

P. Y. Barreyre, of Grenoble University's business school, calls this vertical disintegration 'impartition'. As he explained in a *Strategic Management Journal* article: 'a firm imparts when, in order to allocate its own resources to activities more congruent with its strategic objectives, it contracts out instead of doing in-house.' The French call the choice between in- or out-house *'faire ou faire-faire'*. The English is less euphonious and so became the acronym DIOCO (Doing In-house Or Contracting Out). We also talk of the 'make or buy' decision.

Impartition always involves cooperation. As Barreyre puts it:

'Impartition is not only an economic orientation. Its corollary is a cooperative behaviour towards the outside organisations'. It is done when a firm perceives gain in so doing which is an example, assuming no other firm loses, of a more cooperative style improving the sum of the game. It goes without saying that since impartition, to be successful, requires the imparter to cooperate with the sub-contractor, nice strategies like TFT with an inbuilt propensity to cooperate, are good imparters.

Returning to Porter's 'value chain', one can regard the DIOCO choice as a decision about 'process' as opposed to 'product positioning'. The DIOCO choice determines the size of the segment a company occupies in the value chain. This perspective leads directly to the idea of the 'Value Added Partnership' which we shall consider at greater length in Chapter nine.

THE OTHER PLAYERS

It is important to keep in mind the generality of the theory of corporate evolution. As we saw in the first chapter on business ethics, companies are playing with people as well as other companies.

Most strategy theorists, while acknowledging the interactions between companies and their customers and regulators, see the game of business as strictly a company affair. That may be reasonable enough while competition is seen as not only the dominant but also the natural style of play. But a game theory approach to corporate strategy that allows for a cooperative style of play needs to define the players more widely. It must recognise that human beings and their political institutions also demand a strategic response from companies.

We shall begin to look more closely at the other players in the business game in Chapter Five when we shift our attention to the internal game played between companies and their employees. But before forsaking utterly the old competitive paradigm, we shall investigate in the next chapter its most controversial and most important manifestation – the takeover system.

SUMMARY

- Evolution in the natural world has produced highly sophisticated strategies.

- Modern management theory fails to recognise the importance of a company's history.

- The company is a jury-rig, imperfectly adapted to modern times.

- Porter emphasises analysis and structure.

- Peters stresses creativity and agility.

- Olins and Ouchi introduce the corporate personality.

- The portfolio strategy is an impoverished one.

- Cooperative strategies like TFT do well in positive-sum games.

- An important goal of strategy, in addition to winning games, is to maximise the game's sum. TFT is good at this too.

CHAPTER 4

Having and Eating

Companies are omnivorous and fuel their more or less insatiable appetite for growth in a variety of ways. Their metabolisms reflect the appetites of their current managers but tend to shift between two basic modes. Some companies at some times are vegetarians (herbivores), which forage widely for the human and financial resources they need to sustain 'organic' as opposed to acquisition-led growth.

Other companies at other times are carnivorous and very often cannibalistic. This chapter will look closely at the important phenomenon of corporate cannibalism, more commonly known as the 'takeover'. It will investigate the reasons for its present popularity as the basis of a business strategy (the 'acquisition-led strategy') and discuss the evidence, such as it is, that takeovers benefit shareholders and the economy.

We shall also try to locate within the modern takeover culture the position of the nice company pursuing a strategy similar to (but not necessarily identical with) the 'tit for tat' (TFT) strategy described in Chapter Two.

The takeover culture in general and the acquisition-led strategy in particular are good tests of the TFT strategy. They represent a harsh, carnivorous environment for nice strategies and the present dominance of the takeover culture, and the popularity of the acquisition-led strategy, has the appearance at least of collective stability.

The nice company is not acquisition-led. It may acquire other companies from time to time, but only if they are agreeable. A distinguishing feature of the nice company is that it never makes hostile bids. Indeed, for reasons to do with its internal culture, it finds it hard to make bids of any kind. In Japanese the word for takeover is the same as the word for hijack. The homonym is in tune with the nice company's instincts.

The nice company is also vulnerable during periods of high takeover activity, often being 'taken out' by the nasty, acquisition-led group. The acquisition-led strategy enjoys tax advantages and benefits from an element of self-fulfilment; the market expects acquisition-led companies to do well and so gives them a premium share-rating which helps them to do well.

With the deck so stacked against the nice company, its only protection during high risk periods of so-called 'merger mania' is excellent performance. Only the good survive although the central assertion of this book is that the power of the nice strategy is such that nice companies are good more often than is generally supposed.

We shall conclude the chapter by asking some fundamental questions about the meaning and nature of ownership, and so the significance of acquisitions, in the modern business world.

MERGER MANIA

The first point to note about corporate cannibalism – mergers and acquisitions (M&A) – is that there is no such thing as a merger. The outbreaks of so-called 'merger mania' that occur from time to time in some Western economies are nothing of the kind. For the combination of two companies to rank as a true merger each party would have to exercise equal control over the enlarged organisation following the merger.

This is almost never the case. I challenge anyone to cite one example of a merger in the UK or the US over the past decade where the leadership of the two component companies subsequently shared power in a meaningful way. (It will be recalled that in Chapter two we identified strategies and management teams as the two 'selectable' features in corporate evolution.)

The reason the fiction of the merger has gained such currency is that it is better for tax reasons to describe an acquisition as a merger. Merger accounting confers considerable tax benefits on the enlarged organisation. In the UK, the US and in some other industrialised, capitalist economies, substantial though not always substantive costs associated with the integration of companies following a merger can be written off against tax. Hence the emergence of the 'tax driven' merger where owners (shareholders) in the enlarged company can benefit from an acquisition, in terms of net earnings per share, even though it leads to no real improvement in pre-tax performance.

M&A activity is best regarded as evidence of activity in the 'market for corporate control'. Bids both agreed and hostile are initiated by management teams who believe they can do better for the owners of the target company than the incumbents. This, or so the takeover theory goes, is evolution in action.

As already noted, bidders are frequently aided in this endeavour by tax concessions not available to the non-acquisitive company. It is, however, undoubtedly true that even without such help good managers are able on occasions, but not nearly so frequently as is generally supposed, to deliver on their often explicit promise to target shareholders of better performance.

The market in corporate control is an evolutionary mechanism of the first importance. A successful bid is equivalent to the death of the target company's management team and its strategy or rather its failure to inspire emulators. Ostensibly, it is evidence of a lack of fitness to survive.

The arbiters in these duels are the target company's owners (shareholders) and, to a lesser extent, the owners of the acquiring company. Though management teams, like governments, run things, shareholders are the market in corporate power just as voters are the market in political power. If the takeover is a key evolutionary mechanism in the corporate world, then the shareholder is a key agent of corporate evolution.

The lack of shareholder control over a company's destiny in normal times has been discussed almost as much as the lack of voter power between elections but when a takeover bid is mounted shareholders hold the only cards that matter.

According to modern takeover theory, shareholders decide between competing management teams on the basis of the costs the incumbents and their challengers are respectively imposing or are thought likely to impose. These so-called 'agency costs' of management (management teams are the agents of the shareholders) involve much more than just the salaries, perks and stock options of the executive directors and their senior colleagues, although, as Burton Group's controversial 'super' executive stock option scheme showed, these can become significant in agency cost perceptions.

56

More important than these, however, are management strategy and style. Managers as agents may not always behave in ways that are in the best interests of their principals (shareholders). They may prefer, for example, to run a large company than to run a profitable one. They may sacrifice earnings for growth because they associate their status more closely with the size of the company they run than with its profitability. Or they may prefer a quiet life to a profitable one. Agency costs can be regarded as the value foregone by shareholders because the incumbent management, for reasons of its own, is not exploiting to the full the company's profit opportunities.

The existence of agency costs gave rise to the doctrine that a so-called 'free market in corporate control' is the best and only effective guarantee that shareholders will not be taken to the cleaners (have imposed on them excessive agency costs) by self-indulgent management teams. If management teams try to impose excessive agency costs the company's shares will fall below their maximum theoretical value and so give other management teams the opportunity to buy the company cheaply.

The doctrine was first enunciated in 1965 by Henry G. Manne in a seminal article in the *Journal of Political Economy*, entitled 'Mergers and the Market for Corporate Control'. He declared: 'Only the takeover scheme provides some assurance of competitive efficiency among corporate managers and thereby affords strong protection to the interests of . . . non-controlling shareholders.'

A number of factors have contributed to the escalation of merger activity since then: the relaxation of anti-trust laws, the migration of resources from mature and declining industries, de-regulation and improvements in takeover technology including a plentiful supply of sophisticated corporate finance advice and new financial instruments such as the notorious junk bond.

The original Boston matrix (see Chapter Three) is a bit *passé* now, but the idea of a portfolio mix as a managerial target is still very much alive and remains another important theoretical pillar of the acquisition-led strategy.

It is a nice coincidence that BCG's Bruce Henderson began to develop his matrix at just about the time Henry Manne published his article on mergers and corporate control. As Henderson was providing the strategic logic for mergers, Manne was validating the acquisition-led strategy as a healthy phenomenon, particularly for shareholders.

One of Manne's most ardent and influential intellectual heirs is Professor Michael C. Jensen of the University of Rochester and the Harvard Business School. In an article in the *Midland Corporate Finance Journal* entitled 'The Takeover Controversy: Analysis and Evidence', published at the height of the Anglo-American merger boom in 1986, he said: 'The market for corporate control is creating large benefits for shareholders and for the [US] economy as a whole.'

It creates these riches, argued Jensen, 'by loosening control over vast amounts of resources and enabling them to move more quickly to their highest-valued use.' Jensen is by no means alone in this belief but we shall focus on his work because he is an eloquent and influential spokesman for the pro-merger cause.

But though Jensen claims shareholders *and* the economy benefit from takeovers, he only adduces evidence for shareholder gains. The literature is nonetheless extensive:

- A Morgan Stanley study concluded that total premiums received by shareholders in American target firms in the $239bn worth of acquisitions in 1984 and 1985 amounted to $75bn (31%).
- The US Securities and Exchange Commission (SEC) estimated that shareholders in firms acquired in 260 'tender offers' – these are usually but not always the 'hostile bids' of UK parlance – between January 1981 and May 1985 received immediate gains of $40bn.
- Jensen and Richard S. Ruback showed that hostile bid premiums at the time of the bids had averaged more than 30% historically and in recent years had been running at about 50%. Acquiring firms benefited to a lesser extent – by 4% in hostile takeovers and not at all in agreed 'mergers'.

According to Jensen the prize over which takeover battles are fought is 'free cash flow' – the cash flow that is surplus to the requirements of both day-to-day operations and viable medium- and long-term investment programmes. (What constitutes 'viability' in this sense is a matter of some debate. As we shall see, stockholders tend to judge investment viability indirectly, according to their own investment time horizons.)

In theory all free cash flow should be paid out in the form of dividends. To the extent that it is not, managers are imposing excessive agency costs on owners and, if the evolutionary mechanisms are working properly, they should become vulnerable to a takeover bid.

But how do stockholders actually choose between rival management teams and, more to the point economically, how competent are they to judge what constitutes a company's free cash flow? As far as the free market theory is concerned this is not an admissible question. Officially the competence or otherwise of shareholders is quite beside the point. They are the owners, they decide, and that's the end of the matter.

However, the competence of stockholders to judge what portion of total cash flow is 'free', and therefore to make 'correct' decisions during takeover bids, is of crucial importance for the economy at large. When stockholders regularly get it wrong the performance of the economy suffers and we are all worse off than we would otherwise have been.

ARE MARKETS MYOPIC?

It is not easy to refute or corroborate Jensen's claim that the economy, as well as shareholders, benefits from an active market in corporate control. It may be true, but it is hard to be sure either way because the takeover destroys any possibility of comparing what happens after the takeover with what would have happened had there been no takeover.

But let us suppose, for the moment, that shareholders as a breed suffer from short-sightedness; that they attach too little value to future earnings for the health of the economy as a whole. This is the main argument of the anti-merger camp. If it could be clearly demonstrated that markets are myopic the whole theory of agency costs, and the efficacy of a free market in corporate control as a mechanism for reducing them, would be in trouble.

If shareholders accept bids because they prefer a quick profit to the greater long-term earnings they would have enjoyed had their company remained independent, then it is hard to argue that takeovers reduce agency costs. They may do, but if some bids are accepted because markets are myopic then some bids may be accepted when there are no agency costs. Shareholders, with their defective sight, may simply be denying themselves, and therefore the economy, large long-term gains for the sake of small short-term gains.

This is why Jensen is so anxious to dismiss the idea that

shareholders, particularly the dominant institutions such as pension funds, insurance companies and unit trusts (mutual funds as they are called in the US), are myopic. He cites a study by the Office of the Chief Economist of the SEC which showed that companies with large institutional shareholders are no more prone to being taken over on average; that large institutional shareholdings are not associated with low Research and Development (R&D) spending; that high R&D spenders are not especially vulnerable to bids and that, by and large, share prices respond positively to news of higher R&D budgets.

The pattern of the rhetoric is revealing. The pro-merger camp must not only show that takeovers reduce agency costs but also that they do no harm to self-evidently good things like long-term investment and R&D. (Too much investment — investment that fails to meet target rates of return — is, of course, a type of agency cost.)

The evidence for market myopia is patchy, conflicting and inconclusive but its general drift is not very comforting for the pro-merger camp.

A study by Debra Dennis and John McConnell ('Corporate Mergers and Security Returns', *Journal of Financial Economics*, 1986) showed that most mergers are 'value-creating' for both acquired and acquiring companies which was 'consistent with the "synergy" hypothesis of mergers'. Their data consisted however of gains to shareholders 'around the announcement dates' of 132 mergers. Frederic Scherer of the Brookings Institute pointed out in a *Brookings Review* article that studies showing significant gains for shareholders have all focused on 'stock market reactions during a very short time frame surrounding takeover announcements.'

Scherer said that when the post-takeover interval is extended to two years, the evidence showed that stock prices of the acquiring company decline relative to the levels that would have been expected had they simply mirrored the performance of non-merging companies in comparable risk classes. And he argued that even if initial gains are sustained, that does not mean the predator is running the victim better. The improvement could be due to merger-accounting tax savings.

But in another *Brookings Review* article Douglas H. Ginsburg, Assistant Attorney General of the Antitrust Division of the Justice Department, said the myopic markets thesis 'is not supported in fact any more than it is in economic theory' and 'offers no valid reason to conclude that the wealth created by takeovers is somehow contrary to our national interest.'

Ginsburg argued that studies by John Pound of the Investor Responsibility Research Centre 'refute the hypothesis that there is a systematic flaw in the stock market valuation of takeover targets', show that 'there is no market failure that should cause the government to intervene' and 'clearly point to a net benefit to the economy from takeover activity.'

In Britain a study by Julian Franks and Robert Harris found that in the 30 years up to 1985, UK mergers 'have, on average, been value-creating for both acquiree and acquiror shareholders as measured by equity market prices *around the merger announcement date*' (my emphasis). However, they reached the tentative conclusion that looking over longer post-merger periods would give a very different result.

Another UK study by Professor Stephen Nickell and Sushil Wadhwani concluded that investors value dividends more highly than capital gains and attach excessive weight to current dividends relative to future dividends. This is a powerful refutation of the claim that markets work well. If markets are efficient, shareholders should be indifferent between dividends and capital gains and between current and future dividends, after allowing a normal discount rate. What is one to make of all this?

Let us recapitulate. We began with the Manne thesis that the takeover promotes managerial efficiency and so protects the interests of non-controlling shareholders. We identified management agency costs as the losses incurred by shareholders which an active market in corporate control helps to minimise. We pointed out that the efficacy of an active market in corporate control in reducing agency costs depends crucially on the validity of the efficient market hypothesis (the 'efficient market theology' as Scherer calls it) and we then reviewed research into shareholder gains and market efficiency.

No-one disputes that shareholders do well out of takeovers initially but there is considerable doubt (Scherer, Franks and Harris) about the long-term durability of these gains. Scherer says most of them disappear within two years. If he is right shareholder gains are ephemeral market phenomena, not lasting takeover phenomena.

Moreover, there is also considerable doubt about the validity of the efficient market hypothesis (Nickell and Wadwhani) although the evidence is far from conclusive. This is worrying for the pro-merger camp because even if an active market in corporate control has imposed beneficial managerial disciplines, which it undoubtedly has, it may, if markets are inefficient, have also produced disadvantageous results which offset the disciplinary benefits. The less efficient markets are – and as we have seen there are serious tax distortions in the corporate control market – the less faith one can have in the precision of the takeover discipline.

The two key questions as far as the economy is concerned are: 'what makes for good industrial performance?' and 'is there evidence that market inefficiencies inhibit good performance?' To be more specific, do market inefficiencies and distortions give such an overwhelming edge to a particular style (the acquisitive style) that other styles (such as the nice style), which are inherently more productive, are unable to establish themselves. If so, the nice company is clearly destined for extinction.

But the outlook for the nice company is not as gloomy as the present popularity and tax advantages of the acquisition-led company might suggest. The reason for this is very simple – mergers do not appear to work.

THE PHILOSOPHY OF LAISSEZ FAIRE

Before assessing the evidence, such as it is, for and against Jensen's claim that an active market in corporate control produces significant benefits for the economy at large, I will look at some of the philosophical issues associated with the debate.

Jensen *et al* will argue that as far as performance outcomes are concerned the onus of proof lies with the anti-merger camp because a free market in corporate control is consistent with the prevailing *laissez faire* orthodoxy. A less than wholly free market in corporate control would restrict the freedom of shareholders. Since the balance of the evidence, such as it is, suggests shareholders benefit, at the time of merger announcements at any rate, from merger activity, there have to be very good reasons to limit that freedom.

There is an irony here. The origins of the modern *laissez faire* movement, which has had such a profound effect on Western economic policy over the past decade, lie in the Libertarian movement associated with the Virginia Polytechnic in the US, the Adam Smith Institute in the UK and with such thinkers as Robert Nozick, Murray Rothbard and Milton Friedman's son, David.

Their fundamentalist approach to economics has generated the notion of minimalist government. They argue that with one notable exception *all* functions of modern government, including defence, the enforcement of law and the administration of justice can, in theory at any rate, be supplied by the market.

The one exception they allow, indeed insist on, is a robust anti-trust agency. The Libertarians regard the market in corporate control as a special case, requiring special treatment, because it has implications for other freedoms.

These threatened freedoms are what Sir Karl Popper's 'paradox of democracy' is about. Popper urges that democracy should not be too free otherwise it will permit the establishment of its antithesis, tyranny. The rise to power in Europe this century, through democratic processes, of Fascist and Communist tyrannies were arguably products of this paradox.

There is also a 'paradox of free markets' which states that the market, particularly the market in corporate control, cannot be too free otherwise it will permit the emergence of its antithesis, monopoly.

Thus, on closer inspection, the philosophical basis for a free market in corporate control is much weaker than the pro-merger camp implies. It is by no means clear that the onus of proof should be on those who propose tougher anti-trust laws.

It should also be recognised that the business establishment has a strong vested interest in maintaining a free market in corporate control. The establishment is big business and many (but by no means all) big businesses have become big through mergers. They have acquired political power and it is in their interests to deploy that power to preserve their freedom to make more acquisitions. I am not alleging an establishment conspiracy to frustrate moves to tighten anti-trust policies but I am suggesting there is an unconscious establishment prejudice in favour of a totally free market in corporate control.

Signs of this prejudice are evident in the flawed logic of pro-merger research. For example, to point to immediate shareholder gains as evidence that mergers are a 'good thing' is to employ a circular argument. There would be no mergers if there were no share price gains because it would not be in the interests of shareholders to accept bids. Shareholder gains are an integral part of the merger phenomenon and so cannot be used to show its benefits. Jensen's argument reduces to the claim that mergers are good because they occur.

And as Michael Porter has pointed out (*HBR*, May–June, 1987) 'the short-term market reaction is a highly imperfect measure of the long-term success of diversification,' (or acquisition) 'and no self-respecting executive would judge a corporate strategy this way.' The weakness of the short-term market reaction test of acquisition success was vividly demonstrated in 1986 when UK drinks group Guinness orchestrated an illicit share-manipulation campaign, involving the notorious US arbitrageur Ivan Boesky amongst others, to win the bid battle for Distillers. In the short term both Guinness and Distillers shareholders made substantial gains but these were ephemeral because they were the result of the artificially inflated Guinness share price.

MERGERS ARE MAD
One of the most bizarre features of the merger debate is the disproportionate amount of attention paid to stock price movements as opposed to the actual performance outcomes.

One reason for this, as noted above, is that it is hard, in practice, to confront and compare the merger result with the non-merger result. What needs to be shown to validate the Jensen/Ginsburg position is that mergers generally improve performance. Evidence of this kind is hard to come by and is generally cited very selectively.

Dennis C. Mueller, in an article published after the end of the 1960s/70s merger boom (*Journal of Banking and Finance*, 1977), concluded that though the theoretical debate was still very much alive, 'the empirical literature . . . draws a surprisingly consistent picture. Whatever the stated or unstated goals of managers are, the mergers they have consummated have on average not generated extra profits for the acquiring firms [and] have not resulted in increased economic efficiency.'

Though a recommendation for policy-makers to proceed cautiously 'in view of the conflicting evidence' seemed reasonable, Mueller noted:

it is in fact a recommendation to accept the neoclassical theories of mergers, stick with the *status quo* policy on mergers and accept

64

this policy's underlying premise of an invisible hand guiding the market for control.

We now have almost a century of accumulated evidence as to the effects of a *laissez faire* policy towards mergers. Enough time has elapsed and evidence been gathered that one can say this policy experiment has not been a success.

The time has come to try a new experiment. I think we can now legitimately ask managers to prove prior to a merger, that this merger is likely 'to substantially lessen' inefficiency.

In a book published three years later in 1980 (*The Determinants and Effects of Mergers*), Mueller and others studied the impact of mergers on company efficiency in the UK, the US, West Germany, France, Belgium, Holland and Sweden. The results showed slightly improved net profits in four countries, including the UK, as a result of mergers but uniformly lower growth in all countries. Returns to shareholders were improved in four countries (including the UK) but the difference disappeared after three years.

This corroborates the intuitive conclusion derived from the examples of West Germany and Japan, where the incidence of mergers has, in the past at any rate, been low and non-existent respectively, namely that economic performance and the level of activity in the market for corporate control are negatively correlated.

A study of Federal Trade Commission data by Scherer and David Ravenscraft (*The Profitability of Mergers*, Bureau of Economics, FTC Working Paper 136, 1986) found no evidence that victims of hostile bids were poor performers and little evidence of post-merger profitability gains. Indeed, in cases where post-merger profits fell, they fell more rapidly than those of the non-merging control group.

Scherer and Ravenscraft concluded: 'the society-wide benefits of takeovers have almost surely been exaggerated by their advocates; the risks are real, though poorly measured. The debate needs to be refocused on the fundamental question of what makes for good industrial performance.' And there is plenty more grist for the sceptic's mill.

A *Business Week* article in June 1985 concluded that nearly two-thirds of mergers fail; a *Journal of Business Strategy* article (summer 1986) estimated that a third of all mergers fail because of poor, post-merger integration. As General Electric was contemplating the acquisition of United Technologies, a senior GE executive said nine that out of ten acquisitions 'are a waste of time and a destruction of shareholders' value' (*Business Week*, 20 April 1987).

Unilever chairman Mike Angus remarked in Summer 1988 that 'the takeover used to be the price of bad management. Now it's the price of good management.' Management consultants McKinseys, in a study of mergers between 1972 and 1983 involving America's top 200 companies, found that only 23% were successful (as measured by increases in shareholder value). The highest success rate (33%) was in small acquisitions in related fields and the lowest (8%) was in large acquisitions in unrelated fields.

Scherer says most mergers reduce efficiency because they reduce competition. An SEC economist quoted by Tom Peters said: 'most industries where we have competitive difficulties are not exactly filled with pygmy companies. You don't put two turkeys together and make an eagle.'

Michael Porter, in a study of the diversification behaviour of 33 large US companies, found that 53% of acquisitions in new industries were subsequently divested including nearly three-quarters of acquisitions in areas unrelated to core businesses (*HBR*, May–June 1987).

Porter used shareholder value (capital gains plus dividends during the period 1950–86) as his yardstick. He acknowledged that ideally shareholder value associated with diversification should be compared with what shareholder value would have been had there been no diversification. Since, for reasons we have already discussed, this is impossible, he used the number of diversified business units retained as a proxy. He concluded: 'only the lawyers, investment bankers and original sellers have prospered in most of these acquisitions, not the shareholders.'

A study by *Financial Weekly*, published in Spring 1988, of the nice and nasty members of Britain's top 100 companies (nasty companies were defined as those that had made one or more hostile bids during the past six years) showed that in terms of earnings per share growth, nice companies substantially out-performed nasty companies. This was despite the fact that the market had been acting as if the opposite was the case (see Chapter Six for a fuller report).

Porter tried to explain the poor record of diversification in general and diversifying acquisitions in particular by reference to three of his basic premises about corporate strategy.

We met the first in the last chapter – competition takes place between business units, not diversified companies, and that unless corporate strategy gives priority to 'nurturing the success of each unit' it will fail, however well constructed the business portfolio.

His second premise is that 'diversification inevitably adds costs and constraints to business units'. The units have to comply with the control and reporting requirements of the corporate centre, their strategies have to be consistent with those of their stable mates and they must 'forgo the opportunity to motivate employees with direct equity ownership'.

Porter's third premise is the most telling: 'shareholders can readily diversify themselves.' Why should investors approve of diversification behaviour, in view of its poor record, when they can diversify their portfolios more readily and more cheaply (given the need for corporate diversifiers to pay a control premium) themselves?

Apart from anything else, the merger is a sterile act compared with the building of a new factory. It merely shuffles the pack. It can improve but it cannot create. Business leaders inspired by portfolio ideas and armed with arsenals of modern takeover weapons might make good estate agents in the next life but they would make lousy architects.

Mueller pointed out in his 1977 article that

> mergers compete directly with capital investment, R&D and other investment-type expenditures for cash flows and managerial decision-making capacities. While a manager is perhaps indifferent between whether a given rate of expansion is achieved through internal or external growth, society is likely to be better off through the creation of additional assets.

So although, for reasons that are not clear, acquisition-led companies are popular with investors, they do not appear to have the performance edge. Some do well and doubtless contribute to economic restructuring and a more rigorous managerial culture, but by and large the prospects for the acquisition-led strategy look bleak. It seems to work initially, in that it delivers extra shareholder value (for target company shareholders at any rate) at the time of the merger, but the follow-up is usually poor.

Acquisition-led companies are not, on average, impressive

long-term performers. Within the next decade or so they are likely to become unfashionable as nice companies get into their stride.

In short, the notion that mergers help to improve the corporate species is a more plausible and a more powerful idea than it is a reality. A 1986 study by Holl and Pickering of the University of Manchester Institute of Science and Technology supports this view. They compared a matched sample of 50 abandoned and 50 consummated UK mergers. The results showed that bids that succeed worsen performance but that the threat of a merger, when successfully resisted, leads to improved performance.

It is worth noting that much of the above can be applied to a new variation of portfolio strategy that I have christened 'brand portfolio strategy'. In this, the protagonist, instead of buying other companies, buys brands to achieve some kind of ideal geographical or functional coverage. The argument loomed large at the time of Swiss food giant Nestlé's hostile bid for UK confectionery group Rowntree for £2.5bn in 1988.

The Nestlé bid was motivated by the axiom of marketing theory which states that: 'it's cheaper to buy brands than build them'. Note the absence in this statement, which makes it as silly as it is influential, of any price or time qualifiers. It is equivalent to saying there is *no* price and *no* time at which it would be cheaper to build brands than to buy them. How do any brands get built in the first place if this is the case?

The Rowntree affair is also evidence of market inefficiencies the absence of which, as we have seen, is an integral part of the pro-merger position. Before the Rowntree auction (another Swiss company, Jacobs–Suchard, was also a bidder) the market valued Rowntree at a little over £1bn. Nestlé bought it for more than twice that. Either the Swiss group grossly overpaid or the market had grossly undervalued Rowntree before the bid.

On the subject of market inefficiency another powerful piece of anecdotal evidence was the worldwide collapse of share prices in October 1987. Markets were predicting a major world recession. Its failure to transpire required a modification of a delightfully wry observation by US economist Paul Samuelson some years previously: 'of the last five recessions the market has predicted nine'. The market's score is now ten out of five.

WHO REALLY OWNS COMPANIES?

The purpose of this chapter has been to refute the conventional wisdom about the efficacy of the merger as an agent of economic restructuring and as a discipline on management. I do not deny that mergers, and particularly the threat of takeovers, have contributed significantly to a quite remarkable improvement in management quality over the past decade in both the US and the UK but particularly in the UK.

My point is that these benefits have been won at a cost and that inefficient markets have caused merger mania to escalate to a pathological degree such that long-term business planning is being seriously inhibited. Even if it could be shown clearly that mergers have been of net benefit in the past, that would not necessarily mean they will continue to be so. The corporate environment is changing and may now be emerging from a period in which the merger was even a theoretically effective discipline.

According to Porter in his *HBR* article:

the days when portfolio management was a valid concept of corporate strategy are past. In the face of increasingly well-developed capital markets, attractive companies with good managements show up on everyone's computer screen and attract top dollar in terms of acquisition premium. Simply contributing capital isn't contributing much. A sound strategy can easily be funded; small to medium-size companies don't need a munificent parent.

Moreover, for the takeover to be a good discipline the wielders of the disciplinary instrument, the shareholders, must have the ultimate power. In practice this requires not only that their decisions should be final but also that their scrip (stocks and shares) should always and inalienably reflect and embody the full value of the company.

Five years ago that would have gone without saying but nowadays it looks as if shareholders have begun to lose their grip on the real value underpinning their investments. They do not own companies as unequivocally as they once did. In law their property rights remain inalienable but in practice the value of the companies they 'own' is becoming less and less identifiable with the shares they hold.

Take the case of the UK investment bank Hill Samuel. During the run-up to the liberalisation of the UK securities industry in October 1986 (the Big Bang), Hill Samuel was preparing to become an important player in the new, enlarged securities industry. To this end it bought the respected Scottish stockbroking firm Wood Mackenzie.

Buoyant market conditions carried Hill Samuel through the first year but already, by the spring of 1987, some of its directors had begun to listen sympathetically to representations from Wood Mackenzie that much more capital was needed if the securities division was to stand any chance of making it in the big league.

They therefore responded positively in July to a bid approach from the Union Bank of Switzerland (UBS), already strongly placed in London as the owner of top rank broking firm Phillips & Drew. Hill Samuel's chief executive Christopher Castleman was disgusted. He recalled the occasion in an interview with *Financial Weekly* in early 1988: 'When UBS made their approach I felt that Hill Samuel didn't need to lose its independence. The securities business was too small a part of the group for the rest to be sacrificed for it.' He resigned.

The effect on the Hill Samuel share price was dramatic. Its market value soared from £475m to £710m in the expectation UBS would bid at a price valuing the group at £740m. Five weeks later the talks foundered. The market value plunged from £700m to £600m despite continuing bid speculation and the appearance on the bank's share register of a bevy of arbitrageurs.

A month later another row broke out within Hill Samuel. After the failure of the UBS talks the bank's two star corporate finance executives, Trevor Swete and Chris Roshier, began talking about a takeover to Barclays de Zoete Wedd (BZW), a large, integrated securities house. When they told Castleman's successor David Davies of their discussions he sacked them. The Hill Samuel share price came under severe pressure. The group's market value fell from £630m to £586m.

To what extent can Hill Samuel shareholders be deemed to have been the sole owners of the company if the dismissals of Swete and Roshier could reduce the market value by £44m? What is ownership in this sense if, by merely exercising their right to walk away, two people can inflict such damage on its value?

Merchant banks like Hill Samuel are examples of what I call the 'knowhow company' – a company whose main assets are the talents and experience of its staff. Other examples include advertising agencies, law and accountancy firms, hospitals, universities, newspapers and computer software companies.

But the equivocal nature of corporate ownership is not confined to such companies. Even in traditional industrial companies, where ownership is more closely related to tangible assets such as plant and equipment, there are pockets of knowhow working (I call them 'pro-teams') which account for a disproportionate amount of the company's value.

The main problem with the old concept of corporate ownership is that slavery is unlawful. Shareholders cannot own a company where the value is embedded in able, mobile people, in the same way that they can own a traditional manufacturing company where the value is embedded in plant and equipment bolted to the floor. Until investors acknowledge this and recognise that they must pay with their loyalty for the loyalty of their key employees, they are going to be ambushed constantly by walk-outs.

This divergence of ownership and value is growing and becoming more widespread. Over the past two decades or so a sea change has been taking place in the business world, characterised by the emergence of a financial surplus and the development of a corresponding shortage of human competence and ability.

The old concept of ownership is valid only so long as the contribution of shareholders, which is financial capital, remains the scarce resource. In a situation of financial surplus, where too much money is seeking too few profitable ideas and the ability to implement them, shareholders must lose power. The value of their shares becomes increasingly dependent on the loyalty of their company's value-creating employees and that loyalty is in turn dependent on the way in which the company is managed.

In a *Financial Weekly* article in October, 1987, in the wake of the Hill Samuel affair, I tried to estimate just how dependent the quoted UK investment banks were on their staff. It was a rough analysis but the results were interesting. They are reproduced in Table 4.1, showing net assets and market value. We called the difference between these variables 'people-dependent' (P-D) assets:

Table 4.1

HUMAN ASSETS IN UK INVESTMENT BANKS
(Financial Weekly, 17.10.87)

Company	Market Value £m	*Assets* Net £m	P-D £m	P-D ratio	Staff	P-D/head £'000
SG Warburg	862	506	356	0.41	2164	164.5
Morgan Grenfell	818	371	447	0.55	2675	167.1
Hill Samuel	630	194	436	0.69	5212	83.7
(−Swete/Roshier	586	194	392	0.67	5210	75.2)
Hambros	560	251	309	0.55	4118	75.0
Kleinwort Benson	530	365	165	0.31	2402	68.7
Schroders	402	177	225	0.56	1030	218.4
Guinnes Peat	334	159	175	0.52	1045	167.5
Henry Ansbacher	136	54	82	0.60	319	257.1
Brown Shipley	85	44	41	0.48	733	55.9
AVERAGES				0.52		139.8

(excluding − Swete/Roshier)

Sources: Extel and Datastream.

The wide variation in the right-hand column reflects varying mixes of business. Hill Samuel was actually much less dependent on its key people than other investment banks, largely because it had a substantial retail operation. Banks like Schroders and Henry Ansbacher are more vulnerable to departures and defections because they are more dependent on high value-added business such as corporate finance.

OUT OF SWEETNESS . . .
In an environment where takeovers are fashionable, not only with business theorists but also with investors, the nice company is at a considerable disadvantage.

It is not in its nature to be acquisitive so it cannot exploit the tax advantages associated with mergers and neither can it become the beneficiary of the high share-ratings associated with the popularity of the acquisition-led strategy. The nice company is at risk when merger mania is rampant. It can be, and often is, 'taken out' as the modern parlance has it.

But the nice company is also a tough competitor in the business game. It tends to perform well (see also Chapter six) despite its apparent strategic disadvantage and in any case there is little evidence that the acquisitive strategy delivers durable, incremental value. Indeed, what evidence there is points to the opposite conclusion.

In a changing cultural environment the nice company also has a considerable edge in people management. As we shall see in the next chapter, niceness is an internal style as much as it is an external strategy. It recognises the significance of the shift in the balance of power between financial and human capital and is better at hanging on to the store of value represented by its key people. In short, the nice company has an understanding of the importance of its 'knowhow capital' and puts effort and resources into nurturing it.

Its reluctance to acquire protects it from the serious cultural problems associated with post-merger integration and when it does acquire another company it is invariably a welcome bidder and so less likely to be troubled by the subsequent defections of key people who regret their loss of independence.

Moreover, the nice company's characteristic emphasis on organic as opposed to acquisition-led growth tends to create a more stimulating internal environment which further reduces staff turnover (which is rapidly becoming the most important of all business ratios).

It is not enough to be nice. It is necessary to be nice to succeed in the long run but it is also necessary to be tough. It is worth recalling the four qualities of TFT to which Axelrod attributed its success in his computer tournaments. TFT is nice; TFT is retaliatory in that it punishes nastiness immediately; TFT is forgiving in that it will cooperate as soon as its opponent cooperates, and TFT is clear. Once encountered, the TFT strategy is instantly recognisable.

In the long run the market is likely to realise its mistake and cease to give premium ratings to predatory companies. Though the market is not always right it has an urge to improve itself. It will remain deluded only for so long. This impending change of heart in financial markets about the merits or otherwise of the acquisition-led strategy is one of the features of the changing financial environment I shall discuss in Chapter Six.

SUMMARY

- The theory of takeovers alleges economic as well as corporate benefits but fails to adduce evidence for the former.

- There is some evidence that markets are inefficient (myopic).

- The prevailing *laissez faire* philosophy does not support the case for a totally free market in corporate control.

- Mergers do not appear to add value to companies.

- Ownership rests with shareholders *and* employees.

- The nice company, partly because it is a good employer, has considerable defensive qualities in what remains, for the time being, a hostile environment.

CHAPTER 5

Inside The Nice Company

In an article in *The Guardian* in March, 1988 journalist Paul Fisher described the plight of Mike Gascoigne, a 38-year-old computer programmer who resigned from a well-paid job when he found himself working on a new air-launched missile system.

Gascoigne hated the work. He had made it clear in his interview that he disliked the idea of working on military projects but had been inveigled into the job notwithstanding. He was bitter and deeply concerned about what he described as the Ministry of Defence's 'takeover' of the scientific world.

Fisher also described the case of 24-year-old Peter Keevil, a computer hardware engineer who had left a large defence contractor for similar reasons. Unlike Gascoigne he had quickly found anther job in the area of computer-aided design (CAD) which he liked much better.

Keevil's attitude was less uncompromising than Gascoigne's. He told Fisher he was not a pacifist and was well aware his work in CAD might easily turn out to have military applications. He could not rationalise what he had done but he could describe his state of mind. He said: 'I feel more relaxed now. I was in a dark grey area; now it's light grey.'

Both men were clients of Exchange Resources, a high-tech recruitment agency set up by Tony Willson after a conscience-bruising career working on the Trident and Chevaline missile projects and the Ptarmigan military communications system.

Exchange Resources specialises in non-military, high-tech jobs. Its literature spells out its business idea. It tells potential employers that Exchange Resource people 'want to work on technology that is not repressive or debilitating to the economy and who, when their views are fully considered, are highly motivated and less likely to job-hop.' It promises potential clients that it will try to the best of its abilities, 'to find you suitable employment in organisations which respect your views . . . and to offer individual counselling on career, ethics and other personal issues.'

If Gascoigne's and Keevil's opinions on how well their views reflect those of their peers are anything to go by, Tony Willson should do well. 'Most of the people,' Keevil said, 'have qualms about military work'. Gascoigne believes that 'given the choice, most people would prefer to do something else than work for the military, but they have families to feed and mortgages to pay.'

THE POWER OF SCARCITY

Karl Erik Sveiby and I have argued elsewhere (*Managing Know-how*) that over the past two decades or so a sea change has taken place in the balance of power between human capital on the one hand and financial capital on the other.

The time is past when the game of resource matching in business could be summarised as too many ideas chasing too little money. Nowadays the boot is on the other foot. If it is an axiom of capitalism that financial capital is and will remain the scarce resource, then capitalism's days are numbered.

The world is awash with cash. Companies have mountains of it. The business world is in the process of discovering anew the truth of Bacon's observation four centuries ago that 'knowledge itself is power'.

One sign of this change is the equivocal nature of corporate ownership noted towards the end of the last chapter. As companies become more dependent on able people their value becomes intimately linked to how diligently these knowhow professionals can be induced to work and how long they can be induced to stay with the company. To suppose, in an era which execrates and outlaws slavery, that companies whose main assets are people can be owned in the same way as companies whose main assets are plant and machinery, is manifestly absurd.

The problem, and a cause of much tension and misunderstanding between all players in the game, is that this power shift has so far gone largely unrecognised by the establishment. The presumption that money is scarce and that, as a consequence, the suppliers of

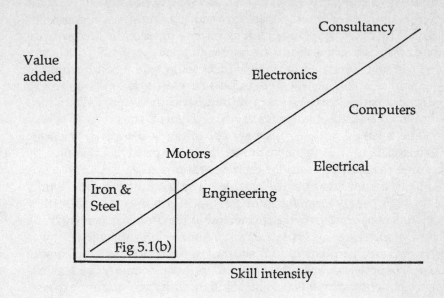

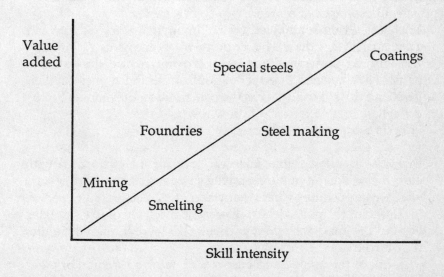

Fig 5.1: The Edge Function
There is a tendency within economies, industries and their various segments for increases in value added to be associated with increases in skill intensity.

money to a company (its shareholders) are its only owners, remains deeply embedded in corporate law (both statutory and common) and is still taken more or less for granted in most of the literature on business management and corporate finance.

Professor Gordon Edge, one of the world's leading authorities on the management of research and development, believes there is a strong positive correlation in *all* industries between value added and what he calls 'skill intensity' (see Figure 5.1).

The business idea of his new consultancy company Scientific Generics is to help its clients to achieve competitive advantage by raising the skill intensity of their operations.

Skill is an attribute of people. The skill shortages, loudly lamented by government ministers and economists because they restrain economic growth, are inevitable at a time of generally rising skill intensity. It is as futile today to bemoan skill shortages as it was yesterday to bemoan capital shortages. That skill, talent, competence, experience, business ideas and innovative ability are scarce is a permanent fact of business life. Skill intensity will continue to rise. It is inconceivable that the situation will reverse itself and so force able people to cede market power back to the financial capitalists. Managers must proceed on the assumption that good people are going to become even scarcer.

Michael J. Prietula and Herbert A. Simon, in a *Harvard Business Review* article entitled 'The Experts in Your Midst' (January, 1989), argued that most companies do not realise the value of experts. They suggest managers should note the names of their experts and should try to assess the contribution they make. Sveiby and I call such an exercise a 'knowhow audit'.

Prietula and Simon said:

Expertise is often found in lower level people who deal with customers (like the employee on the customer service hotline) and who are in positions where many activities meet (like the person in charge of the parts depot). Expertise often encompasses value beyond the job description, particularly where human dynamics play a role.

Think of the nontechnical aspects of being a foreman or plant scheduler. They know you don't put this job on this machine with this person, or else productivity will drop. They are the people who know the inner workings of the company even better than you.

This osmosis and anastomosis (the cross-connections linking tree-like systems) between expert and company are constituents of the company life-form. The expertise of a company's people defines the company's vital functions. Generally speaking, the lower 'down' a conventional corporate hierarchy one goes the more company-specific expertise becomes. It is this company-specific expertise and knowhow – the way we do things round here and the way this particular thing is done – that makes each company unique. So much is automated these days and so much will be automated that human dynamics is more or less all that is left to distinguish a company from its competitors.

An inevitable consequence of this trend is the rise to power in all organisational hierarchies of the personnel or 'human resources' function. Sveiby and I believe there are already a number of industries where the personnel function has become of primary strategic importance and we are so convinced of the generality of this trend that we predict within a few years the very idea of a personnel department will be wholly discredited.

The case of Jaguar, the British luxury car maker, may help to explain the paradox of the disappearing personnel department.

When John Egan (now Sir John) assumed the leadership of Jaguar in 1980 it was state-owned, had a terrible reputation for poor quality and unreliability in its main market of North America and was losing money hand over fist. Egan realised quality was the key to any recovery so he shut down Jaguar's quality control department. He saw in the quality control function not a cure for Jaguar's quality problems but the symptom of a profound malaise in its manufacturing process.

The campaign he embarked upon to 'build in' quality and quality-consciousness to the whole fabric of the company was hugely successful. Within a few years Jaguar had risen from the bottom to the top of the US luxury car leagues of customer satisfaction and Jaguar PLC, privatised but still protected from takeover by a 'golden share', was making pots of money.

The subsequent acquisition of Jaguar by Ford, precipitated by the weakness of the US dollar (which hit Jaguar's US sales hard) and by the British government's bizarre decision to change the 'golden share' goalposts in the middle of the game, was a great pity. But it was not a sign of failure and does not detract one iota from Egan's prodigious achievement.

Just as quality became Jaguar's primary stategic focus in the early

1980s, so people management is set to become the primary strategic focus in most industries by the end of the century. Egan has shown that as soon as an area becomes the primary strategic focus the very last thing it needs is a dedicated department. Everyone is involved, company leaders most of all.

Looked at from this point of view the predicament of people like Mike Gascoigne and Peter Keevil, the two computer experts we met at the beginning of the chapter, seems less poignant. Their distaste for defence-related work seems more of a problem for defence contractors than for them. Computer skills are in short supply. It is a sellers' market.

Companies whose business idea is to sell defence systems must recognise that some people with ability *and* ideals (they often go together) will refuse to work for them while they adhere to their business idea.

In high skill-intensity areas the difference between a company's business idea (what it is in business to do) and its personnel idea (the sort of people it needs to do it) disappears. When a company's main assets are people, the idea of a strategy without a personnel policy makes no sense. Indeed, one can go so far as to say the personnel idea has priority over strategy because a company's 'core know-how', which is represented by the collective skills of its employees is the main determinant of its strategic opportunity set (see Chapter Three).

As soon as core knowhow considerations achieve priority in the strategy-making process, the defence contractors wishing to hire men and women like Mike Gascoigne and Peter Keevil have another way of responding to each individual's fastidiousness.

Instead of looking elsewhere for staff they can reason along the following lines: 'Our core knowhow lies in the design and manufacture of rugged, high-speed, high-reliability electronic data processing and communications systems. We're using that core knowhow in defence work. To maintain competitive advantage in our core knowhow we need to hire people like Gascoigne and Keevil but they won't work for us because of our defence work. Maybe we should stop doing defence work.'

Mike Gascoigne told *The Guardian* that if people like him and Peter Keevil had the choice they would avoid military work. They do have the choice and Gascoigne and Keevil have exercised it. In a business world where the key management skill is an ability to recruit and keep good people, the moral human being has the power to influence the non-moral company. And the wage slaves need no Spartacus to lead them. All they have to do is say 'no'.

GLUE THEORY

Since an ability to recruit and keep good people is, these days, the essence of good management, an organisation's 'stickiness' – the degree to which it holds together in the face of unrelenting disintegrative pressure – is an indicator of management quality.

Stickiness is most easily measured in terms of staff turnover. An organisation in which staff turnover is low, relative to some average for the sector or industry, can be deemed, *prima facie*, to be relatively well run. It is not quite as simple as that though.

A very low staff turnover figure can be as much a sign of poor management as a high one. It can reflect a lack of refreshment; an isolation from the mainstream of corporate development; an insularity that can lead to an arid and querulous conservatism where ageing founders, wedded to anachronisms, would thump their desks in frustration if the bailiffs hadn't taken them away.

But although low staff turnover *can* be a sign of corporate senility (the syndrome also includes the corporate equivalents of such ailments as arterial plaque, obesity, progressive myopia, deafness and chronic neophobia), a relatively high staff turnover figure is a more common symptom of bad management.

Stickiness is a quality not a quantity. The extent to which it is desirable to attract good people and keep them varies from time to time and from industry to industry. In industries where the growth of skill intensity is relatively fast, for example, a high rate of recruitment, which may or may not be associated with a high level of departures, can be appropriate in order to maintain an adequate rate of refreshment.

'Glue theory' is the collective term I use to describe both the principles on which the various components of stickiness are based and the ways and means by which an appropriate stickiness can be achieved and maintained. It involves such matters as capital structure (the extent to which employees are motivated by equity and options, for example); corporate culture (including corporate history); organisational structure; social ambience; the scope for individual self-fulfilment and the potential employees have to be excited, intrigued, enthused and otherwise stimulated by, with and about their work.

An important principle of glue theory is that strategy itself is a component of stickiness. What a company does, how it does it, its manners and general demeanour, all affect its ability to recruit and keep good people. In companies where stickiness is acknowledged to be a priority, strategies must satisfy the precepts of glue theory before they can be adopted.

For example, a company that has just withdrawn from defence contracting for reasons to do with its wish to secure its core knowhow, might consider replacing its military work by buying rather than building related, non-defence businesses. Before deciding on such a course the company leaders would need to be sure the cultural conflicts that attend every merger can be resolved quickly and that stickiness in general will not be reduced.

Glue theory and the elucidation of the principles of corporate magnetism – a company's ability to attract good people in the first place – are the next major challenges for management. Companies will have to learn to resemble 'sticky magnets', or 'magnetic toffees' if you prefer.

We will delve no further into this important subject here (see *Managing Knowhow*) but will take a critical look at a modern rule-of-thumb (I hesitate to dignify it with the title of a theory) that is one of the major obstacles standing in the way of glue theory's development.

CRITICAL MASS

I must confess I once liked the term 'critical mass'. I used it often in the early 1980s when writing about Britain's 'managerial renaissance'. I am fascinated by nuclear physics and catastrophe theory. Though I understand them only a little, the idea implied by the term critical mass in business, of a discontinuity in the managerial culture that could turn an atmosphere of decline and despondency into one of vigorous optimism within the space of a few years, was enormously appealing.

Since then the term has been much abused by business economists and practitioners. In particular the physical principles it describes have been misinterpreted and invoked to explain and justify the lust for size that appears these days to overwhelm every manager with the ambition and political deftness needed to rise to the top of a large company.

The following passage, taken from an imaginary document sent to shareholders to explain their imaginary company's latest bid, is typical:

Your company needs critical mass if it is to compete effectively in the global marketplace and it needs it quickly. This acquisition, and others like it, will take your company from the middle of the world league to a position close to the top. Your directors are all convinced that within a decade the industry will be dominated by half-a-dozen players. This acquisition will help ensure your company will be one of them.

Stirring stuff, and it usually works. There are very few cases of shareholders refusing to sanction bids. The idea that size is desirable, not in its own right but in so many other ways that it might just as well be, is deeply embedded in our financial and managerial cultures.

In recent years I have developed a standard response when the idea of critical mass is proffered to explain an acquisition or an acquisition-led strategy. 'Critical mass?' I ask innocently. 'Isn't that the point just before the company blows up?' Sadly, the implied invitation to discuss the effects of size and acquisitions on the company's culture and integrity, and on the outlook and motivation of its employees, is rarely taken up. Too many managers only see the benefits of size. They see them only dimly, but they see the harm size can do not at all.

The lust for size is a non-rational, human obsession (it is not shared by the corporate species) that equates size in the corporate world with personal achievement and status.

We saw in Chapter Four that mergers are fashionable despite their effects on performance, not because of them, and there is little evidence that size itself produces above-average returns either. Indeed, what evidence there is points to the opposite conclusion. In late 1988, at the time of the joint bid by GEC and the German group Siemens for GEC's smaller UK rival Plessey, I pointed out the operating profit margin of the huge German conglomerate was less than 2%. It earned four times that on its cash 'mountain' which was big enough to buy Plessey *and* GEC.

Some will argue the wafer-thin margins of German companies are attributable to Germany's turbulent industrial history and to its peculiar financial consequences. Maybe so, but that does not alter the fact that critical mass was being invoked to justify Plessey's acquisition by a far less profitable company.

We must be clear about the status of size in this debate. Its advocates cannot admit that size is desired for its own sake because shareholders derive no direct benefit from size. Size can only be pursued as an effective means to some other end and that other end is usually deemed to be the maximisation of profitability or earnings per share.

The implications for the nice company of the prevailing financial climate will be examined in the next chapter, but before we leave the size debate, there is a final structural point to be made.

There are certain attributes of size, like reach and financial strength, that are genuinely advantageous. A global distribution network is invaluable if a company's business idea is to market a global product, and access to substantial funds is essential if the business idea is to undertake major engineering projects.

But a manufacturer can achieve global reach by establishing a global network of independent distributors with business ideas complementary to its own, just as easily as it can by acquisition. We saw in the last chapter how 'unbundling', or what Barreyre calls 'impartition', can increase the 'sum' of business games.

The UK sweets group Rowntree was chided in 1988 by its Swiss nemesis Nestlé for licensing brands like KitKat and Smarties overseas instead of marketing them directly. But Nestlé wanted Rowntree because the UK group's brands were more successful than its own.

Neither is financial strength an exclusive attribute of size. As we noted above the world is awash with cash these days. In 1987 the US investment bank Kohlberg Kravis Roberts financed its $25bn acquisition of the US conglomerate RJR–Nabisco entirely with debt. Banks on both sides of the Atlantic, desperate to replace the big-ticket lending to Third World countries that went so badly wrong, are falling over themselves to finance leveraged bids, buy-outs and buy-ins. When small and medium-sized companies seek finance for half-way decent projects (and for banks decent, these days, mostly means big) hordes of importunate bankers have to be told to form an orderly queue.

As my friend and colleague Jane Wynn has pointed out, the nicest irony of all is provided by the top level meeting that takes place before a big company, pleading the exigencies of critical mass, pounces on its prey. The table is in the offices of the bidder's merchant bank advisers. Also present are the bidder's independent stockbrokers, its independent legal advisers, its independent bankers, its independent accountants, its independent investor relations consultants, its independent management consultants and its independent public relations advisers. As likely as not, the coffee and sandwiches are supplied by the merchant bank's independent catering contractors.

For such consummate cooperative pluralism to be so routinely deployed in the implicit assertion of its own impossibility must surely rank as one of the absurdities of the modern business age. Perhaps it is of such paradoxes that Thomas Kuhn's paradigm shifts are made.

It will be abundantly apparent by now that I am no fan of the term 'critical mass' as it is presently used in business. I now prefer the analogous idea of 'escape velocity' to which I was introduced by Sir John Hoskyns. It has the virtue of avoiding the possibility of confusion between mass and weight of which most business misinterpretations of the term critical mass consist.

Mass is not, as the size advocates seem to suppose, equivalent to weight. It is a function of energy and the speed of light. As an analogy for business the critical mass idea might suggest a small, energetic company is equivalent, in some way, to a large, placid one but it would never propose the existence of a special threshold, where things become different (if not easier), that is attainable by virtue of size alone.

THE CORPORATE ECOSYSTEM

The main trouble with large size in the corporate world, and this applies particularly to size achieved by acquisition, is that it is hard to manage.

I would hazard the guess that if it were possible to measure the number and severity of management problems, they would be found to have a geometric relationship with size – that is to say, both would increase at a faster rate than size and would ultimately reach a critical point beyond which they are collectively insoluble.

Nice strategies, like TFT, offer a solution to the problems associated with a lack of mass (or escape velocity). They lead, as a matter of course, to the accumulation of a wide circle of corporate friends, any or all of whom can be nodes in networks capable of supplying all the truly advantageous attributes of size. TFT is a good network builder and a good network manager.

But these qualities are not merely the result of TFT's prowess in the outside world, they are also the consequence of its way with people. A company employing a TFT strategy is nice inside as well as out. Indeed, it is hard if not impossible to deploy TFT successfully in the outside world if its nice, cooperative qualities do not also infuse the company's internal culture and philosophy. Equally, it would be futile, and rather bizarre, for a company that is internally nice to try to mix it with the nasties externally.

David H. Ingvar, Professor of clinical neurophysiology at the University of Lund in Sweden, advocates a neurobiological approach to management. In an article on 'biological management' in the SE Bank's quarterly review (1984) Ingvar noted: 'in many of the more recent management handbooks there is an element of toughness and cynicism, an idealisation of authoritarian aggressiveness, which is rather casually believed to be part and parcel of the conditions of business life.' Ingvar declares this nasty view of business to be incorrect because it is 'unbiological'.

Though I am not sure I would agree with Ingvar that the quality of being biological is a necessary condition of validity, his assertion that people have psychological needs that should be accommodated by the management style is entirely in tune with the themes of this book and of *Managing Knowhow*.

Indeed, I would go much further than Ingvar. He urges managers to cultivate a sense of group self-awareness and to create a climate in which employees can readily reconcile the facts of a company's past with the feel of its present and the hope of its future. I argue that companies themselves can be defined in this way; that the hopes and fears of employees, their interests and abilities and the direction given to their endeavours by the momentum of their company's history, collectively comprise the metapsyches of corporate life-forms.

Just as colonies of ants behave in ways individual ants cannot (like forming bridges of their bodies during emigrations), so the abilities and behaviour of companies transcend what could be and is done by individuals. And with the metapsyche there is a metabody, the strength of which is the company's *raison d'être*.

The two together, the body and the psyche, comprise an intelligent life-form complete with a mind and an inventory of instincts.

CORPORATE PSYCHOLOGY

What do we know of the corporate life-form? We know it exists in real-time because it has a past and a future, both linked to its present. We know it plans ahead because it has instincts to optimise and survive. We know a little of its metabolism; its blood is money, its nutrients are innovation, skill, enterprise and human energy, that its product is profit, that it has an embryology but no clear maturity and that exsanguination (total money loss) is a necessary and a sufficient condition for death.

We know the company is a symbiote of humanity, a peculiar kind of slave species that employs its owners. We know it is routinely bought and sold and that it regards such servitude as a natural, if sometimes irksome, fact of life.

We also know its psychology consists of, but is not equivalent to, the sum of the individual psychologies of its employees. We know that it recognises and remembers; that it has a governing brain that orchestrates its bodily functions and plans its actions. We suppose that, though each company has its own unique personality, both mental and physical fitness are necessary for success.

City analysts and other corporate critics concentrate almost exclusively on the company's circulatory system. They have nothing to say about corporate psychology. For them the mind of the company is equivalent to the mind of its leaders and they would regard the existence of a heart and soul as a positive liability.

In a sense they would be right. There are attitudes, such as the belief that in Hobbes's 'war of all against all' (*bellum omnium contra omnes*) civilization's tenuous foothold in society is preserved only by the caring professions (humanity's quality control department), that companies should avoid like the plague.

THE POVERTY OF MACROECONOMICS

For most of this century the economic tradition that had ruled from Adam Smith's *Inquiry into the Nature and Causes of the Wealth of Nations* (published in 1776) to the eighth edition of Alfred Marshall's *Principles of Economics* (published in 1920) has been fighting for its survival with a parvenu body of theory known as macroeconomics.

The publication in 1936 of John Maynard Keynes's *The General Theory of Employment, Interest and Money* marked a watershed in the development of the dismal science. It switched the focus of attention decisively away from the firm and onto the economy. The bird's-eye view was dazzling in its grandeur. As the whole body of the economy came into focus, economists felt touched by the sublime. They had achieved parity with the natural sciences because, by looking beyond the ephemera of the market, they had glimpsed something of the fundamentals.

But the spirit of Smith and Marshall survived and it has lately been making something of a comeback. 'Microeconomics', the pejoration thrust upon the earlier tradition by its bumptious usurper, is now, in my view (though I'm biased) much the more vital of the two sub-disciplines.

It is concerned with the supply side of the economy (to distinguish it from the preoccupation of macroeconomics with the Keynesian idea of aggregate demand) and the focus of its attention is the company.

Keynesianism has been a hugely successful body of theory. In the view of most economists it has removed forever the possibility of a recurrence of deep, general and long-lasting depressions. But it has spawned a problem almost as great as the one it has solved – namely 'stagflation', persistent inflation during conditions of less than full employment. Keynes did not consider the possibility of such an equilibrium position and if it had been put to him he would almost certainly have regarded it as so improbable as not to be worthy of consideration.

But stagflation, a legacy of the application of the Keynesian model if not a corollary of the theory itself, has since become an apparently incorrigible fact of life and the main economic problem of the post-Keynesian era. The problem of stagflation needs to be solved. In my view it is no coincidence that the theory of corporate evolution, and the principal role played in it by the nice company, point towards a solution.

To understand why this is so we will look at the work of two men who stand at the cusp of the next paradigm shift in corporate evolution. One is a theorist, the American economist Martin Weitzman, and the other a practitioner, the British businessman Sir Peter Thompson.

THE SHARE SYSTEM VERSUS THE WAGE SYSTEM
The Weitzman thesis, as it has come to be known, is one of those rare economic ideas that remind those who have grown up with the belief that Keynesianism is the crowning glory of economics, that macro- and microeconomics are actually two interacting parts of a larger whole.

Weitzman put the point eloquently in his book *The Share Economy: Conquering Stagflation*. He wrote:

> The principal economic problems of our day have at their core not MACRO but profoundly MICRO behaviours, institutions and policies. The war against stagflation cannot be won at the lofty, antiseptic plane of pure macroeconomic mangement. Instead it must be fought out in the muddy trenches of fundamental micropolitical reform. What is most desperately

needed is an improved framework of incentives to induce better output, employment and pricing decisions at the level of the firm.

The Weitzman thesis states that if the pay of employees were to be linked directly to the revenue of their employer companies, the macroeconomy would be less troubled by inflation. Weitzman's remedy for the disease of stagflation is to substitute for the conventional wage system what he calls a 'share system'. The prescription derives directly from the theory of the firm, a major component of classical, pre-Keynesian economics.

All economists recognise that we live in a world of imperfect or 'monopolistic' competition where prices and wages are relatively 'sticky' and where firms are always eager to sell more of their output. In Weitzman's words: 'modern industrial capitalism is a system characterised by a more or less permanant excess supply of goods'. Against this orthodox background Weitzman compares the responses of employers to the question of whether they should hire additional employees under a conventional wage system on the one hand or under a share system on the other.

Suppose ICI employees earn, with wages and other benefits, an average of £5 an hour. Under a wage system ICI will be willing to hire additional people so long as it can sell the extra output of one more employee working for an hour for at least £5. Since expanding output reduces prices and therefore revenues, there must come a point when the declining marginal revenue from the additional output falls to the cost of one more employee – the point at which the marginal cost equals the marginal revenue. At that point it will not be worth ICI employing any more people and if demand falls, because of a recession for example, causing prices to fall in sympathy, ICI will need to lay off employees in order to bring marginal costs back into parity with the lower marginal revenues.

Suppose, however, that ICI switches to a new contract with its employees based not on a fixed wage but on a fixed proportion of revenue per head. In that event marginal revenues will *never* fall to marginal costs because every time revenue falls, wages will fall in sympathy. If the proportion of revenue per head paid to employees is 60%, for example, it will always be worth ICI hiring more people because marginal revenues will always be two-thirds higher than marginal costs.

The differences between the share system and the wage system are depicted graphically in Figure 5.2. As Weitzman puts it:

A share system looks very much like a labour-shortage economy. Share firms ever hungry for labour are always on the prowl – cruising around like vacuum cleaners on wheels, searching in nooks and crannies for extra workers to pull in at existing compensation parameter values. Such an economy inherently resists recession.

The share system is what Weitzman calls a 'natural enemy' of inflation because of the downward inflexibility of consumption and wages. The theory of the 'consumption function', one of the key components of the Keynesian model, states not only a commonplace, that consumption rises as income rises, but also that consumption rises more slowly than income. The richer you are, the less valuable the next £1 of income seems, so you are less likely to spend it. Saving is the difference between income and consumption and it is fortunate that it rises as income rises because saving finances the investment needed to create wealth.

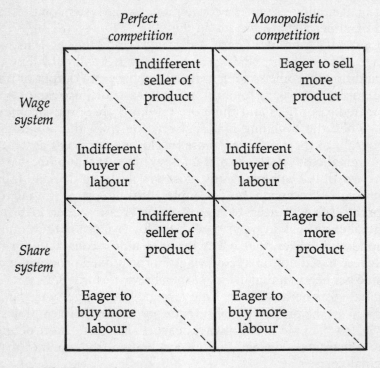

Fig 5.2: The Wages of Sharing
Martin Weitzman's share economy looks the most attractive under standard conditions of monopolistic competition.

But the consumption function has a sting in the tail. Another way of putting it is that consumption today is influenced by consumption yesterday as well as by income today and that is true for decreases as well as increases in income. It takes us time to adjust our consumption to a change in our income. And this stickiness of consumption is reflected in a corresponding stickiness in wages. The 'ratchet consumption function' has been translated into a general expectation that nominal incomes can rise but not fall.

That means companies suffering a fall in sales cannot, because of the unions and general expectations, preserve their profits by reducing wages. Their only other recourse is to raise prices which has the same effect in the end because it cuts 'real' (inflation-adjusted) wages by reducing the purchasing power of nominal wages.

This simply transfers the ratchet to prices. The expectation that wages will rise but never fall is transformed, by profit preservation behaviour, into the fact that prices rise and never fall. This asymmetry can generate very high rates of inflation given only moderate volatility in company profits. Ratchet functions are driven by oscillation. Profits do not have to rise at all in the long run to generate inflation, they just have to go up and down a lot.

In this way the demand-side problem of inflation, with which governments all over the world have been struggling ever since Keynes said recessions could be cured by printing money, can be seen to have its origins in the supply side. It is the downward inflexibility of wages, coupled with the variability of profits, that is the main cause of inflation.

Weitzman's solution is to improve the flexibility of the labour market by linking wages to revenues. He suggests governments should use the tax system to encourage companies to introduce so-called 'profit-related pay' (PRP) schemes. A number of Western governments, including Britain's, have already dabbled with PRP tax concessions, albeit half-heartedly. I have no doubt they will become an indispensable tool of economic management over the next decade.

But the importance of the Weitzman thesis lies not so much in its originality (profit-sharing has been commonplace in most professions for centuries and the tradition of producer cooperatives in industry goes back at least as far) as in its provenance. The proposal comes from the demand side and is couched in language the demand side understands. The thesis has even been mentioned approvingly in recent years by that citadel of macroeconomics, the Organisation for Economic Cooperation and Development (OECD). Weitzman has transformed profit-sharing from one of those wishy-washy nostrums peddled by pink-tinted idealists, into a theoretically respectable policy option.

SIR PETER'S 'HIDDEN PLUS FACTOR'
I suppose Sir Peter Thompson seems a bit like a pink-tinted idealist sometimes but he is far too much of a pragmatist to have any patience with the wishy-washy. He was born and bred in Yorkshire, after all, where patience with the wishy-washy has always been scarce and his idealism was kindled by a left-wing history teacher at Bradford Grammar School.

By the time he went to read economics at Leeds University he was fully persuaded of the virtues of state-ownership although his working life began in the private sector. After graduation he was hired by Bird's Eye Foods, then still a small company, to run its transport section.

He left in 1962 and then, after brief stints at GKN and the Rank Organisation, he joined state-owned British Steel in 1968. From there, in 1972, he went to run British Road Services, part of the huge National Freight Corporation (NFC), assembled during the Labour government's campaign to bring 'the commanding heights of the economy' into state ownership. In 1976, following a major shake-out at NFC, Thompson was appointed Chief Executive (Operations).

He loves lorries. He told Maureen Cleave in an interview for the *Observer Magazine* (January 1989) that it was not the engines that fascinated him but 'the fact that without them the kind of society I want just couldn't work. Trains can't pull up at your front door or run behind every supermarket'.

He likes the immediacy too: 'you can be day-to-day effective. In the morning your warehouse is full of soapflakes and by the end of the day it is empty, with fleets of lorries loaded with Persil going all over the country, and you can start again.'

NFC was to flourish hugely under Peter Thompson's leadership but it was a close run thing. He nearly gave up. 'When I joined,' he told me, 'I believed totally in nationalised industries, but by the mid-70s I'd become disillusioned. The way it was controlled by politicians, it was not a good system. If the opportunity had presented itself in 1979, I'd probably have left.'

92

But the world was changing. In 1977 the Tory opposition outlined its transport policy in *The Right Track*. The document included the following fateful passage: 'Our preferred solution . . . is to seek private investment in the NFC, and provide a corporation similar . . . in make-up to British Petroleum.'

In April 1979, with a general election a month away, the party manifestos appeared. The Liberals promised a halt to, but not an undoing of, the nationalisation process; Labour wanted more of it, and the Tories were bent on privatisation. A major watershed had been reached in Britain, the economic and philosophical elements of which were to turn Peter Thompson from an able, idealistic businessman into a paradigm shifter.

But his conversion was not complete. He had rejected the idea of state ownership but had yet to find a new path. 'The Conservative manifesto delayed my departure,' Sir Peter recalled. 'It committed the Tories to selling NFC shares so as "to achieve a substantial private investment in it".'

What was Thompson to make of it all? He was leader of a large, state-owned enterprise but no longer believed state capitalism worked; he felt 'people would work better if they didn't have to work for shareholder profit' and yet he was confronted by the probability that within the foreseeable future shareholder profit would be the NFC's *raison d'être*.

An idealist might have resigned, a pragmatist might have changed his ideals, Peter Thompson, being both, did neither. He allowed the conflict to chafe in his mind. He worried it, nudging its irreconcil-abilities towards a dimly perceived resolution. He had time because the onset of recession in 1980, as the Tories put the squeeze on their enemy number one – inflation, hit the NFC hard, deferring the date of privatisation.

Thompson described the moment of his personal paradigm shift in his interview with Cleave. He was on a golfing weekend in Wales with senior colleagues in the spring of 1980. He recalled (giving a flavour of his leadership style):

We often used to do this. We played golf and shared the cooking and drank a lot and the atmosphere was mellow.

A merchant banker had told me the company was worth about £55 million and I began to wonder if we shouldn't buy it ourselves. At first we thought of a management buy-out and then, in a flash, all my old political antennae were working.

By God, if we could involve *everybody*, if I could go to Sainsbury or whoever and say – the guy who delivers to you owns part of this company. He will be much more willing and more diligent and much less likely to go on strike.

We'd have in our locker something else nobody else had, the hidden plus factor, *employer enthusiasm*.

There was a long road ahead but green lights illuminated the critical path at the right times and the right places and on 22 February 1982, at a London Transport depot, Peter Thompson, on behalf of the National Freight Consortium, gave transport minister David Howell a cheque for £53.5m in return for 100% of the National Freight Company.

Employees, many of whom had taken out second mortgages, put up £6.5m. The remaining £47m came from the City in bank loans. The financing was a remarkable tribute, not only to the enthusiasm of NFC employees but also to the impact NFC's management, and the whole idea, had made on bankers. The City had met the nice company and was favourably impressed.

It was even more favourably impressed by the time NFC began to prepare for its flotation on the stock market in February 1989. So much so that, as we shall see in the next chapter, it was willing to abandon one of its most sacred principles to make room for what had become Britain's largest and most rapidly growing transport group.

The NFC's importance lies not in what it is and not even in what it has become, although both are remarkable. Like the Weitzman thesis, its significance in the theory of corporate evolution lies in how it has been perceived.

The John Lewis Partnership retailing group, the Scott Bader specialist chemicals company, Baxi Heating, Geographers' A–Z (publisher of the London street guide), the Kalamazoo office equipment concern and FI Group (the computer systems company) are all older, and in some ways purer, examples of successful, employee-owned companies.

The crucial difference with the NFC is that it has breached the orthodoxy and, in so doing, has modified it. The original buy-out had to overcome the scepticism of the City's banks and the flotation seven years later forced the stock market and the financial institutions to modify one of their basic principles.

The NFC is the nice company *par excellence*. It is also very visible (in 1988 a sample of financial editors voted it their favourite company), it is in a basic industry and so must rank as a core holding for many institutions and it is superbly run. It is corporate evolution in action; strategy as rhetoric; perhaps even the embryo of an Axelrod cluster that will grow and come to dominate the global population of companies.*

THE SHARE SYSTEM

Sharing is important to the theory of the nice company. We have seen how powerful a strategy cooperation can be in the outside world and how a sense of partnership is its natural and even its necessary internal corollary. And we have also seen how Weitzman's share economy attacks the endemic illness of modern economies; stagflation.

The NFC, with its employee shareholdings and profit-sharing schemes, exemplifies the micropolitical benefits of the sharing principle. The system works in the economic microcosm as well as in the macrocosm. It is much more than a mere dream.

The sharing idea is becoming more important because of the shift in the balance of power between people and capital discussed earlier. Companies are selling jobs as well as goods and services. When someone joins a company he or she is incurring the opportunity cost of being unable to join another company. Recruits are buying jobs with the difference between the value they can add and the compensation they are paid.

A share system reflects the nature of this trade because it links compensation to value added and so endows the employment contract with the flavour of parternship. The conventional wage system, where there is no link between compensation and revenues, gives the employment contract more of the flavour of exploitation.

Sharing, partnership, cooperation and collaboration are all nice company words. Part of the ultimate victory of the nice strategy will be the widespread adoption of Weitzman-like share systems. For governments struggling with the recurring curse of stagflation, there is a strong incentive to bring about the onset of the share economy sooner rather than later.

But the establishment and the City are still at the beginning of the nice company learning curve and old habits die hard. Many hazards lie in wait for the nice strategy as it approaches the City. The NFC,

* See Sir Peter Thompson's book *Sharing the Success*.

though it has succeeded in forging for itself a novel and potent defence against hostile takeover (see Chapter Six, pages 100–7), has entered a dangerous place where strategies go in and out of style and where dreams are manifestly mortal.

THE NICE SHAREHOLDER

Dr John Randall, chief executive and architect of the UK food group Avana, left in disgust when Avana's shareholders ignored the advice of their board and accepted a hostile bid from rival food company Ranks Hovis McDougall. He felt betrayed by shareholders who had done extremely well out of his stewardship during the previous decade, enjoying one of the most sustained and substantial increases in share value of any UK company.

Tony Craven-Walker, leader and main architect of Charterhouse Petroleum (one of the most successful of Britain's small oil companies), felt similarly betrayed when institutional shareholders refused to back an agreed merger with Saxon Oil that would have created a medium-sized UK oil company. Many had been lamenting the lack of such companies, arguing that it was in the national interest that groups capable of operating internationally should develop in the UK oil sector as a result of the exploitation of the North Sea oil province.

Saxon was acquired by Enterprise Oil instead and soon afterwards Charterhouse fell victim to the Belgian oil group Petrofina. Craven-Walker and his colleagues dispersed. Within a few months of the Petrofina takeover it was as if Charterhouse Petroleum had never been.

Randall and Craven-Walker are just two examples of the numerous able and creative managers who leave Britain's quoted-company sector each year because they feel the City is a gluttonous ass. Some go on to do good work in the unquoted sector but others turn to less creative pursuits like consultancy and golf and so are lost to our body corporate entirely.

The institutional shareholders do not seem to care very much. They continue to vie with each other for the best portfolio performance, apparently quite oblivious of any effect their treatment of managers and their strategies might have on overall company performance and the general quality of management.

There is a contract between managers and shareholders. One hears a great deal about breaches of that contract by managers (see Chapter three) but very little about the other kind of breach. The inalienable rights of shareholders are sacred totems that are taken for granted. 'Managers?' the City inquires loftily, 'they're ten a penny. You lose one, you hire another.'

In the theory of corporate evolution shareholders are part of the company. Their power and the way they use it determine important internal features as well as the company's fate in the outside world. And it is as true for shareholders as it is for company leaders themselves that recruiting and keeping good people is the new imperative.

Sympathetic and supportive shareholders are a boon. They permit a company to be more adventurous, more innovative, more forward-looking and so more attractive to able men and women keen to commit themselves to a search for profit through building and strengthening rather than through buying and pruning.

In the beginning Randall and Craven-Walker both had the support of their shareholders. They returned the favour by delivering substantial shareholder value. Then the City defected. TFT's response to a defection is automatic – it defects. In all likelihood if Randall and Craven-Walker had been treated more kindly by the City they would still be in there now proving just how positive the sum of the business game can be.

It remains to be seen whether the NFC, with its new defensive arsenal, will survive in this hostile environment long enough to end the lesson it has taken from the gospel of the nice company.

SUMMARY

- The balance of power has shifted away from financial capital towards human or knowhow capital.

- This focuses management attention on human resource management and renders extinct the personnel department.

- People are the key to competitive advantage because in them resides the company's core knowhow.

- Core knowhow takes precedence over strategy because it defines the strategic opportunity set.

- Glue theory concerns the stickiness of companies and is the next major management challenge.

- An obstacle inhibiting the development of glue theory is a misplaced belief in the business idea of critical mass.

- The benefits of size can also be achieved through cooperation (eg TFT).

- An internalised TFT helps to define the personality of the corporate life-form.

- The economist Martin Weitzman and the businessman Sir Peter Thompson are agents of a paradigm shift (an evolutionary change).

- The significance of their ideas lies not in themselves but in how they have been perceived.

- Shareholders still have a lot to learn.

CHAPTER 6

The Financial Environment

The species company, like other life-forms, inhabits a number of environments. Just as the scorpion's habitat differentiates into elements such as the meteorological, the geological, the topological, the botanical and the zoological, so the environment of the company differentiates into the social, the technological, the governmental, the economic, the competitive and the financial.

If the company can be said to be the native of any one of these sub-environments it would have to be the last. The company is a financial creature. Limited liability, the characteristic which distinguishes it from other commercial organisations is, first and foremost, a financial quality.

We have already questioned whether a company's equity (its ordinary shares) is these days as identifiable as it used to be with the company's underlying value, in view of the damage that can be inflicted on that value by the departure of people. In this chapter we shall look at how the constantly changing financial environment is not only being required to adapt to the rise of the nice company but is also, in a variety of ways, positively encouraging it.

It need not have done either. As we have already seen the path of evolution does not always run smooth. Adaptations are just that — they are not tailor-made accommodations of specific changes in the environment. The company is a jury-rig. It takes with it into tomorrow the adaptations of yesterday and by no means all of them turn out to be assets. It so happens that by and large, and right now, the tide of change in the financial world is running with the nice company.

THE CITY'S DILEMMA

The National Freight Consortium (NFC), examined in the last chapter, is a nice company. It has not made, and nor is it likely under its present management ever to make, a hostile takeover bid. Such a move would be inimical to its internal culture. The charismatic leadership of its chairman Sir Peter Thompson has imbued the NFC with a style of working that is both competitive and compassionate and there is every indication that this style will survive Thompson's retirement as chairman at the end of 1990. The style constrains strategy. There are things NFC's competitors can do that NFC cannot.

But in return for this unilateral disarmament NFC has acquired strengths that more than redress the imbalance of competitive advantage, or so Sir Peter and his co-owners believe, and so the NFC's record, relative to those of other transport companies, suggests (see below).

Sir Peter is very happy with the bargain. The dilemma he faced when his belief that 'people would work better if they didn't have to work for shareholder profit' was confronted by the inevitability of privatisation has been resolved very simply – by making the people the shareholders. The nice company thereby acquired the nice shareholders.

Though NFC's employees have done extremely well out of their investment in their company (the value of their shares rose from 4p at the time of the buy-out in 1982 to 250p at the time of flotation in early 1989), their humanity remains uncompromised. As Sir Peter put it in his interview with Maureen Cleave (*Observer Magazine*, January 1989):

> The motives of our shareholders are neither greedy nor short-term. They spend a lot of their money on charity and they are capable of absorbing business concepts much faster and to a greater depth than I had thought. What I've learned is that people are both shrewd and basically nice.

And because all concerned were anxious to conserve as far as possible the identity of employees and shareholders after flotation, the NFC became the carrier of a strategic mutation. As the limitations of the internal market in NFC's shares, coupled with its wish to grow by acquisition as well as organically, began nudging the company towards public flotation a new clause, giving employee shareholders double voting rights in takeover bids, was

100

added to the articles of association (equivalent to the company's written constitution).

Nothing could have been better designed to provoke the financial establishment. There is an old Jewish story about a man and wife being woken up one Sunday morning by the abusive demands of one of the man's creditors. The wife endures the harangue for a while and then loses her patience. She goes to the window and shouts 'he's not going to pay you!' Sir Peter did something similar. He made his problem – how to preserve the 'hidden plus factor' of employee ownership after flotation – the City's problem. The NFC said to the financial institutions: 'We know you don't like restricted and variable voting rights but we've got them and we're coming to the market anyway.'

The NFC, by carrying the double voting rights clause with them to the stock market, is provoking an historic confrontation of modern 'niceness' with the old paradigm, based on the divorce of ownership and employment and a free market in corporate control.

The champions of the old order included the International Stock Exchange (formerly the London Stock Exchange), which could have denied the NFC's shares entry to the market, and the powerful investment protection committees (IPCs) of the Association of British Insurers (ABI) and the National Association of Pension Funds (NAPF), the representative bodies of the two main types of financial institution. The ISE and the IPCs are key regulators of the market in shares. They have power, through the sanctions at their disposal, to insist on certain standards of corporate behaviour.

The IPCs in particular abhor restricted voting rights, of which the NFC's controversial article is an example. The reason for their distaste is that privileged shares make it more difficult for the company to be taken over. This, so the theory goes, robs holders of non-privileged or 'junior' stock of a speculative element in the share price. Other things being equal, the shares of a company that can be taken over will trade at a higher price than the shares of an identical company that cannot be taken over or that cannot so easily be taken over.

The IPCs, acting as the champions of shareholder rights, have waged a long and successful campaign against restricted voting rights. It is impossible for them to be sanguine at the prospect of the emergence of a new kind of restricted voting stock just as their victory over the existing breed seemed to be nearing completion.

But the pension funds and insurance companies have other duties apart from those they owe to their unions, the ABI and the NAPF. The most important of these are the fiduciary responsibilities they owe to the beneficiaries of the funds they manage, namely the holders of insurance policies and pension rights.

This fiduciary duty requires fund managers to do all in their power to maximise the value of the funds in their care. If it can be shown the performance of companies with restricted voting rights, of the kind in the NFC's articles of association for example, is better on average than the performance of companies without such rights, then fund managers face a dilemma.

If they accede to the demands of their IPCs to vote down proposals for restricted voting rights and to decline to invest in companies that already have them, they risk being in flagrant breach of their fiduciary duty to maximise performance.

At the root of the dilemma is a trade-off. The sanctity of the principle of a free market in corporate control derives from the belief that shareholder value resides in that freedom. But shareholder value also resides in good performance and the NFC says its good performance derives, in part at any rate, from employee ownership and control.

The stock exchange and the financial institutions seem unaware of the Trojan horse in their midst. When the NFC duly came to the market in early 1989, with a price-tag of £900m (remember, the consortium only paid £54m for it in 1982 and £47m of that was a bank loan), the stock exchange insisted it was a special case and that its tolerant attitude to NFC's variable voting rights should not be seen as a precedent. Indeed, the ISE told me that after it had signed its listing agreement with the NFC a number of other companies had asked leave to introduce similar voting restrictions but had been refused on the grounds that they were nothing like the NFC.

But the City is deluding itself if it supposes the NFC example can be isolated in this way. If companies are not sufficiently like the NFC to win the concessions they want they will become more like the NFC. Restricted and variable voting rights seem certain to become more common from now on.

Some companies, seeking competitive advantage in nice strategies and Sir Peter Thompson's 'hidden plus factor', will follow the NFC's lead and establish privileged classes of employee shareholders. Others, frustrated by what they see as the City's short-termism, will seek to erect defences against hostile bids to give themselves the time they need to bring their strategies to fruition.

Division in the ranks of institutional fund managers over the issue also seems probable. Fund managers succeed or fail on performance. If they do worse than average in the long run – if they discharge their fiduciary duties less well than most other fund managers – they will lose business and if they do better they will gain business.

Imagine what would happen if an Axelrod cluster of nice companies succeeded in invading a population of nasty companies by achieving above average earnings per share growth. Assuming the market acknowledges the superior performance of the nice companies as, for reasons explained below it is bound to do eventually, the shares of the nice companies will reflect this out-performance.

Let us suppose, for the sake of argument, that each member of the nice cluster has, for reasons to do with internal niceness, adopted restricted voting rights, and let us further suppose the IPCs are urging their members to boycott companies with restricted voting rights. This is a powerful threat because the quality of the market in a company's shares will be very low (prices will be lower than they would be otherwise and it will be hard to buy and sell) if the financial institutions refuse to hold the stock on principle.

The fund managers have a choice. They can elect to abide by the IPC's proscription and decline to invest in the out-performing nice companies, thereby surrendering some performance, or they can ignore the exhortations of the IPC in order to discharge their fiduciary duties more fully. In this way two investment strategies will emerge; the IPC-compliance strategy which will tend to under-perform and the rebel strategy which will tend to out-perform.

The latter strategy, because it is better, will come to dominate the fund management industry, leaving the IPCs with a dwindling band of under-performing loyalists steadily losing market share in fund management to their rebel rivals. The IPCs will no longer represent their industries. They will be confronted by a stark choice; either cease to proscribe restricted voting rights or cease to exist.

Before exploring in more depth the reasons for the inevitability of the rebel victory, I must make one final point about the significance of the NFC precedent. It is to do with its effect on the City's vision.

The idea that employee-owned firms have a special, beneficial quality not enjoyed by other, conventionally owned companies is hardly a revolutionary one for an industry that has itself been dominated, until very recently, by the partnership model and which has always had close links with the accountancy and legal professions which remain employee-owned. But the distinction between the ownership pattern of City firms and the pattern common in the companies that were the object of their professional interest, could be safely ignored while most quoted companies were industrial.

The old paradigm, in which the scarcity of financial capital is the system's centre of gravity, was a fair reflection of the power balance in manufacturing industry. It became manifestly less satisfactory when, thanks partly to the persuasive powers of the brothers Maurice and Charles Saatchi, the City acquired a taste for high-growth, high-profitability knowhow businesses in areas like advertising, design, public relations, estate agency and even architecture.

New kinds of analysis became necessary when firms like these began to come to the stock market. The old yardsticks, like return on capital, operating margin and return on equity, are pretty meaningless in companies where there is hardly any capital and where the price of this year's huge profits growth is next year's collapse as frustrated staff leave *en masse* to set up their own businesses or to join rival companies less obsessed with maximising short-term shareholder value.

A striking example of this kind of trade-off occurred in the summer of 1989 when London Weekend Television, holder of the must lucrative of Britain's independent TV franchises, announced plans for a capital restructuring designed to 'lock in' senior employees. The independent TV companies were approaching the end of the current franchise period with some trepidation because the new franchise round was to be an auction.

The market in senior TV executives – the sort of people needed to make winning the franchise possible in the first place and profitable thereafter – had become very active as the companies jockeyed for position. LWT had lost some senior people already so it decided on drastic action. It said to its shareholders: 'Your company is worth £200m today. If we don't retain the franchise it will be worth less than £50m. We need people like Greg Dyke, our managing director designate, and Melvyn Bragg, head of Arts and Current Affairs programming, to ensure we keep the franchise. We're asking you to give these people 15% of the company to encourage them to stay.'

The proposal was dressed up a little. Shareholders were to get a large, debt-financed cash pay-out and the senior people had to pay something for their shares, but the essence of the deal was a gun at the head of shareholders: you give part of your company to the senior employees or they'll leave and the value of your shares will collapse.

The example of NFC, and of other industrial companies trying to tap Sir Peter Thompson's 'hidden plus factor' of employee enthusiasm, suggests the importance of such 'people factors' is not confined to 'people businesses' and knowhow companies. The shift in the balance of value-creating power from money to men and women is making *all* businesses people businesses.

TOWARDS A MORE EFFICIENT MARKET

We saw in Chapter Four that the theoretical case for an active market in corporate control, often dubbed merger mania when it is very active, has been weakened in recent years by mounting evidence that mergers do not work and that the so-called 'efficient market hypothesis' is just that – an hypothesis that is only an imperfect reflection of reality.

But the belief that the market is always right is more than just a truism. In a House of Commons speech in 1947 Winston Churchill said: 'democracy is the worst form of Government except all those other forms that have been tried from time to time.' The same can be said of the market. It is a very bad way of allocating resources but it's a damn sight better than anything else that has been tried.

The reason for this is that unlike the deliberate mechanisms employed in centrally planned economies, it is inherently self-critical. It makes mistakes but it has the ability and the will to correct them once they become apparent.

An example of this learning process at work is the emergence of the concept of value-added and of employee-based measures as important tools of company analysis. The following analysis of the UK's three largest transport companies, Christian Salvesen, the NFC and Transport Development Group (TDG), illustrates the point.

The key measure used here – value added per £1 of pay – has been pioneered in Britain by Geoff Smith. (All the figures are taken from the latest accounts.)

The old profitability paradigm ranks the trio according to return on assets and margins:

Table 6.1

Company	Sales £m	Profit £m	Assets £m	Margin %	ROA %
C. Salvesen	298	47	232	15.8	20.3
TDG	549	44	254	8.0	17.3
NFC	1255	67	425	5.3	15.8

Value-added and employee analyses present a different picture:

Table 6.2

Company	Value+ £m	Assets £m	Staff '000s	Pay £m	V+/ £pay	Intensity index(*)	Adjusted V+/£pay
NFC (**)	496	425	30.5	383	130p	100	130p
TDG	298	254	13.4	185	145p	136	107p
C. Salvesen	166	232	6.9	95	175p	241	73p

(*) Intensity index = assets/capita (NFC = 100)
(**) NFC's pay and Value added included £12m of profit-sharing.
Value+ = Value-added = Pre-tax profit + pay + depreciation + interest payable.

The old system takes no notice of the efficiency with which each company uses its employees. It looks only at the efficiency with which companies use their financial assets. But though NFC's margins are barely a third of Christian Salvesen's, its value added per £1 of pay is three-quarter's of Salvesen's and is almost twice Salvesen's figure after adjusting for the latter's much greater use of capital.

Value-added and employee-based analyses help to illuminate the significance of the internal 'hidden plus factors' enjoyed by nice companies. Their results are often very different from those of conventional analysis and the market, intent on self-improvement, has begun to recognise that these novel measures have an important contribution to make to its understanding of companies, particularly in the area of risk analysis.

It is important to recognise how catholic markets are in their constant search for self-improvement. The more sensitive the market is to all relevant information the more efficient it is. As we have seen, relevant information these days includes a company's ability to recruit and keep good people, so it was with some interest that Wall Street analysts studied a book published in 1984 by Addison Wesley (now part of the nice British conglomerate, Pearson) entitled *The 100 Best Companies to Work for in America* by Robert Levering, Milton Moskowitz and Michael Katz.

An implication of the book was that the 100 companies mentioned should be better than average at recruiting and keeping good people and so deserved a higher than average share rating. Five years later the British publisher Fontana produced a volume identical in form to the American book entitled *The 100 Best Companies to Work for in the UK* (though with no attribution to its US precursor) by Bob Reynolds. The list included, amongst others, the NFC, Virgin Group, ICI, The Body Shop, BP and Pearson, all of which are mentioned elsewhere in this book as exponents, to a greater or lesser extent, of the nice strategy.

There were ironies in both the timing and content of the British version's publication. On the eve of publication the owner of the Fontana imprint, Collins, was acquired, after a hotly contested bid battle, by Rupert Murdoch's UK publishing group News International (controlled by Murdoch's Australian master company News Corporation). News International was not listed among the 100 best employers, whereas Pearson, of which Murdoch owned a threatening 20%, was.

Since the quality of being a good employer is clear evidence of a nice internal strategy, and since a key argument of this book is that nice companies are good performers, I was intrigued to see how a group of companies selected on a good employer basis had actually performed. Conjecturing that nice employers would do well *Financial Weekly* looked at the relative performance of the 43 public companies in the Fontana sample. The results of the study were published in *Financial Weekly* in March, 1989 (no. 517).

They showed that the average growth in earnings per share (EPS) over a four-year period for the 43 good employer companies was 109% against an EPS growth for the market as a whole of only 68% during the same period.

It follows from the argument presented here that in the knowhow business of publishing nice strategies endow companies with a significant competitive advantage. If this is so, Pearson is likely in the long term to out-perform News Corporation. City analysts, by incorporating the judgement of the Fontana book in their assessments of Pearson and News International shares, may help to bring this out-performance about.

THE ENLIGHTENED LENDER
The importance of analytical methodology is not confined to the assessment of equity. Lenders too are motivated to become better informed about their corporate customers. Their value judgements are made on the basis of reports on companies and their various debt issues or bonds by credit rating agencies like Moody's, and Standard and Poor's. The agencies try to assess the likelihood of the debt being serviced and repaid. They rank the security of debt on an AAA–D rating scale – hence the 'triple A' ratings of financially sound companies.

Debt ratings are arrived at in the same way as equity ratings. Analysts investigate the company according to criteria that vary from industry to industry but which usually include such things as cash flow, inventory control and the management of equipment, plant and human resources.

Ratings analysts have just as much of an appetite for new and better methodologies as equity analysts. If they come to believe that a certain kind of company, like the knowhow company, is peculiarly vulnerable to mass defections of talented people, their ratings will reflect their judgement of the likelihood of such defections, which is really an assessment of management's ability to prevent them. In this way the cost of debt to a company will also be affected by the niceness or otherwise of its internal management style.

But as we have seen, niceness is a strategy for all dimensions. It is a way of relating to the outside world as well as a way of managing a company's own ecosystem. The City also needs to devise ways of measuring these external factors.

NICENESS AT LARGE
In the spring of 1988 *Financial Weekly* published the results of a study of Britain's largest 100 companies (the constituents of the stock market's main index, the FT-SE 100) that indicated the existence of a market mistake.

The companies were classified as nice or nasty according to whether or not they had made one or more hostile takeover bids in the past six years, irrespective of whether the bids had been successful. This was by no means a rigorous test of niceness because a willingness to make hostile bids is not a necessary condition for nastiness. It is, however, a sufficient condition because nice companies, as I have begun to define them, never make hostile bids.

After winnowing the FT-SE of recently privatised groups (because their track records were too short), oil companies (because the impact on their earnings of oil price movements drowns all other influences) and an investment trust (because it is not really a company), 91 companies remained. Surprisingly, in view of the popularity of the acquisition-led strategy, 57 of them were nice according to the working definition and only 34 were nasty. The financial sector, including banks, property and insurance groups, was particularly nice – 15 of its 18 members satisfied the niceness criterion.

The performance of each group was measured according to the average growth of the earnings per share of its members over a five-year period. The results were startling. The nice group outperformed the nasty group by no less than 60% (see table). The out-performance was even more marked when the financial group was excluded because financial companies had performed poorly over the period. The 42 nice companies in the industrial group out-performed the 31 nasty companies by 86%.

Table 6.3 How Nice and Nasty Compared, 1982–86

Sample	——EPS%growth ——				——P/Es——			
	No.	%	Avge	Premium	No.	%	Avge	Premium
FULL	91	100	156.5		84	100	17.0	
Nice	57	63	181.9	60%	50	60	18.1	15%
Nasty	34	37	114.0		34	40	15.7	
INDUSTRY	73	100	178.2		73	100	17.4	
Nice	42	58	221.8	86%	42	58	18.6	18%
Nasty	31	42	119.1		31	42	15.8	

The study went on to investigate how efficiently the market had been tracking this out-performance. We did this by looking at how the stock market had rated the nice and nasty groups during the survey period. If the market was efficient in this respect, that is to say, if it had noted hostile bidders were relatively poor performers, it should have rated the nice group more highly than the nasty and the rating should have been higher by the same percentage as the nice group's out-performance.

The price/earnings ratio (P/E) is the conventional measure of the market's expectations of growth in earnings per share. If the market had been efficient the nice group should have had an average P/E 60% higher than the nasty group in the full sample and 86% higher than the nasty group in the industrial sample. It did not. The nice groups in both samples had higher average P/Es but not that much higher. The P/E premium for the nice group in the full sample was 15% and the P/E premium for the nice group in the industrial sample was 18% (see Table 6.3).

Table 6.4 The rating anomaly – a market mistake exposed

Ratings using nice as standard:

Sample	Nice		Nasty			
	EPS% grth	Average P/E	EPS% grth	Actual P/E	Implied P/E	Anomaly (%)
Industrial	201.3	18.6	119.1	15.8	11.7	4.1 (26)
Financial	69.9	15.8	57.0	12.1	12.9	−0.8 (7)
FULL	166.8	18.1	114.0	15.7	12.4	3.3 (21)

Ratings using nasty as standard:

Sample	Nasty		Nice			
Industrial	119.1	15.8	201.3	18.6	26.7	−8.1 (30)
Financial	57.0	12.1	69.9	15.8	14.8	1.0 (1)
FULL	114.0	15.7	166.8	18.1	23.0	−4.9 (21)

The market had been getting it wrong. For some reason it had been giving nasty companies higher P/Es than seemed to be justified by their performance. I do not propose to offer an explanation for this blindness beyond noting that the Nickell and Wadwhani study referred to in Chapter Four found some evidence that stock markets are periodically visited by fashions and fads which lead to nonrational judgements.

My point is that markets have been misjudging nice companies, that markets are motivated to become more efficient and so it is inevitable in the long run, as the market corrects its mistake, that nice companies will be afforded ratings that more fully reflect their performance.

The advent of a more efficient market in this respect is bound to help nice companies even though they are less acquisitive than nasty companies. A high P/E enables its possessor to buy other companies cheaply but it also reduces the cost of capital in a general way. A high P/E makes it cheaper to raise money through a rights issue, for example. The reciprocal of the P/E – the earnings yield – is a measure of the company's cost of equity capital. The higher the P/E the lower the earnings yield.

This means that when the market corrects its mistake about nice companies, as its hunger for efficiency will force it to do, the nice company's relative cost of capital will fall. Since the cost of capital helps define the opportunity set for investment – the lower the cost of capital, the larger the viable set – the nice company will perform even better.

Furthermore since the higher ratings of nice companies will also make it more difficult for nasty companies to acquire them, the survival chances of the nice strategy will be improved. True, these differences are very marginal, but it is precisely on such marginal differences that natural selection works.

There is an intriguing footnote to this study. When researching the good employer study mentioned above (based on the Fontana book *The 100 Best Companies to Work for in the UK*) *Financial Weekly* decided to apply the same hostile bid criterion to the sample of good employer companies. We found that good employer companies are, by and large, nice in their bidding behaviour too. In our adjusted sample of 91 companies, 37% were nasty whereas only 19% of the good employer sample failed the niceness test. And if they were excluded from the good employer group, the average EPS out-performance was even better – 121% against 109% for the whole good employer sample and 68% for the market as a whole.

THE ETHICAL FINANCIER

In June, 1984 the UK unit trust group Friends Provident launched Britain's first 'conscience fund', the Stewardship Unit Trust. By the end of 1988 it had £82m under management and had spawned a dozen emulators. Altogether Britain's twelve 'ethical' unit trusts (the equivalent of US mutual funds), and one 'ethical' bond fund, had £145m under management by Christmas 1988, 45% more than a year previously against an advance of only 22% for unit trusts as a whole.

True, the ethical share of total unit trust investment had risen from only 0.29% to a fractionally less insignificant 0.34% but that was not at all bad after only four years, and the trend was clear. A cloud the size of a man's hand had risen above the horizon of UK capital markets and it was growing.

The ethical unit trusts are by no means the only investment funds in Britain subject to screening according to ethical criteria. The Church Commissioners manage about £100m and there are many local authority pension funds that are conspicuously subject to ethical screening in their investment.

In America the phenomenon of the ethical trust or conscience fund is more firmly established. Some estimates put the amount of ethically screened investment as high as 10% of Wall Street. And in America moral human beings have been considerably more successful so far in pressganging their political and legal institutions into service in the crusade against the nonmoral company.

Scores of state and local governments have passed laws requiring public funds to divest South Africa-related stocks. Total assets affected by such laws and similar voluntary guidelines were estimated in *Business Week* in July 1987 to be about $400bn. Membership of the Social Investment Forum, a national group of fund managers, tripled between 1983 and 1987 and according to the New York-based Council on Economic Priorities (CEP), a non-profit research group, there was $40bn of ethically and socially screened investments in 1984, $100bn in 1985 and $200bn in 1986.

The execration of South Africa's apartheid policy dominates the ethical investment scene in the US. It is a category on its own that dwarfs all the others put together. And it does not seem to carry a financial penalty. A study by Wilshire Associates of California found that between 1979 and 1984 South Africa-free portfolios out-performed unrestricted portfolios by an average of 7% each year. *Barrons*, the US weekly financial newspaper, calculated that in 1984 and 1985 South Africa-free stocks in the 'Standard and Poor's 500' had out-performed the S&P 500's South Africa stocks by 61% to 48%.

The ethical fund performance picture is mixed on both sides of the Atlantic but so far there is not a jot of evidence that they underperform. The ethical investors are therefore getting a bargain. They are paying for a clearer conscience by restricting their choice of companies to invest in but are not incurring a financial penalty for their fastidiousness. That they make the choice before they know it costs them nothing, indicates that they would have been prepared to pay but they do not need to. Being an ethical investor is costing them nothing.

112

Furthermore, nice companies, as well as faring no worse than average on investment criteria, appear to out-perform nasty companies quite significantly on financial criteria. An unpublished study by Robert H. Terpstra and Robert A. Olsen compared the performance of the 18 'best' companies and the 20 'worst' according to a 'Social Responsibility Classification'.

It found that between 1974 and 1980 the best firms, on average, grew faster than the worst (14% versus 9%), were more profitable (net margins of 7% versus 5%) and achieved a higher return on equity (15% versus 10%).

The emergence of the ethical investor as a significant supplier of corporate finance is a development of fundamental importance for the corporate species. It is an example of a process I call 'extrusion' – the fabrication of human attitudes, like ethics and moral prejudices, into substantive features of the corporate environment. The extrusion process will be looked at more closely in the next chapter when we discuss the role of government in the theory of corporate evolution. The key point here is that investors, by extruding their preferences into ethical screening systems, are changing the financial environment in ways which favour strategies that are in tune with their prejudices (Figure 6.1).

It is easy to see how this works. There is a sum of money, M, available to companies. A proportion of it, P, is ethically screened. Companies that pass the ethical tests have access to all of M but companies that do not only have access to $M-P$. The effect this has on the cost of capital depends on how large P is and on how many companies pass the screening test. If P is large and there are only a few ethical companies, the cost of capital advantage is likely to be significant. But even when P is small and companies are generally ethical there will be a cost of capital advantage at the margin and it is mostly the marginal advantage, the edge, that drives evolution.

One can regard the ethical investor as an external, symbiotic member of an Axelrod cluster of nice companies. Working together the nice company and the ethical investor can give leverage to the power of the nice strategy in its struggle for survival and dominance. And there is a positive feedback loop at work too. The ethical investor gives a cost of capital edge to the nice strategy which enables it to perform better, which makes it more attractive to a larger number of investors, which further reduces its cost of capital . . . and so on.

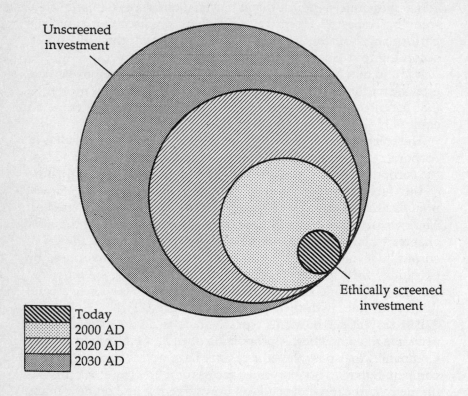

Fig 6.1: The Rise of the Ethical Investor
Ethically-screened investment is still only a tiny fraction of the total but its share is growing.

THE CASE OF SOUTH AFRICA

In the summer of 1987 the State of California's $34bn retirement fund was preparing to comply with a law passed the previous year requiring the fund's divestment of $6bn worth of South African investments. Basil J. Schwan, one of the fund's officers, was reported in *Business Week* to have deep misgivings about the divestment. Proponents of the divestment bill had argued it made financial sense to withdraw investments from a country heading for trouble. Schwan complained that 'they provided an economic argument for what's really a social issue'.

Schwan was wrong. South Africa is not just a social issue. It is also an economic and financial issue because the corporate world is subject to political institutions. South Africa became, through the process of ethical extrusion, a financial issue as soon as the divestment law was passed.

The loathing Californians and other Americans feel for South Africa's most notorious political institution also has economic significance for South Africa itself. It raises the local cost of capital and, by encouraging companies to respond to demands to sever links with South Africa, it also weakens the economy.

According to the March 1989 bulletin of the Council on Economic Priorities (CEP), over 100 resolutions concerning South Africa, ranging from the withdrawal of operations from the country to the termination of sales to the South African Defence Force, had been filed by shareholders for consideration at annual meetings. Resolutions tabled for annual meetings of US companies in 1989 also concerned other international justice issues, nuclear and conventional arms contracting, equal opportunities, smoking and health and corporate funding for agencies that support abortion.

Altogether, according to the CEP report, there were 214 social resolutions filed with 142 companies, an increase of 66% over the number filed in 1986.

Political pressure on further divestment is also becoming more intense in the US following the passage of the Anti-Apartheid Act in 1986. Although the election of George Bush as President in 1988, rather than the more hard-line (at least as far as South Africa is concerned) Michael Dukakis, was something of a relief for South African investors, few doubted major sanctions legislation would ultimately be passed in the US if the policy of apartheid was not abandoned.

Warburg Securities of London, in a report on the effect of US sanctions on South African investments published in August 1988, expressed the view that sanctions 'should not bring an immediate tidal wave of US disinvestment, but would be more likely to lead to the gradual erosion of an increasingly illiquid market.' The report estimated that US investors held about $4.5bn or some 12% of the South African mining share market and 16% (worth about $2.5bn) of the gold share market.

For South African mining companies, threatened by the prospect of the withdrawal of such vast sums from their local capital markets, Basil Schwan's assertion that the anti-apartheid lobby is a social rather than an economic phenomenon is cold comfort.

The process of ethical extrusion, sometimes exploiting political and sometimes financial institutions, bridges the gap between our two ethical domains. The South African economy, companies that have links with it and all other companies that, in one way or another, inspire the execration of large numbers of people, are becoming increasingly aware of the power the moral human being has over the nonmoral company.

NICENESS AND SHORT-TERMISM

As we have seen, the sanction imposed on companies by ethical screening of investment is financial. Companies which fail to pass the various tests have to pay more for their money and so can do less with it.

A company's cost of capital is amongst the most significant of its commercial attributes. And it is not just the relative cost that is important. As we saw in Chapter Two, Axelrod's iterated version of the prisoner's dilemma produces the odd result that general standards of business conduct are affected by the level of interest rates.

This conclusion is a consequence of the requirement in Axelrod's system that for cooperative behaviour to evolve the future must cast a shadow of minimum length over the present. We saw that if a player is so keen to win the current play that he or she cares hardly at all about what happens subsequently, he or she will play dirty. A high discount rate for future plays can turn an iterated game into a one-play game, so producing the orthodox gambit of defection.

The critical level of discount rate above which an iterated game plays like a single-play game depends on the probability of more encounters with the same player and on time preference. It seems reasonable to assume, however, that the discount rate would have to be very high for the future to cast so short a shadow that the results of subsequent plays are wholly immaterial.

The interest rate is a convenient proxy for the discount rate. At the time of writing (Summer 1990) UK base rates are 15%. This is historically high and reflects an exclusive reliance by government on interest rates in the seemingly incessant war against inflation. As we saw in the last chapter, stagflation is the most vexing of modern economic problems.

The higher the interest rate the shorter the shadow cast over the present by the future and so the weaker the evolutionary pressure for the development of nice strategies. The impact of the interest rate on corporate and financial time preference has yet to be fully appreciated. High interest rates not only limit the set of viable investment opportunities through the cost of capital constraint; they also affect the *type* of investments undertaken.

I believe the main cause of the so-called 'short-termism' of our financial markets and corporate strategists is the excessive use by government of the interest rate weapon in the battle against stagflation. High interest rates make companies more reckless of the future. They favour the fast buck merchants, who tend to be nasty, at the expense of cooperators and collaborators who need time to demonstrate the superior wealth-creating qualities of the nice strategy.

The short time horizons of institutional investors induce them to defect (by accepting hostile bids) too readily in their games with managers. Some able managers are so alienated by such breaches of faith that they desert the quoted sector.

Those that stay are forced to adapt to the City's short-termism by becoming short-termist themselves. In this way the economy loses the habit of planning ahead and of undertaking the collaborative, long-term projects that have given the Japanese and West German economies (where interest rates have been far lower) such structural strength.

We seem to be locked in a vicious circle where the solutions we find to one set of problems create more problems. Keynesianism was a solution to the problem of deep economic depressions but its implementation spawned the problem of stagflation. And because artificially high interest rates (there should be no need for them in conditions of financial surplus) address the symptoms rather than the cause of stagflation they have spawned the problem of short-termism.

It is time to look critically at the indiscriminate use of the interest rate weapon in the war against stagflation. Government should accept that the long-term economic damage inflicted by persistently high interest rates is too great a price to pay for a spurious price stability. Some other solution to stagflation must be found and by far the best candidate is Weitzman's share economy.

Because financial markets, as we have seen, are constantly seeking to improve their efficiency, City economists will be in the forefront of the next paradigm shift in economic orthodoxy.

Denis Healey, the most able of the Labour Party's post-war crop of finance ministers, acknowledged the power of City economists when Chancellor of the Exchequer in the 1970s. Frustrated in his early attempts at monetary policy management by accurate second-guessing by the City, he petulantly complained that 'the economy is being run by bright young men writing brokers' circulars'. A subsequent Tory Chancellor was less respectful. He called the City economists 'teenage scribblers' but they were hurting him too. The City became monetarist before the government and they are likely to be first with Weitzmanism too.

SUMMARY

- The company inhabits several different environments but is a native of the financial environment.

- The NFC has caused the financial environment, the City, to adapt to it as much as the NFC has had to adapt to the City.

- Markets are self-critical and self-improving. They have an appetite for more precise analytical methodologies.

- The growth of ethical investment and conscience funds has cost of capital implications which favour nice strategies.

- The case of South Africa is a striking illustration of the power of the phenomenon of ethical extrusion.

- High interest rates encourage short-termism and inhibit the evolution of nice strategies.

- The City, driven by its urge to improve itself, is likely to lead the way towards Weitzman's share economy.

CHAPTER 7

Tuning the Game

The subject of this chapter is the role of government in a world inhabited by moral human beings and nonmoral companies.

Government represents a bridge spanning the gap between our two ethical domains – of human–company relationships on the one hand (domain one) and of company–company relationships on the other (domain two). We shall begin our discussion of the shape of this bridge, and of the kind of traffic it carries, by describing its foundations in ethical domain one from which it originates.

John Rawls, in his book *A Theory of Justice*, which is widely regarded as one of the major post-war works on moral philosophy, divided government into four branches:

- The allocation branch, responsible for keeping the price system 'workably competitive' and preventing the formation of 'unreasonable market power'.
- The stabilisation branch, responsible for maintaining reasonably full employment such that those who want to work have a free choice of occupation and that the 'deployment of finance is supported by strong effective demand'.
- The transfer branch, responsible for ensuring the social minimum, taking needs into account.
- The distribution branch, responsible for preserving 'an approximate justice in distributive shares by means of taxation and the necessary adjustments in the rights of property'.

We are concerned here only with the first two which, according to Rawls, are responsible for maintaining 'the efficiency of the market economy generally'. Branches three and four play only an indirect role in the government/company game as important sources of ethical extrusion into the corporate environment.

The success with which government discharges its responsibility to maintain the efficiency of the market economy depends on three things; how well it understands the corporate species, the mutability of companies and strategies (how prone they are to vary), and the precision with which policy can encourage desirable variations and inhibit undesirable ones.

The first point to note about governments and their institutions is that they are themselves intermediate life-forms that exhibit both human and corporate qualities.

THE ECONOMICS OF POLITICS

Companies do not like government. Much more so than their human symbiotes, their deepest wish is to be free. The great engineer Isambard Kingdom Brunel expressed this basic hunger, which he shared, in his evidence to the Commission on the Application of Iron to Railway Structures (quoted in *Isambard Kingdom Brunel* by T. Rolt):

> They will embarrass and shackle the progress of improvement tomorrow by recording and registering as law the prejudices and errors of today. No man, however bold or however high he may stand in his profession, can resist the benumbing effect of rules laid down by authority. Devoted as I am to my profession, I see with fear and regret this tendency to legislate and to rule.

But since this tendency to legislate and to rule is endemic in human societies, companies have to live with it. The corporate habitat is littered with the detritus of the ethical human being in the form of law (statutes and the courts), regulation, tax systems and various forms of licensing. Companies, though they do not share the human ethical sense, are obliged to deal with the ethical manifestations extruded into their environment by the political process.

Fortunately these extrusions have evolved in ways that make them perfectly intelligible to companies. This is because the evolution of the main policy-making institutions, namely the political parties, is driven by forces very similar to those that drive corporate evolution. Companies and political parties speak the same evolutionary language.

120

The correspondences between companies and political parties has been thrown into sharp relief in recent years by a bold invasion of political theory mounted by a group of economists led by Professor James Buchanan of the Virginia Polytechnic Institute. They claimed politics was not, as most political theorists supposed, a subject in its own right but was rather a sub-discipline of economics. The claim is grand one. It embraces not only the democratic process but also bureaucracy, lobbying, regulation and constitutional theory. Collectively these sub-disciplines are known as the 'theory of public choice'.

Notwithstanding the fond imaginings of some politicians there is no 'natural party of government'. Political parties compete with each other by differentiating their products. That the political process is competitive rather than convergent on an 'ideal' set of policies, is because of a rather surprising discovery by the Nobel laureate economist Kenneth Arrow. The 'Arrow paradox' states that it is logically impossible to construct a 'social welfare function'. In other words there is no set of policies that will satisfy everyone.

The 'economic imperialists', as Buchanan and his followers were christened, addressed an important political question that had been neglected in the pre-Arrow era, namely 'according to what pressures, given the impossibility of a social welfare function, do the policy product lines of parties evolve?'

The usual pre-Arrow answer is that a political party consists of a group of people with a common philosophy and that it therefore derives its policies directly from philosophical precepts. Thus policy-making is entirely explicable in terms of the development of a preexisting set of core doctrines. External events are only significant when they generate new problems. They cannot change the core doctrines, they can only be accommodated by them. Votes are beside the point. Keeping faith with the shared philosophy is the only imperative.

This view is consistent with the self-image of the left-wing of the British Labour Party. There is a certain nobility in such a fundamentalist approach to politics but because it refuses to recognise the impossibility of a social welfare function there is precious little else.

The doctrine-driven model may help to explain policy-making in certain parties at certain times but it is not a plausible model for a political party although it may be for a church. Since political parties resemble companies more than they resemble religious organisations it seems reasonable to begin seeking an answer to the question of what forces drive the process of policy formation by asking what it is that political parties are trying to maximise.

According to the economic imperialists political parties and companies both sell desirable things to customers (human beings and their various institutions) in return for currency. The difference is that whereas companies sell products and services for the currency of money, political parties sell philosophies and policies for the currency of votes.

We decided in Chapter Two that companies are optimisers. They seek more than mere survival. They try to maximise profits, market value, sales or some mixture of these within time horizons of varying length. And we saw in the last chapter that some modern companies behave as if they are driven by an urge to maximise their knowhow capital.

The metabolism of political parties feeds on votes because votes are the currency of power. Buchanan and his followers proposed that the rational political party is motivated by the wish to achieve or retain the status of government and that its adoption and abandonment of policies is entirely explicable in these terms.

The party manifesto at the time of a general election is the main marketing document. Its purpose is to maximise the votes cast for the party because only in this way can the probability of election or re-election be maximised. No rational party will persist in offering for sale, in return for votes, policies for which there is no demand because such a course would jeopardise the party's survival and so its chances of achieving, or being returned to, power. One implication of this model is that in a two-party system the policy packages offered by each party will be very similar because the incremental votes each party is seeking to win were cast for the other party last time.

There is not the space here to do full justice to the theory of public choice. It embraces much more than mere politics. There is a sub-discipline devoted to the theory of bureaucracy which shows that bureaucrats are motivated by the desire to maximise the size of their departments, there are models for lobbying and what the Americans call 'log-rolling' (the trade-offs that take place as part of the lobbying process), and the Chicago school has shown that in the US transport, broadcasting and electricity industries at any rate, regulators have tended to end up on the side of the industries regulated.

For our purposes the theory of public choice contains a number of important insights:

- Political parties and the institutions of government such as bureaucracies and regulatory authorities are similar to companies in that they are optimisers.
- They are different from companies in that the variables they try to maximise are non-monetary.
- The constitutional framework within which political parties, bureaucracies and regulatory authorities operate has a profound effect on outcomes. For example, if unchecked, bureaucracies tend to become much too big and regulatory authorities tend to 'go native'.

The first two points define the relationship between companies and regulatory agencies. They identify the political party as an expression of popular will and the policies it implements when in power as extrusions of that will. Insofar as these policy artefacts affect the corporate environment, the political system establishes a presence in what I call ethical domain two (see Figure 7.1). In the UK these outposts of government in the corporate world are mostly garrisoned by agents of the financial and industrial ministries, namely the Treasury and the Department of Trade and Industry.

The first two points also show that although the principles and language of human ethics are unintelligible to the company, their manifestations in policies are not. Law and the legislative process are meaningful to companies. Political parties process human ethics, transmute them into policies and, when they achieve power, they extrude them into artefacts of the corporate environment. Because the process is the creature of evolution and not of deliberate design, it is both elegant and effective. In contrast its artefacts – the laws and regulations themselves – *are* the products of deliberate design and have therefore been, for the most part, both clumsy and ineffective.

The lesson of the third point is that, the regulatory frameworks in which companies operate have as much, if not more, influence on policy consequences as the policies themselves. Good policies are frequently frustrated by inappropriate (usually excessively elaborate) frameworks. And like companies, industrial policies are diachronic (covering the whole of their history) rather than synchronic (just here and now). They carry into the present the residues of the past. Regulatory styles, prejudices (especially of tax

123

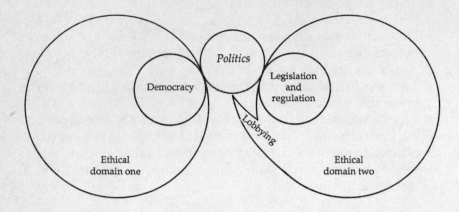

Fig 7.1: Man, Politics and the Company
Politics extrudes domain one ethics into domain two, but domain two extrusions
feed back into politics through lobbying.

authorities), bureaucratic rules of thumb, anachronistic legal
precedents and the litter of past policies, all infuse the corporate
environment with a kind of sclerotic nostalgia which goes largely
unnoticed even by the companies themselves.

Government has a responsibility to clear up this mess and to
ensure new mess is prevented from accumulating. It is no easy task
because there are always consequences of regulatory and de-
regulatory acts that are unexpected. The safest course is to do as
little as possible and to undo as much as possible. If it is felt that
something must be done, industrial policy-makers should first seek
to understand the nature of the corporate game and then they
should try to influence the direction of corporate evolution. The
essence of good policy is the refinement of the game's rules, not
direct interference in the game itself.

THE CONSERVATIVE ROLE
An industrial policy based on the theory of corporate evolution
should recognise that natural selection conserves as well as
liberates.

Indeed, in its original, pre-Darwin form, the idea of natural
selection played *only* a conservative role. The geologist Sir Charles
Lyell and the naturalist Edward Blyth, both known to Darwin

124

(Lyell's *Principles of Geology* gave natural selection its clock), had shown how 'wild nature' polices the integrity of species by weeding out monsters in the same way as plant and animal breeders eliminate undesirable variations.

This conservative role of natural selection is the basic model for industrial policy-making. The goal of policy is to maintain the quality and integrity of the corporate species. Ministers should acknowledge that the wild nature of the market is a control of this kind and so should interfere with the process of natural selection only when wild nature, perhaps because of the detritus of the past, is getting it wrong. They should be vigilant but usually passive, stepping in only when mutations emerge within the corporate species that prevent the market from discharging its proper allocative function.

CORPORATE CONTROL
An entomologist friend of mine, Dr Gavin Robertson, spent three years in Cambridge studying greenflies. The aphis, as the greenfly is known to naturalists, is a voracious plant pest that multiplies at an alarming rate by parthenogenesis, a form of asexual reproduction.

Gavin was trying to establish the ground rules for a war between the aphis and one of its predators. The ladybird is the best known aphis-killer, but for reasons I forget Gavin had chosen a wasp as the protector of his cucumber crop. (It may even have been one of the ichneumonidae, the parasites with the grisly life-style we encountered in the first chapter.)

The technique is known as biological control and, in principle anyway, it is a very elegant idea. Farmers, instead of spraying expensive and sometimes poisonous insecticides over their crops, induce nature to do the de-infestation for them. At first sight it seems very simple. If the farmer has a pest, he finds one of its natural predators, introduces the insects to each other and then sits back and watches the inevitable entomological mayhem.

But there is one small problem. If there are too few wasps the aphids, with their inordinately prolific reproduction, will be coming at the predators faster than the wasps can kill them. For the wasps it will be great, like shooting fish in a barrel, but for the cucumbers it will be murder.

So, why not simply introduce more wasps? That is not quite the answer either. If there are too many wasps they wipe out the aphids in short order and then die of starvation, leaving the cucumbers with no protection from the next band of marauding aphids, gravid with their innumerable progeny.

The trick is to try to get the numbers just right so that there are enough wasps to prevent the aphid population from exploding but not so many that it starts to decline.

It is a matter of matching the vectors of aphis and wasp reproduction rates and of calculating wasp kill rates at varying aphis densities. There is much more to it than that, of course. Reproduction rates of both insects vary according to temperature and humidity and there are any number of other variables to take into account.

But the principle of biological control remains elegant despite the complexities of its application. It is a much neater form of pest control than pesticide for three reasons: it is cheaper, it is, in theory at any rate, more effective in that it poses fewer re-infestation problems and, most important of all, it is non-invasive in that unlike the blunderbus of pesticide, the rifle of biological control leaves innocent bystanders unharmed.

A method of control that is cheap, effective and precise is as much to be desired in the field of industrial policy as it is in a field of cucumber.

I should state again that I am no fan of government control. My belief in the allocative virtues of the free market economy is quite passionate. I take the view that as far as industrial policy is concerned, and most other policy too, government is better employed when repealing and removing statutes and regulations than when passing and imposing them. But as we saw in Chapter four, the idea that a free market needs to be protected from its own excesses has a very respectable libertarian pedigree.

My 'paradox of free markets', the form of which I borrowed from Popper's paradox of democracy, states that **if markets are too free they will permit the emergence of monopoly.**

Government has a duty to ensure the allocative mechanism of the free market economy works effectively. It must try diligently to protect the free market from the monsters of monopoly and the cartel, and it must seek means of attacking and killing the pests of corporate complacency, inefficiency and slothfulness without affecting healthy tissue. The corporate equivalents of Gavin's wasps have an important part to play in this essentially conservative process of market de-infestation.

One of my favourite corporate 'wasps' is the UK conglomerate

Hanson (formerly Hanson Trust). Over the past two decades or so this London-based group has been the world's leading exponent of the acquisition-led strategy. My infrequent but invariably enlightening conversations with Hanson's leaders – Lord Hanson, Sir Gordon White and Martin Taylor – have played an important part in the development of my views about agency costs and the takeover (see Chapter four).

The key point about Hanson's aggressively acquisitive nature (as we might expect, it is mirrored by an internal style that has been called harsh but fair though never comfortable), is that it is hard-wired. There is no blood-lust in Hanson's unrelenting hostility. It is not just like a wasp; it *is* a wasp. It cannot stop itself unsheathing its stinger when it sees a corporate aphis. Its hostility is purely instinctive.

The coding for the instinct lies embedded in the Hanson strategy which, though anything but nice, shares with TFT the qualities of simplicity and clarity. 'Companies exist' Hanson might say in its mission statement, if it had any patience with such things, 'to create shareholder value. Many companies appear not to be aware of this. Our business idea is to create value for our shareholders by taking these delinquents over and getting their minds right.' Hanson makes no secret of its waspishness. It is proud to be a predator and though there is no atom of altruism in its strategy, Martin Taylor is quite sincere when he says 'economies need companies like ours. We're useful to them.'

But if the government is Gavin and the economy is his cucumber crop, it is not enough to abominate aphids and approve of their predators. Like Gavin, government must tackle the intricacies of vector analysis. They must ask such questions as: 'how many wasps should there be?'; 'should they have long stingers or short ones?'; 'should the aphids be allowed to develop wasp defences and, if so, to what extent and of what kind?' and 'what is the minimum number of aphids needed to ensure the wasps don't eat themselves out of prey?'

There is a tendency among politicians who believe in *laisser faire* to assume that what happens is right, but this is only reasonable if the original situation is right. As we have seen, the corporate habitat is littered with the detritus of past policies and prejudices.

The conventions of merger accounting, the chronically suspicious attitude of the tax authorities, the high degree of corporate integration in some Western economies (particularly Britain's), striking cross-border differences in market freedoms (in the market for corporate control for instance) and the 'faddy' nature of the securities industry all conspire to frustrate allocative efficiency.

So although the theory of corporate evolution, when applied to policy-making, has a strong prejudice in favour of laisser faire it is a prejudice tempered with pragmatism. It cannot be indifferent to existing distortions embedded in the corporate habitat. The wasps of natural selection need an adequately competitive environment if they are to fulfil their allocative role well.

EVOLUTIONARY POLICY-MAKING

The differences between conventional and evolutionary policy-making can be illustrated by word contrasts:

Evolutionary	Conventional
Environment	The economy
Climate	Political philosophy
Catastrophes (*)	New governments
Corporate ecology	Economic theories
Corporate control	Regulation & law
Variation potential	Competition policy
Gene pool maintenance	Mergers policy
Corporate taxonomy	Standard Industrial Classifications (SICs)

(*) *Catastrophe is used here in its technical sense – a sudden shift from one equilibrium to another.*

Let us look at each of these in turn:
Environment/economy
Corporate life-forms need a relatively stable environment in which to operate. It should not be *perfectly* stable because that reduces the potential for evolution, but the main parameters, such as interest and tax rates and aggregate demand should be sufficiently stable, in terms of their rates of change, for long-term planning.

Climate/political philosophy
The climate for corporate life-forms should be clement. That is to say that, subject to the constraints of social and political priorities such as minimum living standards and what seems to be a fair distribution of wealth, government should subscribe to an econo-

mic philosophy that recognises the needs of companies, in terms of the fiscal and monetary conditions under which they prosper, and the fact that the corporate life-form is the major wealth-creating species on the planet.

Catastrophes/new governments (philosophies)

It should be recognised that sudden and substantial changes in philosophy, as when governments change in relatively polarised political systems, are very destabilising for the corporate life-form and therefore involve significant adjustment costs. New philosophies should therefore be introduced gradually, in order to minimise disturbance.

Corporate ecology/economic theories

Political tactics (the expressions of philosophies in policies) should be based on an understanding of the physiology of the corporate life-form and of its propensity to evolve. There is a law of government that states that each new policy produces unexpected outcomes, some of which are counter-intuitive, i.e. the opposite of what was expected. Theory states, for example, that when a country's currency strengthens in foreign exchange markets, its world competitiveness falls. But in post-war Germany and Japan, microeconomic responses to the macroeconomic fact of higher exchange rates, have caused competitiveness to *rise* as the Deutschemark and Yen have strengthened. No theory that fails to recognise the needs of companies and their ability to adapt is a suitable basis for policy-making.

Corporate control/regulation and law

Governments should recognise that since control systems demand a compliant response, the manner in which a policy is applied often has as much influence on outcomes as the policy itself. The idea of corporate evolution, by focusing attention on the compliance behaviour at the policy-making stage, helps to avoid mistakes that are the results of good policies badly applied.

Variation potential/competition policy

Since free markets contain within them the seeds of their own destruction (the paradox of free markets), the maintenance of competition ranks as the highest policy-making priority.

The corporate life-form is motivated to preserve, as far as it can, the prevailing conditions of its environment. A government, when introducing 'natural enemies' of anti-competitive behaviour to the corporate environment, must ensure they are sufficiently well-armed and equipped to frustrate the inevitable attempts of the existing corporate order to preserve the status quo.

Gene pool maintenance/mergers policy

Though the overriding need is to preserve stability, there is also a need to maintain variability. An economy must have a minimum degree of evolutionary potential if it is to retain its ability to adapt to changing circumstances. That requires the corporate population to be large and heterogeneous. The more varied the corporate population, the more adaptable it is. There should therefore be a prejudice against mergers because mergers reduce heterogeneity and therefore adaptability. One of the great policy conundrums of modern times is how to preserve the invaluable disciplinary effects of a free market in corporate control without reducing unduly the richness of the corporate gene pool.

PRIVATISATION – A TAXONOMIC CHANGE

Since, as we have seen, corporate evolution proceeds according to the law of natural selection working on strategies, there is a need for a system of corporate taxonomy based on strategies rather than on industrial classifications.

For example, the key qualities for policy-makers of the UK conglomerate Hanson lie not in the industries in which it operates but in the fact that it is pursuing a relatively short-term, acquisition-led strategy that preys on mature, brand-rich companies that are imposing high agency costs on shareholders.

The importance of strategy and strategic change is nowhere more strikingly illustrated than in the phenomenon of privatisation that has been one of the major features of industrial change in the UK economy over the past decade.

The act of privatisation is tantamount to the emigration of a commercial organisation over the political bridge from ethical domain one to ethical domain two. Since the natural habitat of companies is ethical domain two, such migrations are generally beneficial for the organisations concerned. Privatised groups usually end up healthier after a period of acclimatisation but they also end up very different.

By and large people trust state-owned organisations more than those in the private sector because they seem, at any rate, to be subject to direct control through the political processes of ethical domain one. This control is also often reflected in nice strategies because it would be plainly incongruous for a state-owned organisation, wedded by its nature to the ideal of public service, to be avaricious and predatory.

When the same organisations are privatised this direct control is lost and the company becomes inherently less trustworthy. It is hard to overestimate the significance for the organisation's culture and its relationships with its customers and suppliers, of this shift of allegiance from the ideal of public service to the interests of shareholders.

But the bargain is a good one, particularly now, when evolutionary pressures are encouraging all companies, not just state-owned ones, to adopt nice strategies. And it may be that the public service tradition in some of the major privatised organisations, if it survives the initial exorcisms, will help them to lead the way in the adoption of nice strategies. After all, a belief in the ideal of public service is not so different, in practice, from a conviction that it is better for business, in the long run, to pursue a nice strategy.

From the point of view of government, however, the significance of the privatisation act is allocative. By exposing inefficient state-owned organisations to the disciplines of the market, it is helping to discharge its duty to make the economy efficient. It is a classic example of evolutionary policy-making.

STREET-PARKING – A CASE STUDY
To show how evolutionary policy-making works in practice we shall look at a quasi-hypothetical case study.

The central theme of evolutionary policy-making is that the best way of dealing with monstrous phenomena like stagflation, merger mania, fraud, inefficiency and conservatism is to identify or devise natural enemies of the monsters and then to introduce them into the corporate environment. For example, Weitzman believes his share economy is a natural enemy of stagflation, and Hanson-type companies are widely regarded as natural enemies of corporate inefficiency and other agency costs of management.

In the following case study the problem for which we, as policy-makers, must find a natural enemy is the vexing phenomenon of illegal parking in our congested inner cities.

It has been estimated that the average speed of travel through central London has recently fallen below the 11mph estimated to have been the average for the horse-drawn era just before the arrival on our streets of the internal combustion engine.

The main reason for this striking regression in the speed of urban travel is that the effect of the technical increase in the speed of vehicles, which, other things equal, would have tended to reduce congestion, has been more than offset by the effect of higher vehicle density. Most of the city's roads and streets were not designed for such density in the first place and have been rendered even less adequate by a kind of arterial plaque, consisting of the growth of on-street (and on-pavement) parking. Despite the application of parking laws and the liberal use of yellow paint this problem has grown inordinately.

Parking laws and yellow lines make the city environment legally more hostile to the on-street parker but they need to be policed, and direct policing by the regulatory authorities has resource implications. Traffic wardens initially proved quite effective natural enemies of the on-street parker but, as average living standards rose and the scale of the problem grew (thus reducing the probability of getting a ticket), the on-street parker acquired a tolerance to parking fines in much the same way as pests tend to acquire a tolerance to pesticides.

The effectiveness of the parking ticket system was rejuvenated when it began to be routinely supported by the vehicle removal activities of the police, but after a while resource constraints again allowed on-street parkers to acquire sufficient tolerance to resume their growth.

During the past couple of years a new and potentially much more powerful natural enemy of the on-street parker, in the shape of the wheel-clampers, has been let loose on London's streets. The licensed wheel-clamper is, in theory anyway, the perfect natural enemy of the on-street parker. I admire the wheel-clamp system enormously. It cannot eliminate on-street parking because if it did the licensed wheel-clampers, like Gavin's wasps, would go out of business and so allow the on-street parker to make a comeback, but it can keep it under control.

The wheel-clampers, the knights of the yellow lines, are properly regarded as the franchisees of London's parking laws. They have no need to be aware of the elegance of the system they operate to be effective (it is probably better if they are not) – all they need to know is that the more illegal wheels they clamp the more money they make.

The reason the system is so effective is that its operational features attack the on-street parker where it hurts most – not in his or her pocket primarily but in his or her mobility. Time is more precious than money these days and the dilemma of the urban traveller, similar in form to the prisoner's dilemma game described in Chapter two, is that for an individual for whom time is precious, the best way to cope with congestion is to add to it, namely to have his or her car parked outside the office.

Wheel-clamping is effective because the greater the chances that on-street parkers will find their wheels clamped, and so have to wait to be unclamped (and miss appointments), the greater their reluctance to rely for their mobility on their cars.

But the system would work better with a number of refinements suggested by the principle of natural control advocated here. It is mostly a matter of establishing the goals of the policy and of designing the system in such a way that the agents of the goals, in this case the licensed wheel-clampers, are motivated, by the exigencies of the system rather than by an understanding of its purpose, to behave in a way that achieves those goals.

Wheel-clampers should be regarded as both a source of licence revenue and as providers of social amenity (namely, clearer streets). Local authorities should decide on the balance between their revenue and social amenity priorities and should reflect the latter in a 'clear streets' bonus rate arrangement with the licensed wheel-clampers such that, for example, a higher proportion of unclamping revenue is retained if the incidence of on-street parking (perhaps measured in terms of the estimated average speed through the borough) is kept below an agreed minimum.

No other constraints on wheel-clampers are necessary. I believe they should be free to charge what they like for unclamping and to take as long as they like to do it.

Imagine you were a wheel-clamping licensee with a high clear-streets bonus-rate arrangement and imagine, further, that you begin your operations at a time when congestion in your area is severe. You are strongly motivated to trigger the bonus rate so you are inclined, initially, to charge heavily for unclamping and to take a long time doing it. You are in punishment mode. Once your penal charges (in terms of unclamping costs and, more importantly, waiting time) have reduced congestion to near the level at which the bonus rate is triggered you are likely to reduce unclamping charges and speed up the unclamping process.

It would be folly to continue to charge too much and take too long once the bonus rate was achieved because your prey would become too scarce. It would be in your interests to switch to 'cull' mode so that the balance between the revenue retention rate, fixed by the bonus, and the number of hits, determined by unclamping price and time, is such that revenues are maximised.

Thereafter the wheel-clamping business would be a matter of keeping a close watch on density and of being ready to correct any signs of divergence from the optimum by adjustments to unclamping prices and times.

In my view the best way to decide which companies should do the unclamping is to offer for sale at auction licences with clearly specified clear-streets bonus arrangements. A wealth of fascinating information for industrial psychologists about the value to modern men and women of time and mobility would be a purely incidental by-product of the operation of such a system over time.

But that is not the end of the story. With no further action by the authorities, the wheel-clamping 'industry' evolved in a way that brings to mind Jonathan Swift's witty poem:

> So, naturalists observe, a flea
> Hath smaller fleas that on him prey;
> And these have smaller fleas to bite 'em,
> And do proceed *ad infinitum*.
> (*On Poetry*, 1733.)

Hardly had the parasitical London wheel-clampers got into their stride than there appeared, quite spontaneously, a second-order parasite. On returning to their illegally-parked cars, victims of the clampers soon began to find a second communication on their windscreens alongside the dismayingly strident 'Halt! Do not attempt to move this vehicle . . .'. It had a more friendly tone, something like 'Don't Panic. You've been clamped but we can help you. Ring this number and for a small additional fee we will arrange for your vehicle to be unclamped and we will let you know when this has been done.'

Imagine you had decided to go into business as an unclamping arranger. What would be your *modus operandi*? You would not want, if you could help it, to spend your time rushing around town looking for clamped cars. You would be motivated to acquire information about where the clamped cars were as quickly as possible because you would know competitors would be hunting the same prey. It would be in your interests, therefore, to try to find out which vehicles were about to be clamped so that you could be waiting around the corner, ready to slap your solicitation on the immobilised vehicle before anyone else.

One way of gathering such commercially useful information would be to tip off the clampers about illegally parked cars. In this way you would be entering into a symbiotic relationship with the clampers by acting as a freelance intelligence system for them.

It is even possible to imagine that after such a symbiosis had been at work for a while the clampers would decide to save search costs and just rely for their business intelligence on tip-offs from the unclamping arrangers. It would be a bit like a hyena with a taste for offal, tipping off lazy and more fastidious lions about the availability of antelope.

Moreover, it would be perfectly logical (and entirely in the spirit of the business school prescription that you should try to sell more products to your existing customers) for wheel-clamping firms to go into business as unclamping arrangers (and for the latter to bid for clamping licences).

Indeed, it might appear to be inevitable in a free market for these two businesses to converge into partnerships or even integrated companies. In any case, since both business ideas share the same information base it would be logical, in the long run, for them to specialise. The unclamping arrangers would cease to fulfil their original function and would concentrate, instead, on intelligence gathering (finding the illegal parkers). The licensed clampers would assume all operating duties – clamping, posting both kinds of notices and arranging the unclamping.

But logical though such collaborations and business integrations might seem, nice company considerations might easily frustrate such evolution.

The unclamping facilitator is selling convenience. Clamp victims do not *have* to use their services and in the heightened emotional state of being clamped they might resent deeply the knowledge, or even the suspicion, they had been shopped by the company now offering them an unclamping service.

Nice strategy considerations in this strange, parasitical marketplace might persuade unclamping arrangers that it would be prudent to take great pains to distance themselves from any suggestion of collusion with wheel-clamping licensees.

The principles involved in this kind of control system have very general application. One possibility policy-makers might consider, for example, is the use of licensed, freelance inspectors to police emission-control regulations.

Suppose a safe maximum for the emission of a particular gas from an industrial process was established. The normal way to police such rules would be for an invariably understaffed inspectorate to make random checks on the industrial plants involved, and to issue proceedings against owners if they find the maximum levels have been exceeded.

Adaptive behaviour by the owners involves establishing a pattern for the checks and ensuring emission levels are legal at around the time the next check is expected. They are motivated not to comply with the regulations but to minimise the probability of being caught not complying.

Now suppose the inspectorate is sold to its inspectors and that the privatised company is licensed to continue its work and is paid for it out of the fines resulting from successful convictions. Suddenly the inspectors, from being overworked and underpaid civil servants companies can get on the right side of and otherwise manipulate, are transformed into ravening wolves, highly motivated to catch polluters and bring them to book. The probability of getting caught breaking the rules would soar and, if the fines were large enough, the owners of the plants would become motivated to comply permanently with the emission-control regulations.

THE LIMITED CREATIVE ROLE

We have been dealing here mostly with the conservative role of natural selection in the corporate environment and the use to which it can be put by government in its disciplinary mode, but natural selection's most celebrated role, the one identified by Darwin, is as the cause of selection and so the driving force of evolution and here the case for government intervention is weak.

It is one thing to identify and attempt to eliminate behaviour patterns that are clearly undesirable but quite another to try to identify and help to promote behaviour patterns *thought to be* desirable. Governments do it all the time though. They try to stimulate more investment, encourage research and development and motivate managers (by giving tax relief on option schemes for example).

Some of this 'positive' policy is the result of lobbying by the companies themselves and when it contains, as it often does, ground-clearing qualities, it is reasonable enough.

By and large however, governments should be extremely wary of second-guessing natural selection. The counter intuitive result lies in wait for those inclined to embark on grand corporate breeding programmes. Government should be content with the conserver role and should sternly resist the temptation to play the evolver.

The most important task of government in the theory of corporate evolution is the preservation and promotion of competition.

THE IMPORTANCE OF SCEPTICISM
Adaptive change in industrial policy is as necessary as adaptive change in corporate strategy. Government needs to be aware of shifts in the thinking of industrialists and business economists such as those associated with the size debate described in the next chapter. And policy-makers must at all times maintain a deep scepticism about the conservative arguments put forward by those with a vested interest in maintaining the status quo.

Government and its agencies, such as the Office of Fair Trading and the Monopolies and Mergers Commission, must always be conscious of the fact that the big business establishment is inherently conservative. It dislikes changes in the theoretical environment, just as biological creatures dislike changes in their habitats. The establishment is, by definition, perfectly adapted to the status quo. *Any* change is a potential threat.

The British government has, in recent years, been persuaded on several occasions, to collude with big business in the latter's voracious search for greater size. The acquisition of Times Newspapers by Rupert Murdoch's News International group (*The Sun, The News of the World* and now *Today,* as well as *The Times* and *The Sunday Times*) should have been blocked in 1981. More recently the competition agencies should not have been persuaded by spurious 'global carrier' arguments to permit the acquisition of the British Caledonian independent airline by British Airways.

The sort of argument put forward by GEC during its first bid for its rival Plessey in 1986, including the claim that the next generation of digital telecommunications switches would cost so much to develop that even bigger companies were necessary, should also have been treated with much deeper official scepticism. I suspect that, given the chance, small, entrepreneurially run companies, with

137

tight research and development budgets would be capable of developing a new digital switch, incorporating revolutionary design features, for a tenth of the money the large companies claim will be needed. The costs of new product development are linked directly to the size of the organisation undertaking the development.

I suggest that before British Telecom orders its next switch it should hold a competition, open to all, for a new design concept, and that the development contract should be given to the company which offers the most cost-effective solution.

Far too much taxpayers' money has been wasted since the war on feathering the nests of the big companies. They might have had a case for some special consideration had their period of hegemony been associated with a relative improvement in the performance of the economy. But it has been associated with the opposite. It is high time the government, as a purchaser of public goods, withdrew its patronage from the big business establishment and gave the other guys a chance.

AN INTERNATIONAL MERGERS POLICY

To end this chapter I want to consider briefly the implications for policy-makers of the increasing internationalisation of business in recent years. It is a process that is almost certain to continue as communications improve and as national cultures are progressively absorbed into a single, global culture.

From the point of view of the managers of a national economy the globalisation of business is a worrying trend because it allows the corporate giants, bent on gaining ever more mass, to escape the strictures of merely national competition agencies.

There is even a body of doctrine within merger policies that acknowledges the fact of supra-national integration and concedes that it has implications for national policies. As we saw above, the argument that an anti-competitive merger should occasionally be allowed because without it the national industry in question will be too fragmented to be competitive internationally, has met with sympathetic consideration by Britain's Monopolies and Mergers Commission.

It should not have been. There is one necessary and sufficient condition in an economy for the evolution of internationally competitive companies and that is a competitive domestic market. Size has very little to do with competitiveness. If the various national governments do not acquire a greater scepticism about the size argument, and if they do not soon begin building the framework for a strong, supra-national competition agency, the world will be dominated by a hundred or so global corporations.

The paradox of free markets is always there waiting to frustrate the trust-busters. An unregulated, supra-national marketplace is the perfect breeding ground for anti-competitive corporate leviathans able and willing to dispense their investment patronage in return for the favours of national governments. The emergent global corporations are the greatest threat so far to the principle of national sovereignty.

Not before time there are signs that the conventional wisdom about size is beginning to change. In March 1989 the US magazine *International Business Week* ran a cover story headlined 'Is your company too big?' It began with what was, for corporate evolutionists, an evocative quote from the English geneticist J.B.S. Haldane:

For every type of animal there is a most convenient size, and a large change in size inevitably carries with it a change of form . . . just as there is a best size for every animal, so the same is true for every human institution.

We shall look in some detail at the *Business Week* article, and at the wider philosophical debate of which it was part, in the next chapter.

SUMMARY

- Government has a responsibility to maintain the efficiency of the market economy.

- The theory of public choice shows that political parties are analogues of companies.

- The principle of biological control offers some important policy opportunities.

- Corporate wasps should be used by government to help natural selection fulfil its conservative role.

- Evolutionary policy-making employs a new language.

- Wheel-clamping to control on-street parking is a good model for policies based on the natural enemy principle.

- The potential for directing corporate evolution towards predetermined goals is very limited.

- Governments should be sceptical about the arguments of the business establishment.

- International collaboration between the various national mergers and competition agencies is urgently needed.

140

CHAPTER 8

The Origins of Niceness

An evolutionary mechanism that employs Darwinian selection as well as Lamarckian 'instruction' needs a source of variation. Trial-and-error processes of this kind cannot rely on learned solutions to the problems of survival and propagation. In the theory of corporate evolution, as in Darwinism, the death of one strategy is a consequence of the selection of another. In this chapter we shall investigate where such superior strategies come from, paying particular attention to the philosophical and economic provenance of the nice strategy.

Once again we shall begin with a look at how biological nature is believed to have solved its problems – in this case, the problem of the provenance of novelty.

In one sense the answer is simple – biological variation comes from genetic mutations, but there must be more to it than that. To be the inspirations of evolutionary change mutations must be accompanied by behavioural changes. As we saw in Chapter two, a mutation is equivalent to the appearance of a strategic 'shell' consisting of a new set of behavioural opportunities. An opposed thumb, enabling a hand to grasp objects, would have been of little evolutionary interest had it not led to the emergence of a tool-using culture.

Sir Karl Popper has proposed various classes of genes for this purpose. His genetic taxonomy includes 'a-genes' that control anatomy and 'b-genes' that control behaviour. Popper further subdivides b-genes into 'p-genes', controlling preferences and aims, and 's-genes', controlling skills, and he proposes that p-genes change first, selecting s-gene change which then selects a-gene change.

Modern evolutionists find Popper's search for direction in the evolutionary process futile and his idea of genetic taxonomy meaningless. It cannot be tested and, like all good Popperians, they are reluctant to waste time on non-testable conjectures.

But Popper's licence to violate his own principles derived from his conviction that Darwinism is not a testable scientific theory but is, rather, a 'metaphysical research programme'. He argued that Darwinian theory had achieved its successes on one planet and was therefore an exploration of a 'situational logic' rather than fundamental science.

But he underestimated natural selection's generality. As Popper himself realised, it is a trial-and-error elimination process identical in form to his own theory of the growth of knowledge. A. G. Cairns Smith argued in his *Seven Clues to the Origin of Life* that natural selection must have preceded biology. One of his speculations concerned randomly flawed crystals of clay selected according to their effect on the formation of silt in streams.

Richard Dawkins believes 'all life evolves by the differential survival of replicating entities'. My assertion of natural selection's generality is that all life, including corporate life, evolves by the differential survival of strategic themes (or stremes). Just as genes propagate themselves in the gene pool via sperms and eggs, so stremes are propagated in the streme pool by the propensity to emulate winning strategies.

But Popper's conjecture that evolutionary change is the product of mutagenic clusters, affecting skills and propensities as well as anatomy, is perfectly reasonable as a logical description of what evolution does. It may not be true in a scientific sense but it is accurate. In terms of corporate evolution it means, amongst other things, that changes in the aspirations, aptitudes and belief systems of managers are necessary if not sufficient preconditions for strategic change.

So natural selection is both inevitable and inexorable. If one accepts that companies, if not alive, are at least life-like, or even clay-like, one has to acknowledge the strategies they use are being selected according to their differential survival. An evolutionary process of some kind *must* be at work within the corporate species and its logical constituents must include changes in attitudes and skills as well as substantive changes in strategic themes.

But where do these changes come from? What is the equivalent in corporate evolution of genetic mutation? We need to find pools of new strategies, complete with supporting philosophies and theories, to make the theory of corporate evolution a useful and plausible model for business economics.

RECULER POUR MIEUX SAUTER

An evolutionary mechanism known as neoteny, identified by the Dutch anatomist Louis Bolk in the 1920s, is a promising candidate for the position of an important if not the main source of novelty required by the theory of corporate evolution.

In the process of neoteny (literally, holding youth), organisms become sexually mature at a stage equivalent to the embryonic stage of their ancestors. This offers not novelty itself but the possibility of novelty because a creature's embryo is more plastic than the adult form and so returning to it, or retaining its features, can provide a wider developmental opportunity set.

The evolution of the ostrich is said to be an example of neoteny because the animal has some of the characteristics of a foetal bird, like its scrawny neck and its flightlessness. The latter quality has, by removing the weight constraint imposed by flight, allowed the ostrich to become the largest bird on Earth.

Man too may be the creature of neoteny. Our rounded, bulbous cranium, containing our large brain, is shared by the embryos of apes and monkeys. In their case subsequent brain growth is slower so the cranial vault emerges smaller and lower in adults. It is probable we achieved our large brains by retaining rapid foetal growth rates.

The human face, distinguished from those of other primates by a straight profile, small jaws and teeth and weak brow ridges, is reminiscent of the face of the juvenile ape. The similarity fades as the ape's jaw accelerates its growth in relation to the rest of the skull, producing the adult's characteristic muzzle.

The *foramen magnum*, the hole in the mammalian skull from which the spinal cord emerges, is beneath the human skull pointing downwards, just as it is in the embryos of most mammals. This is important because it means that when we stand upright we look forward. In other mammals the *foramen magnum* rotates to a point behind the skull, pointing backwards, as the animal matures, a position appropriate for four-footed life.

If, as seems probable, corporate evolution also employs neoteny, it should be possible to trace the origins of a new dominant strategic theme (or streme), like niceness, back to the ideas and experiments of earlier times. Just because such precursors failed to survive or prosper in their original environments, does not mean they would not work now. Times change. Yesterday's heresies have a habit of becoming today's orthodoxies.

STRATEGIC ANTECEDENTS

Key elements of the nice strategy have been sculling around the streme pool for centuries. The idea that people matter, for example, has inspired countless experiments on the common-ownership theme, dating back to well before the 19th-century evangelists like Robert Owen and Charles Fourier, and surviving to the present day.

Modern day UK companies like the John Lewis Partnership stores group, the Scott Bader specialist chemicals company, the quoted office equipment supplier Kalamazoo and the Baxi Partnership, as well as the much-studied Mondragon movement in Spain, show the tradition of the common-ownership strategy is far from extinct.

As candidates for species dominance such enterprises have their limitations, but their survival as a corporate subspecies proves the inherent viability of the common-ownership strategy.

More robust common-ownership survivors from the corporate past include the partnership model that still dominates many of the knowhow professions like law and accountancy, and the 'mutual' tradition that evolved from the friendly societies and retains a firm foothold in the insurance industry and the building society movement.

Corporate vestiges survive of the honest, socially responsible and philanthropic Quaker economics inspired by the teachings of the 17th-century mystic George Knox. The Rowntree Trust, for example, still supports a number of UK charities and socially concerned pressure groups like Friends of the Earth, despite the consumption of its original corporate patron by the voracious Swiss foods group, Nestlé.

PHILOSOPHICAL ANTECEDENTS

Most people would agree that the two most powerful political ideas in the modern world are equality and liberty. Though liberty has, for the time being, acquired dominance in the Western world and is becoming more important in the Eastern bloc too, equality remains influential. It is natural to regard some changes in business strategy as attempts by managers to reconcile the twin ideals of liberty and equality.

144

One might suppose, for example, that the insertion of the mutant clause in the NFC's articles of association about the voting rights of employee-shareholders was the consequence of Sir Peter Thompson's attempts to reconcile his egalitarian ideals with his belief in capitalism.

The long history of the common-ownership idea, traces of which survive in Clause Four of the UK Labour Party's constitution (though as a commitment these days to state rather than employee ownership), still exerts some influence over corporate evolution, particularly in France and Spain.

Syndicalism, which the Russian thinker Peter Kropotkin said was the industrial manifestation of anarchism, remains deeply embedded in the ideology of the left.

In the early 1970s the publication by the Oxford historian Christopher Hill of *The World Turned Upside Down*, an account of the tumult of political and philosophical ideas that swept Britain during the civil war, reawakened considerable interest among young idealists in the 'Leveller' movement of that time, and in the writings of its leading thinker, Gerrard Winstanley.

There are some curious correspondences between ideas that have emerged from the ultra left-wing on the one hand and from the ultra right-wing on the other. Ignoring the terrorist aspects of Mikhail Bakunin's anarcho-syndicalism, its underlying vision is not dissimilar to that of the 'anarcho-capitalists' of modern times. In recent years the latter have been an influential source of ideas for the new political right, exemplified by Thatcherism.

THEORETICAL ANTECEDENTS

Theoretical developments in business economics also help to pave the way for strategic change. We have seen how Bruce Henderson's idea of portfolio strategy inspired the widespread adoption of acquisition-led strategies, and management books like *In Search of Excellence* and *Managing Knowhow* influence the evolution of corporate strategy too.

Structural developments like the progressive divorce of company ownership and control pose new problems and so beg new strategic solutions. And changes in the way the performance of companies is measured can also stimulate adaptations.

Earnings per share has been the key target variable for companies in recent years so they have adopted strategies designed to maximise EPS growth. When value-added per employee, intellectual property or knowhow capital become common yardsticks of company measurement, strategy will adapt to them. Managers will seek new ways to maximise the new variables by which they are judged.

Business theory and techniques of measurement (metrology) exert their influence on corporate evolution by either corroborating (selecting for) strategies or by falsifying them (selecting against). And usually business theory leads changes in strategy.

To illustrate the point we shall look at two of the most lively contemporary issues in business theory – the size debate and the discussion about valuing so-called 'intangible assets' like brands. Both are helping to prepare the ground for the emergence of the nice company as the dominant corporate species.

THE SIZE DEBATE

I have argued elsewhere (*Dinosaur & Co.*) that the advent of an era of rapid and accelerating technological change is a major discontinuity in the corporate environment requiring adaptive behaviour by the corporate species, one result of which will be a reduction in the average size of companies.

The argument went as follows: during periods of stability size is an advantage because economies of scale enable companies to exploit what is known as the 'L-shaped cost curve' – the more you produce of a product the lower the marginal cost becomes. This means that in stable conditions competitive advantage is to be sought in large-scale manufacturing.

It was recognised there were also diseconomies of scale, such as the bureaucracy associated with size and the sense of alienation inspired in people by the feeling of being tiny cogs in huge machines, but these were not thought to be sufficient to offset the cost advantage associated with size.

By shortening product life-cycles, rapid technological advance altered the trade-off between the economies and diseconomies of scale. It denied scale the time it needed to exploit the L-shaped cost curve. There came a point, if change was fast enough, when big companies became the lowest cost producers of obsolete products.

Competitive advantage, from being a function of cost and so of size, became instead a function of speed and agility. Low cost production ceased to be the secret of success. Its place was taken by the ability to keep ahead – to be the first rather than the cheapest.

146

This suggested a new model of competition. Companies still seek competitive advantage but at times of rapid change this becomes a matter of producing new products quickly rather than existing products cheaply. Having established a lead a company 'milks' it and recycles the quasi-monopoly profit into R&D to produce the next leading product.

The argument can be summarised by saying companies are competing these days by becoming smarter rather than stronger. In this way they are recapitulating the evolution of *Homo sapiens*.

This general approach has become quite popular of late. In early 1989 the US magazine *International Business Week* ran a cover story headlined 'Is your company too big?'. It was an account of the debate between writers like Tom Peters and George Gilder who detect a trend towards the 'de-massification' of business, and the modern advocates of the big is best theme like Charles Ferguson of the Massachusetts Institute of Technology and Ted Levitt of Harvard Business School.

Ferguson claims small firm startups have weakened the economy's competitiveness. He explained, they:

> shoot up like meteors for five years and then fall down to earth [and this] fragmentation and instability is not a sign of well-being. Sure, large firms have been screwing up in a massive way. But funding startups is not our salvation. You need large firms or collectives of firms that cooperate efficiently against the Japanese. Small companies can't survive against Japan's stable, concentrated and protected alliances. Most of these startups disappear after the first five years.

He predicted the American personal computer group Compaq 'will either disappear or become a Japanese or Korean company. I give them two to five years.'

Ted Levitt, author of *The Marketing Imagination*, former editor of the influential *Harvard Business Review* and inventor of the so-called 'law of dominance', claims some things can only be done by large organisations. He asks:

> Who's going to be the general contractor to go to the moon or to build a massive pipeline in Alaska? If you had to commit money for a project that takes five years to complete, like building a plant, would you turn it over to a small company? Some things inherently require scale.

And Levitt says large companies are more attractive to investors too:

> Where would you prefer your pension fund invested? General Electric, IBM and Philip Morris, or Widget Semiconductor Corp and some new hamburger establishment? The obvious answer says something important about the stability of large organisations. If the so-called dinosaurs are going to be extinct, why would anyone invest in them?

But even Roger Smith, chairman of the huge General Motors, does not believe size is a sufficient condition for success. He told *Business Week*: 'being big doesn't guarantee that you're going to be good.' He feels a need to foster an entrepreneurial spirit and knows from personal experience how hard it is these days for big groups to recruit and keep good people. 'Where are all the hotshots right now?' he asked. 'They're in Microsoft [IBM's PC software supplier] and other things where people can innovate on their own.'

The entrepreneur T. J. Rodgers, founder/president of specialist microchip maker Cypress Semiconductor, claims large companies are bad innovators and worse venture capitalists. As he put it in the *Business Week* article: 'the big guys will always tell you how it's impossible to capture the hill. Small companies look at the challenge, figure out what's needed to take the hill and to limit the casualties, and then attack it.'

Tom Peters believes it is in companies like Cypress rather than in the GMs, AT&Ts, IBMs and GEs, where the real strength of the US economy lies. 'When things get very big,' he explained, 'they tend to get very sluggish. The only real card the US holds in global competition is the combination of our entrepreneurs and our financial markets'. He admits it looks messy but claims the only reason US car makers like Ford and GM are getting better is because 'pipsqueaks like Honda scared the pee out of them'. He sees two forces driving out 'cholesterol' in big companies: small, entrepreneurial US companies and foreign competition, and he thinks the former are the most powerful agents of industrial regeneration.

George Gilder, America's most eloquent and influential business philosopher, agrees wholeheartedly. He says the strength of the US computer industry is not because of IBM but because of the 'hundreds of computer and software companies that have been growing five or six times faster than IBM for the last 10 years'.

Gilder also dismisses the notion that Japan's success is attributable to its huge companies.

He points out that General Electric is bigger than Hitachi and has plenty of money to finance large-scale R&D. 'Instead,' Gilder complains, 'it chose to withdraw from televisions and semi-conductors. Our large companies haven't maintained our competitiveness.'

There is a basic difference of outlook between the protagonists in the debate. The 'giantism' of Ferguson and Levitt is based on what they see as historical fact. For them business is as it was when Joseph Schumpeter wrote half a century ago that the modern way of life 'evolved during the period of relatively unfettered "Big Business"' and when Paul Samuelson insisted that 'large size breeds success, and success further success.'

Their outlook is both retrospective and static. They seek to understand the present and divine the future by reference to the past. There is no room in their vision of business for dynamic ideas such as change, transformation and corporate evolution. Had they been naturalists 65 years ago they would have found it inconceivable that the dinosaurs of the Cretaceous period would be displaced by the tiny warm-blooded mammals scuttling around their feet.

The giant UK advertising group Saatchi & Saatchi has based its strategy on Ted Levitt's idea of the global corporation, that exploits scale economies 'in marketing, management, distribution and production . . . and operates with resolute constancy – at low relative cost – as if the entire world or major regions of it were a single entity' (*The Marketing Imagination*).

Since I could hardly disagree more with Levitt in this debate and since I have been outspokenly critical of the Saatchi & Saatchi strategy, I was naturally delighted to give Saatchi & Saatchi permission to quote, in a subsequent annual statement, from an article of mine about how companies were investing more these days in becoming smarter than in becoming stronger. Saatchi did not, for obvious reasons, go on to observe that this shift rendered obsolete most of the so-called 'economies of scale' on which its strategy, and Levitt's ideas, were based.

Levitt says some major projects, like moon shots and the Alaska oil pipeline 'can only be done by large organisations'. But he knows very well that both these projects were undertaken by groups of relatively small organisations. Most large companies, and this is particularly true of Japan's giant conglomerates (zaibatsus), make

149

extensive use of subcontractors. There is no shortage either of liquidity to finance major scientific and civil engineering schemes or of project management skills (except, perhaps, in large companies). Britain's end of the Channel Tunnel project is being managed by a new company, Eurotunnel, put together for the purpose. Big projects do not need big companies.

And Levitt's assertion that investors need large companies to produce stable returns is nonsense. Modern portfolio theory says that a portfolio, invested in a large number of small companies is less risky than a portfolio containing a few investments in large companies. Levitt ignores the 'small company effect', the well-documented fact that for most of this century small firms have been consistently better investments than large firms.

GM's Roger Smith knows, from bitter experience, that small firms are becoming increasingly attractive places to work for the able people all companies need to achieve and maintain competitive advantage. GM's Saturn plant in Spring Hill, Tennessee (at the time of writing the plant was on time and under budget for the launch of the Saturn car in 1990) is a major element in Smith's campaign to reverse the 1980s decline of GM's share of the US auto market from nearly 50% at the start of the decade to less than 36%.

A host of other huge companies throughout the Western world are also engaged in a frantic devolution of power down through top-heavy bureaucratic hierarchies to their operating units in a desperate bid to staunch the haemorrhage of talent to companies like Cypress Semiconductor.

The *Harvard Business Review* (HBR), the primary antenna of the business world in its search for enlightenment in the firmament of ideas, declared George Gilder's article 'The Law of the Microcosm' (HBR, March–April, 1988) as the opening shot 'in an important debate on the role of small *vs* large enterprises in the nation's future competitiveness.' Ted Levitt, editor of the *HBR*, said the policy implications of the debate were 'enormous'.

Most of the diseconomies of scale, the growing recognition of which is the inspiration of the size debate, are associated with human factors. Healthy and coherent corporate cultures are hard to create and maintain in large organisations.

Equity, which in these days of highly liquid capital markets is the 'hard' currency of business talent, is a weak motivator unless it is linked to local as opposed to group profitability (but see Chapter Ten for the discussion on federations and 'phantom stock'). Most

150

important of all, agility and risk-taking, the crucial business qualities in a rapidly changing world, are derived directly from the human qualities of creativity and inspiration.

The nice strategy, operating in internal mode, confronts these issues as a matter of course. It is seldom ambushed by sudden defections of frustrated research staff or by abrupt collapses of corporate morale. It is attuned automatically to the undercurrents of dissatisfaction and gratification in a company because it recognises the company's knowhow capital is its most important asset.

An important sub-theme of the size debate concerns the role in the theory of innovation of corporate structure and of the so-called 'make or buy' decision in particular. What, for example, is the optimum size for the research and development departments on which some companies depend for new products, and does R&D, and for that matter any and all of the many other functions of a business, really have to be done in-house?

The nice strategy also scores here. Because of its basically positive view of business and other companies, it is far less inhibited in its search for the right mix of make-or-buy arrangements by a jealous and untrusting approach to control. The nasty strategy insists on control and avoids collaboration because it knows that if its partners are anything like itself they will try to cheat.

THE ENIGMA OF THE BRAND
The other contemporary debate out of which are emerging strong arguments in favour of the nice strategy is the so-called 'brand valuation' issue.

The background to the debate lies in the UK accounting standard that requires 'goodwill' to be written off on its acquisition. This is seen by the accountancy profession as a necessary application of Occam's razor. It was, and remains, an axiom of accountancy practice that a company's audited accounts must represent an unequivocally objective statement of the company's affairs at the balance sheet date.

Since there was no agreed method of valuing intangibles it was deemed necessary to exclude them entirely from audited company accounts. It was a neat solution, in the short term, but its effect was to bottle up a growing pressure for change in the way companies are valued and so to deny intangible assets the professional attention they needed. The result was that the market took matters into its own hands and began to make a mockery of standard company accounts.

Two alternative valuations of companies emerged – the value put on them by the stock market and the value put on them by takeover bids. Table 8.1, taken from a working paper for a Coopers & Lybrand study group on intangibles (of which the author was a member), indicates the scale of the discrepancy between standard accounting valuations and the valuations of bidding companies.*

Table 8.1

Company	Bid value	Net assets per accounts	Goodwill amount	Goodwill % bid value
	£m	£m	£m	%
Pilkington Bros.	1,052	998	54	5
Glass Glover Group	59	33	26	44
Guthrie Corp.	209	107	102	49
County Properties	34	12	22	65
Birmid Qualcast	253	65	188	74
West Yorkshire Independent Hospital	9	2	7	78
Rowntree	2,500	409	2,091	84
Abaco Investments	127	1	126	99

Figures like these worry accountants. The profession is deeply concerned by the widening gap between their audit valuations, undertaken on behalf of shareholders, and 'exit' valuations in bids, because it is fearful that if nothing is done auditors may open themselves up to charges of professional negligence. The valuation anomalies indicate a systematic failure on the part of auditors in their duty to shareholders to render an accurate account of the company's net worth.

The official, audited, £409m valuation of the Yorkshire sweets group Rowntree was clearly anomalous in early 1988, when the market was valuing the company at about £1bn. When the Swiss food giant Nestlé paid £2.5bn for Rowntree, investors who had sold shares earlier had every reason to question whether the £800,000 they had agreed to pay their auditors Price Waterhouse

---

* The Study group's conclusions have been published by Coopers & Lybrand Deloitte as *The Corfield Report.*

for validating the previous year's accounts had been money well spent.

Financial markets have been struggling more positively to get to grips with the intangibles anomaly. Every quoted UK company has to sign a 'listing agreement', known as the 'Yellow Book', with the International Stock Exchange (ISE). Part of the agreement obliges the company to communicate with shareholders if they wish to do a deal involving more than a fixed percentage of the company's value.

The system of classification is officially based on audited net assets. A deal worth more than 15% of net assets is deemed to be a 'class one' transaction requiring a descriptive circular to be sent to shareholders. A deal worth more than 25% of net assets is a 'major' or, more commonly, a 'super' class one transaction requiring the approval of shareholders in general meeting. The growing significance of intangibles has made a nonsense of the system. Whereas Pilkington Brothers would need shareholder approval for any transaction worth £250m or more (some 24% of its bid value), Rowntree would have needed shareholder approval for any deal worth £102m or more (some 4% of its bid value).

The ISE became aware of the problem and has recently changed the Yellow Book rules to allow certain types of intangible assets to be added to net worth for the purposes of class calculations. This formal recognition by the ISE, not only of the existence of intangibles but also of their importance, has exerted even more pressure on the accountancy profession to put its house in order. There is now considerable momentum behind the move towards official recognition of intangibles in a company's financial statements.

But though most of the attention on the intangibles issue has so far been focused on the value of brand names, the process of making visible the 'invisible balance sheet' that we encountered in Chapter six will not stop at brands. The brand valuation debate has opened what seems to some to be a can of worms but to others a veritable cornucopia of exciting possibilities for modernising the archaic structure of contemporary accountancy.

Already there have been calls for the principle of intangibles valuation to be extended. 'If brands are to be included in balance sheets,' the new corporate metrologists ask, 'then why not other intangibles like patents and copyrights?' And if intellectual property is to be included, they why not other assets like corporate reputation (see Chapter 10) and knowhow capital?

153

This lifting of the carpet under which accountants have traditionally swept everything they could not measure with any accuracy, is an important change in the corporate environment which is certain to elicit adaptive behaviour. Companies are coming to be seen as consisting of at least two kinds of assets – intangible and tangible – and their management teams will need to be seen to be taking good care of both. The management of intangibles will be the more important for two reasons: because intangibles already account for most of the average company's value and because they are much more easily damaged by bad management.

THE THREE WORLDS OF VALUE

In an attempt to bring some order to this important but still rather fuzzy area of corporate valuation I have suggested that all corporate assets consist, in varying proportions, of three kinds of value. My model is based on Sir Karl Popper's division of objects into three worlds. World 1 is the physical world where tangibles live; World 2 is the world of experience and thought; World 3 is the world of objective thought, consisting of things like copyrights, patents and brand names (though not brands themselves, or at least not all of them).

The idea is depicted in Figure 8.1. Initially I thought Popper's three worlds were the wrong way round – that there should be a progression from tangible to less tangible to hardly tangible at all. But the order was right. When the model is pictured the central role played by World 2 assets becomes readily apparent.

Apart from indicating that brands and corporate reputation are two important assets that live in all three worlds, the diagram contains two further arguments. It suggests, first, that in addition to the sum of the value of individual assets there is a value in the 'corporate system', the quality that enables the company to continue to do what it does for a living.

Secondly there is, in addition to this 'system value', 'competitive advantage', which is the quality a company needs to maintain and improve its market position. Bot these 'meta-assets' rely heavily on access to World 2 assets. System value lies in the skills and experience constituents of World 2 and competitive advantage lies both in the creative constituents of World 2, and in the World 3 assets which are the products of World 2.

I have used this model in the brand valuation debate to expose the weaknesses of valuation methods based on the net present value of

154

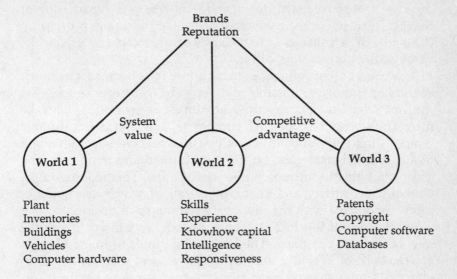

Fig 8.1: The Three Worlds of Value
No system yet exists for valuing World 2 objects properly and yet they are crucial to the more tangible objects in Worlds 1 and 3.

discounted revenue flows such as brand profits and royalty income. I have argued that the true value of a brand cannot be transferred from one company to another unless the facilities supplied by World 2, such as marketing knowhow and distribution skills, come with it. Nestlé, for example, will have substantially overpaid for such Rowntree lines as Kitkat, Smarties and After Eight if the people who are intimate with the marketing and distribution intricacies of *these particular brands* leave the company.

The analysis has an interesting strategic implication. If brand value is dependent on World 2 assets which cannot be bought and sold (because they live in the minds of human beings), it makes sense for a company pursuing a brand portfolio strategy to do all in its power to link the necessary World 2 assets directly to the brands rather than to the company. The more this can be done the greater will be the tradable value of the brand.

One way of linking brands more closely to the World 2 assets they depend on is to subcontract as much of the World 2 work as possible. If the distribution of Kitkat, for example, were to be subcontracted to a distribution company like the NFC, the contract could be transferred with the brand. And when the marketing of Kitkat is farmed out to an advertising agency and a sales promotion company, these contracts also constitute transferable or 'separable' value as the accountants call it.

As we have seen, companies that choose to subcontract as much of their operations as possible in order to be free to concentrate on the area where their competitive advantage is greatest, need to be nice. The strength of the TFT strategy tells us that good, durable relationships with subcontractors, essential for companies pursuing highly focused strategies, can only be formed and maintained by companies able to form corporate friendships. This requires trust, empathy, sensitivity and adaptability, all of which are qualities rarely associated with the old, nasty paradigm of business.

But the idea of World 2 assets has a much more direct link to the idea of the nice company. The hearts and minds of human beings are the stuff of World 2 and, as we have seen, when it comes to effective people management nice strategies are way out in front.

HOPEFUL MONSTERS

The last chapter showed how, in Buchanan's theory of politics as economics, two-party systems tend to produce policy packages that are close together. The incremental votes a party needs to improve its political market share were previously cast for the rival party. They are therefore unlikely to be enticed away by policy packages that are markedly different from those of the rival party.

Much the same kind of incrementalism applies in evolutionary biology. Monsters, or macromutants as they are often called by evolutionists, almost invariably die before they can pass on their novel heredity. They cannot be too different because, by definition, they will not be well-adapted. Generally speaking, evolutionary change proceeds in a series of small steps.

There is a lively debate in evolutionary theory right now about just how general this principle is. All evolutionists agree that most macromutants are flashes of exotic novelty in the tree of life that are extinguished almost as soon as they appear.

But some evolutionists, called saltationists (from the Latin *saltus*, meaning 'jump'), argue that a tiny fraction of hopeful monsters get very lucky indeed and turn out to be just what the environment ordered. And, of course, if even a tiny fraction survive, monsters –

because they can cover a lot of evolutionary ground very quickly – are important agents of change.

Both incrementalism and the hopeful monster idea are of interest to corporate evolutionists. The former establishes the principle that small changes are important because they are more likely to survive and propagate (they do not challenge the status quo with sufficient vigour to be rejected out of hand) and the latter suggests that sudden jumps, though usually doomed, can sometimes catch the spirit of the times and thereby survive and prosper.

It seems to me that the unorthodox clause in the NFC's articles of association (see Chapter Six) is a small change from the point of view of the company's financial environment.

It has been digested, with some reluctance, by the International Stock Exchange and by most financial institutions without too much evident difficulty. It gives employee shareholders extra rights only in the event of a takeover, and now that the NFC is quoted these rights will become progressively less significant as founder shareholders sell their shares or retire (and thereby lose their privileged voting rights).

In contrast, the idea of the producer cooperative – a company wholly and inalienably owned by its employees – has proved to be too far away from the mainstream of corporate evolution to be much of a challenge to the dominant species. The tradition of common ownership has survived, but only just. Its credibility as an alternative corporate form was seriously damaged in the 1970s when Tony Benn, Industry Minister in the Labour government, used taxpayers' money to finance the formation of two common-ownership ventures, the Kirkby central heating firm and the Meriden motorcycle cooperative. They both failed.

Common ownership, because it exemplifies some of the qualities of niceness, is a powerful industrial idea and variations of it may yet come to play a major role in corporate evolution. For the present, however, the need for ready access to capital markets and for clearer and more effective management control systems than producer cooperatives tend to permit (too much industrial democracy can be as bad as too little) make common ownership an interesting rather than an important variation on the company theme.

If it is ultimately to transcend these limitations, it will be because of a series of much smaller evolutionary steps, like the step the NFC has taken, which, because they constitute gradual, incremental change, are able to pull the mainstream with them.

SUMMARY

- Corporate evolution needs a pre-existing source of potential variation.

- Neoteny (holding youth) is an important evolutionary mechanism in both the business and biological worlds.

- Cooperatives and the common-ownership ideal contain certain elements that continue to influence contemporary corporate evolution.

- Developments in business theory help to prepare the ground for strategic change.

- The size debate is questioning strategies based on ideas like critical mass and the theory of dominance and is tending to favour the nice strategy.

- The brand valuation debate puts the spotlight on *all* intangible assets, including knowhow capital which is best managed within the context of a nice internal strategy.

- Hopeful monsters rarely survive. Most evolutionary change consists of small steps.

CHAPTER 9

The Essence of Niceness

In an article in the *Harvard Business Review* in July 1988 Russell Johnston and Paul R. Lawrence told the curious story of McKesson Corporation, a US distributor and wholesaler serving independent drugstores.

In the mid-1970s McKesson was confronted by a problem that was typical of the time. The powerful, integrative trend that has been one of the most striking features of corporate evolution since the Second World War (and which I believe is now drawing to its close) had produced large drugstore chains. They were squeezing McKesson's independent drugstore customers to death. McKesson knew that if its customers failed, it would fail too. It was therefore in its interests to try to help them to survive.

Its search for ways to defend the distributor/store symbiosis focused on efforts to replicate the advantages of the large chains, particularly in the area of stock control. McKesson represented an 'un-bundled' function of the integrated groups so it was quite logical for it to feel obliged to be at least as good at wholesaling and distribution as its bundled counterparts within the big chains.

It developed an order entry system, the data collection devices of which were initially powered by car batteries wheeled round its customers' stores in shopping carts. The system cut the costs of order entry dramatically and greatly accelerated other steps in the supply chain such as inventory checking, order calling, order recording and, eventually, packing and shipping.

In addition to making the symbiotic pair more agile, this sudden infusion of information to the system also liberated substantial

159

amounts of capital previously tied up in inventory, so allowing the independents to compete more effectively with the chains. As the Information Society develops, this kind of transformation is becoming commonplace. Companies find that as they improve their information systems they reduce their working capital needs. In this way information is everywhere being substituted for money.

But McKesson didn't stop there. It realised it could do a lot more with the rich flow of data it had gained access to. It used its computer to extract information from the data to help its customers set prices and design layouts so as to maximise sales in each store. It began to use the data to supply its customers with accounting services such as producing balance sheets and income statements, and it was not long before McKesson realised that by processing prescription history data it could warn its customers about potentially harmful drug combinations.

The independents began to do better in their war against the big chains. They offered better prices, a more targeted product mix and better service, and they did it without sacrificing any of the advantages associated with autonomy, such as their greater responsiveness to local needs and their close links with the community. They had an edge over their chain store competitors whose managers never stayed long in one place and always had to comply with the constraints and bureaucracies associated with large groups.

McKesson prospered too. Since the introduction of the first, rudimentary order entry system in 1976 its annual sales to its drugstore customers have risen from $900m to over $5bn. Profits have risen faster still because the information enrichment has enabled McKesson to reduce the number of its warehouses from 130 to 54, eliminate 500 clerical jobs, strengthen its customer base from 20,000 drugstores averaging $4,000 of orders a month to 15,000 averaging $14,000 a month and reduce the average number of shipments per customer from two a day to two a week and at the same time cut its own and its customers' inventory costs.

But the potential of McKesson's data was still not exhausted. It was of value, the company realised, to its own suppliers, the product managers of consumer goods manufacturers. The latter began to buy the data from McKesson and use it to improve their own delivery scheduling. And the advent of computer-to-computer ordering from suppliers allowed McKesson to cut its staff of buyers from 140 to 12. Similar economies were enjoyed by its supplier companies.

McKesson has also used its information system to help process insurance claims for prescription reimbursement (you pay for your prescriptions in the US and then claim the cost back from your medical insurance). This has established for McKesson links with insurance companies and consumers as well as strengthening them with its drugstore customers.

Johnston and Lawrence call this kind of multi-function network or chain, which in McKesson's case involves consumers, insurance suppliers, retailers, distributor (McKesson) and manufacturers, a 'Value Added Partnership' (VAP). It is a concept comparable to, but much richer than, the 'value chain' idea which plays such a key role in Michael Porter's book *Competitive Advantage* (see Chapter three).

'What makes McKesson so powerful' Johnston and Lawrence suggest 'is the understanding that each player in the value-added chain has a stake in the other's success.' McKesson saw the entire VAP as a competitive unit and was therefore highly motivated to bring as many value-adding functions into the chain as possible.

WHAT IS A VAP?

One way of looking at a VAP is as a simulation of an integrated company – an attempt to exploit the economies of scale that are the alleged justifications for large size in the business world, without incurring the diseconomies associated with bureaucracies and control relationships.

It would, however, be wrong to equate the VAP brain (McKesson in this case) with the bureaucracy of the integrated group. Although VAP brains listen, look, help and advise, they never direct. They are careful to keep their customers and suppliers at arm's length. They have no wish to consume them because they know that if they did the VAP would fail. Conflicts of interest would arise, cultural clashes would break out, customers would defect and both the quantity and quality of the data with which the VAP had been built would fail.

Another way of looking at a VAP is as a stage in an evolutionary process. The giantists will see it as the embryo or precursor of an integrated group destined to fuse together at a subsequent stage.

The demassifiers, on the other hand, may see in VAPs the process of neoteny at work – the emergence of a new species from the embryology of its ancestor. I will go further and hazard the guess that the VAP, though it appears to be just a closely-knit federation of the parts of an integrated group, glued together by a common interest and a shared niceness, is actually in the process of emerging as a new species.

A VAP is a corporate life-form – a seeing, listening, thinking and communicating organism. One of its strengths is its natural alertness to threats and opportunities. The interdependence of its various parts on the health of every other part motivates each member to scan the chain constantly for weak links and to help to strengthen them when they are found.

Johnston and Lawrence give examples of other VAPs in the Italian textile industry and the US film and book publishing industries. They suggest that Japanese car companies, regarded by observers like Charles Ferguson (see Chapter eight) as epitomes of the case for size and integration, are actually VAPs and so epitomes of the opposite. They point out that Toyota, the world's largest car maker, directly produces only 20% of the value of its cars against 70% and 50% for GM and Ford respectively.

Chrysler's recent comeback has been attributed, in part, to its formation of VAPs with its suppliers. It now contributes only 30% of the value of its cars, and Ford's gains at the expense of GM are thought to be partly associated with similar adjustments to its make-or-buy strategy.

The growth of VAPs, often at the expense of their integrated competitors, is a powerful corroboration of my assertion in Chapter three that 'the sum of the (business) game will be maximised when cooperation is maximised.'

It is hard to imagine a prosperous VAP where every part is not employing a nice strategy. A single company in a VAP cannot afford to be greedy because any short-term success it might have in claiming a larger share of the chain's value added is bound to weaken the chain and so damage its long-term interests. Niceness is an integral part of the glue that keeps the chain together.

The VAP demonstrates the power of the nice strategy and shows that niceness can often be a substitute for size. The VAP is an unbundled route towards achieving the positive attributes of size without incurring the negatives.

NICE COMPANIES AT WORK
Amstrad
Amstrad, the British consumer electronics company, is a VAP brain. It looks, from the outside anyway, to be a conventional manufacturing company but Table 9.1, prepared in the autumn of 1987, shows that in terms of market value per head it is anything but conventional.

Table 9.1

Company	Employees	Market value	MV/employees
		£m	£
Amstrad	1,009	1,072.9	1,063,330
Saatchi & Saatchi	10,000	868.6	86,860
Pearson	28,000	1,940.4	69,300
Barclays Bank	80,300	4,460.9	55,553
Vickers	16,000	572.2	35,763
NEI	26,480	247.9	9,362

Source: *Financial Weekly*

Amstrad stands for Alan Michael Sugar TRADing, and Alan Sugar, the entrepreneur who started his meteoric career by selling car radio aerials from a small van, is its most important piece of knowhow capital.

Since Amstrad came to the market in 1980 its sales have risen from £9m to £625m in 1988 and profits have soared from less than £2m to £160m. In the process Amstrad has frustrated IBM's wish for dominance in the UK personal computer market and has set new 'bang for buck' standards for PCs throughout the world. It is the arch-cloner of IBM microcomputers but Sugar is constantly exploring the possibilities in the audio and video markets, and most recently satellite TV receivers and facsimile machines, as well as in computers.

Amstrad is what some Americans call, sometimes disparagingly, a 'hollow' corporation. It subcontracts almost everything, acting as a VAP brain alongside muscular manufacturers and component suppliers in the Far East and the US. With the help of outside design and software specialists it conceives of a new product, buys components in bulk, arranges for manufacture and organises and manages marketing and distribution.

Its greatest asset is its speed. It can be into a market within months of identifying it and out again as soon as volume begins to fall below what it considers to be a satisfactory level. Such companies are major evolutionary threats to large, integrated groups which depend on high margins to pay for their complex and slow-moving bureaucracies.

The emotive term 'hollow corporation' was first used in a scaremongering polemic in *Business Week* in early 1986. It was based on a remark by Akio Morita, chairman and co-founder of Sony, who said:

> American companies have either shifted output to low-wage countries or come to buy parts and assembled products from countries like Japan that can make quality products at low prices. The result is a hollowing of American industry. The US is abandoning its status as an industrial power.

Business Week said Morita was right and that the development was 'a phenomenon our economy cannot afford' and a 'national crisis'. Others take the view that if South Koreans can make computers more cheaply than Americans, it is in the interests of consumers and the economy at large that Korean computers should be imported.

Elementary economics (international trade theory to be precise), tells us that if the Koreans have an absolute and a comparative advantage in making computers, they should specialise in so doing and that America, which has an absolute advantage in the design and development of computer software, should concentrate its efforts in that area. As we have seen with VAPs, and as Adam Smith pointed out two centuries ago in his *Inquiry into the Nature and Causes of The Wealth of Nations* (1766), everyone gains from specialisation.

The emergence of the hollow corporation, which is really just a special kind of international VAP, is corporate evolution in action.

It is a strategic response to global shifts in cost patterns. It is far better for an economy to breed companies like Amstrad, able to cream off large slices of value added from international VAPs, than for it to persist in doing things it does badly behind tariff barriers.

But at the time of writing Amstrad's reputation had taken a knock. Sugar forecasted a sharp drop in profits for the year to the end of June 1989 because of delays in introducing its PC 2000 range of personal computers, weak markets in other product areas and overstretched management: his predictions were proved correct; Amstrad's 1989 profits fell from £160m to £77m before tax. An aspect of the latter problem was the management of distribution. Over the previous year Amstrad had embarked on a programme of selective vertical integration.

Vexed by what Sugar saw as the failure of Amstrad's distributors to maximise sales in certain territories, he started buying them up. They were friendly acquisitions but the addition of the distribution function to a group which until then had studiously avoided acquisitions (apart from the Sinclair brand name Amstrad bought when Sir Clive Sinclair's pioneering home computer group ran into trouble) increased the complexity of the business. And arguably the purchase of a 9% stake in a US memory chip maker in response to a dire shortage of DRAMs (Dynamic Random Access Memories) had reduced Amstrad's purchasing flexibility too.

In VAP theory the creation of ownership or control relationships up or down the value chain damages the democracy of the VAP and makes it work less efficiently. Conflicts of interest arise and the acquirer can often become so distracted by the new pattern of relationships that it takes its eye off the ball.

Notwithstanding such growing pains, Amstrad remains an object lesson for those who believe success is to be sought in the buying and selling of businesses. It is also a striking demonstration of the power of the narrowly focused, non-acquisitive strategy, supported by a skilfully managed policy of subcontracting.

Virgin Group
Virgin Group is another kind of nice company. Its strategy has few of the qualities of a VAP and yet its general demeanour, its corporate manners and the qualities that comprise its reputation are unmistakable signs of niceness.

When Richard Branson opened his first record shop on London's Oxford Street in 1971 you would have got very long odds from contemporary business economists that 15 years later he would bring his company to the stock market on a price-tag of £250m.

He was a hippy – an hirsute aficionado of the trendy, drug-taking, love-making youth culture of the baby-boomers whose contribution to the revival of British industry seemed likely, at the time anyway, to be confined to handmade leather belts and bangles, the import of Indian perfumes and the insolvency of innumerable barber shops.

But Branson knew his market. He imported the good American music first and carried sufficient stock of the big selling records to establish and maintain customer loyalty. The ambience of Virgin shops reflected his sense of oneness with his clientele – it was 'laid-back' and in tune with the gentle and positive spirit of the times. The Virgin 'vibes' were good as they used to say. People still say of the modern Virgin megastores that compared with their rivals like HMV and Tower, they have a slightly noisy, 'avant-garde' feel to them. Branson, by somehow imbuing his shops with the engaging aspects of his own personality, managed to differentiate the record retailing product. By all accounts he has managed to do the same with air travel.

And as a company leader he was also good-humoured and charming. People liked working with him and still do. One imagines the man's incorrigible entrepreneurialism can be very frustrating for colleagues trying to consolidate what has already been achieved, but boring Virgin ain't and has never been. The company has been built on opportunism and no more so than in music. When Mike Oldfield was finding it hard to win a record contract for his haunting electronic compositions, Branson was ready to try his hand at adding a record company to his retailing group. Oldfield's 'Tubular Bells' album could have bombed and consigned Branson's recording ambitions to oblivion. Instead, profits on Oldfield's album became the basis of Virgin's modern prosperity.

By the end of 1987 music accounted for well over half Virgin Group's turnover and nearly three-quarters of profits.

With the help of friendly acquisitions Branson had by then added television services to the quoted part of his empire and the incorrigibly entrepreneurial founder had found time to start a trans-Atlantic airline and nearly kill himself twice crossing the Atlantic in other ways; by speedboat and hot-air balloon.

Branson has often been criticised, particularly in the City, for his evident relish for publicity but it is part of his strategy as well as his style. His aura is both a promotional tool and a cement, helping to win the loyalty of the people he needs to help him run the business. He is generally recognised as being a gifted leader.

His friend, and Virgin Group's former managing director, Don Cruickshank told me of the occasion when the board was discussing the seasonal pattern of business at the Fuji photo labs that had recently been installed in some of the megastores. Branson rang the minilab manager at the Oxford Street store to check the details. The manager was out at lunch and so was his number two. It fell to 18-year-old Gary to answer Branson's questions. Branson, very conscious of how stressful the conversation must have been for Gary, was delighted by the lad's competence and conscientiousness.

This skill with people helps with acquisitions too. Branson has great empathy with entrepreneurs. He knows how hard it is to surrender control of one's own creation and he makes it as easy as he can.

Godfrey Pye and his partner Roger Hoare became rich men after the sale of their Rushes Post Production company to Virgin – they had what is known in the trade as 'two-fingers' capital (enough money to walk out whenever they wanted). Instead they have stayed and given Virgin the management resources it needs to turn TV and video services into a major growth area.

The nice style is particularly valuable in the music division. While other record companies employ top-down planning systems – they establish a sales target first and then work out what is needed to achieve it – Virgin derives forecasts from album-release schedules. There is no attempt to force the artists to adapt to the company's rhythm as is common elsewhere in the industry. 'That introduces tensions between the artists, their managers and the recording executives,' Cruickshank explained. 'As a private company we took the view that it was the long-term relationship with artists that mattered and took the conscious decision to stick to that when we went public.'

Virgin's culture and corporate persona are important assets. They make it easier to attract and keep good people, whether employees or artists, and they endow the company with an ambience that, in the music industry in particular, constitutes a significant competitive advantage.

The style is both appealing and highly sensitive to the shifts of public preoccupation. In May 1989, after Virgin Atlantic's inaugural flight to Japan, Branson banned tobacco advertising and sponsorship on his airline. He said he had found the tobacco ads screened during the flight 'sickening' and said he had 'believed for a long time that it is immoral for tobacco companies to be seen encouraging young people who don't smoke to take up the habit.' The advertising press estimated the decision would cost Virgin

Atlantic £2m in lost revenue over the next five years and likened the move to Branson's launch of Mates condoms at the height of the AIDS scare and his involvement in the government's anti-litter campaign.

The implication was that, once again, Branson had allowed ethics to rule good business sense. There was no recognition that quite possibly the effect of the ban would be to make the airline more attractive to the thousands who shared Branson's distate for tobacco advertising and so would generate, indirectly, far more than £2m of extra revenue.

Branson's decision to take his company private again after less than two years as a publicly quoted company was further evidence of his commitment to the nice style. It was not so much that he was disappointed in the City's treatment of Virgin Group, though that came into it. It was more that many of his friends – Virgin Group colleagues and artists under contract, like Phil Collins – had bought shares in the company when it went public and had lost money as a result of what he and others saw as the market's failure to recognise the company's true value.

That was why Branson offered to buy back the 47% of the company he did not own at the 140p-a-share flotation price. It was a lot to pay – some 70% more than the market price – but that didn't matter to Branson as long as his friends broke even.

City people argued it was Virgin's fault its flirtation with public status was so unrewarding. They said Branson should have courted the City more assiduously, explained in more detail the rationale of the attack on the US market, and refrained from risking his neck in speedboats and hot-air balloons on behalf of his privately owned Voyager group (Virgin Atlantic's parent).

Branson pointed out that compared with the $2bn Sony had recently paid for the CBS record company, Virgin Group had been seriously under-valued before his going private bid. The comparable but larger Warner Communications was valued on the US market at the time at 1.3 times its 1987 turnover, whereas Virgin's market value was less than four-fifths of sales. Branson's assertion that the City was incapable of valuing his music business was strikingly corroborated when, in Autumn 1989, he announced that Fujisankei of Japan had agreed to pay almost £100m for a quarter share in Virgin's music division.

Branson was not without City sympathisers. They recalled how he had been urged before the float not to include his airline and then came under pressure to include it when Virgin Atlantic was successful. Most irksome of all, when Branson responded to City criticism of the low return on Virgin's small shops by selling them for £23m, the shares promptly fell.

The Virgin 'going private' buy-out was the first of its kind and so became something of a City *cause célèbre*. Some said Branson would miss the City more than the City would miss Branson. 'If Virgin wants to be the Warner Communications of Europe,' a top leisure analyst opined at the time, 'I can't see how it can achieve that without the City.'

But by then Warner had ceased to be Branson's corporate model. The company he admired most was the owner of RCA records, the privately owned West German group, Bertelsmann.

Bertelsmann

Bertelsmann AG began its life in 1835 as a printer of religious books and hymnals. For some time, though still privately owned, it was the world's largest media group. It is now the second largest after the recent merger of Time and Warner Communications. It employed 42,000 people worldwide and had annual sales of DM12bn ($6.4bn). Its book clubs had 22m members in 22 countries. It owns 75% of the company that publishes *Stern* and 19 other magazines in Germany, and 25% of *Der Spiegel*.

In 1986 it spent $800m in the US to buy RCA music and records and Doubleday publishing. These deals added to an already substantial presence in America, including Bantam Books, one of the world's largest and most innovative publishers.

Reinhard Mohn, great-grandson of founder Carl Bertelsmann, rebuilt the company virtually from scratch after it emerged in tatters from the Second World War. His commitment to an unusually decentralised management style is said to have been acquired while he was a prisoner of war in the US. After 40 years at the helm he retired as managing board chairman in 1981 at the age of 60, yielding the leadership to Mark Wossner. He is now chairman of the company's supervisory board. He has agreed to hand the position over to Wossner when the latter retires in the late 1990s.

Mohn's success is based on a management strategy informed by a coherent personal philosophy and a good, intuitive grasp of the theory of corporate evolution. In the English translation of his book *Erfolg durch Partnership* (*Success Through Partnership: An*

169

entrepreneurial strategy) he asserts that 'the ability of organisational systems to evolve in current times is a decisive factor for success.'

He believes running a modern business is much too difficult to be left to authoritarian bureaucracies and argues that the rapid evolution of working methods requires creative and inspirational management at the business unit level, as well as at the centre.

In Mohn's system, management and entrepreneurial training occurs on the job. The centre sets goals and monitors results but must listen to the line managers. Mohn recognises that ownership alone no longer confers the right to lead. In the future, he predicts, 'only ability will decide who has management responsibility'.

Mohn thinks managers should be paid only a small proportion of their income in the form of a monthly salary and that the rest should come from profit sharing. He says managers should first optimise the performance of their units and give only secondary consideration to the overall interests of the company. This, he believes, reduces friction 'at the vertical and horizontal seams of a decentralised organisation'.

In Mohn's partnership system the representatives of capital and labour are responsible for articulating the goals of their constituencies. He believes the primary objective of a company is to make a contribution to society and the secondary objective is to give all employees the opportunity to fulfil themselves.

But he dislikes the income-levelling effects of collective-bargaining over the past few decades. His partnership idea demands not equal incomes but a 'consensus concerning the principles of appropriate compensation'.

Perhaps the most interesting aspect of Bertelsmann, and this may be a characteristic that could have evolved only in Germany, is the financial manifestation of Bertelsmann's business philosophy. Employees, by buying non-voting stock with their profit-sharing income, contribute nearly half the company's equity.

Dividend policy is miserly by Western standards. Only a quarter of attributable earnings are paid out to shareholders, giving the company an unusually high rate of capital formation. These days non-voting shares can also be issued to outsiders but this is regarded as a reserve facility, to be used sparingly.

Mohn says the capital supplied by stockholders and employees is,

170

in normal trading conditions, enough to finance annual growth of 15%. Thoroughgoing industrial democrats will cavil at the lack of votes on employee shares. Mohn argues that management's mandate to manage is so crucial to the company's success, and the company's success is so important to the well-being of employees, that the lack of this aspect of corporate democracy is a price worth paying. He also argues that since Bertelsmann's capital structure is merely an aspect of a general partnership philosophy, votes on employee shares are superfluous. The company's success, and its enviable reputation throughout the world for enlightened and sympathetic management, suggests he is right.

Bertelsmann's niceness is based on a profound understanding of the nature of the working relationship between a company, its customers, its employees and the communities where it operates.

Our next case study shares many of these qualities and is one of Bertelsmann's most formidable rivals in the global publishing market. It also shares with Bertelsmann another quality: it has the appearance but not the substance of a family company.

Pearson

Early in 1988 journalists on the French financial daily paper *Les Echos* went on strike in protest against Finance Minister Edouard Balladur's refusal to sanction an agreed £88m purchase of the paper by a British company. It is extremely unusual for journalists to strike in support of the acquisition of their paper by another company. It is even less common for them to strike in support of a bid by a foreign company, but for *French* journalists to strike in support of a bid by a *British* company is a rarity indeed.

The answer to the mystery lies in the nature of the company. It was Pearson, owner of the *Financial Times*, Penguin, half of *The Economist*, Royal Doulton, half of Château Latour (since sold to Allied–Lyons), Madame Tussauds, part of Lazards and a number of other only slightly less illustrious enterprises in fields ranging from oil services to property. Its story spans one-and-a-half centuries and is one of Britain's most remarkable corporate lives.

Pearson's story began in 1844 when Samuel Pearson joined a small Yorkshire building contractor specialising in water, sewage and railway work for local authorities. It was renamed S. Pearson & Son Ltd when Samuel's son George joined the firm, but it was not until George's eldest son Weetman arrived in 1872, at the age of 16, that things began to hum.

171

Weetman Pearson was one of Britain's truly great entrepreneurs. By the time he moved to London in 1884 the 29-year-old Weetman was firmly in the driving seat. By the end of the century he had established S. Pearson & Son as the largest civil engineering contractor in the world.

A dry dock contract in Halifax, Nova Scotia in 1886 was followed in 1888 by a £950,000 contract to build the Avila and Salamanca railway in Spain. In 1889, Pearson won contracts to build the Grand Canal in Mexico and the Hudson River tunnel in New York.

Mexico soon became a major customer. The £3m Vera Cruz harbour contract was won in 1895 and the following year Pearson won a £1.4m contract to construct the port at Coatzacoalcos. In 1898 work was begun on the £2.5m Tehuantepec railway linking Vera Cruz on the north coast with a new £3.3m harbour, also built by Pearson, at Salina Cruz in the south.

Other major contracts included docks in Southampton, London, Cardiff, Port Talbot, Hull, Liverpool and Malta; railways in Britain, China and Colombia; tunnels under the Thames at Blackwall and under the East River in New York; harbours at Dover and Seaham and a huge £9m munitions factory at Gretna.

Weetman's achievements were honoured by a knighthood in 1894, a Baronetcy in 1910 and a Viscountancy in 1917. During the First World War he was president of the Air Board and played an important role in the formation of the Royal Air Force.

Historians attribute his success to his organising ability, his grasp of technical matters and his financial acumen. He was also an unusually enlightened employer who did his best to maintain a continuous flow of work, so minimising the need to lay people off at the end of contracts.

The first diversification occurred in 1901 when, with inspired opportunism, Weetman invested in Mexican oil properties. He sold them soon after the War at a large profit and with the proceeds founded Whitehall Petroleum to seek oil opportunities elsewhere in the world. S. Pearson & Son became a holding company to which Weetman, by now the first Lord Cowdray, added a third operating company, Whitehall Trust, owner of a large stake in the Lazard Brothers merchant bank.

In the meantime Weetman was withdrawing from civil engineering. He took the view that growing nationalism throughout the world heralded the end of international contracting. He decided to

172

concentrate on oil and soon turned Whitehall Petroleum into a pioneering exploration company. It found the first British oil in Derbyshire and created the Amerada company in the US which found oil in Oklahoma, Kansas, Louisiana, Arkansas and Texas. But oil too soon became the focus of nationalism and by the time Weetman died in 1927 most of the Amerada holding had been sold.

The emergence of the modern Pearson from this hugely successful civil engineering group was gradual and opportunist. Weetman had been Liberal MP for Colchester for some years when he was asked to help an ailing Liberal paper, the *Westminster Gazette*. This later became, with the help of some judicious acquisitions, the regional newspaper chain Westminster Press. The interest in fine china began similarly when Weetman responded to his brother-in-law's request to help a struggling pottery company in Stoke.

After Weetman's death his son Clive was too busy forging the new businesses into a coherent group to have much time for new initiatives of his own although he did have a little flutter in civil aviation when he helped to form British Airways in 1935. The airline was compulsorily acquired by the government in 1940 and merged with Imperial Airways to form the British Overseas Airways Corporation. The War also saw the compulsory acquisition of Pearson's remaining US oil interests.

The second, postwar phase of the modern group's development was under the leadership of the third Lord Cowdray. He was 44 when he became chairman in 1954. Annual profits were less than £1m. By the time he retired at the age of 67, the company had gone public, profits had risen to £45m and the group included most of its current portfolio of 'quality' companies including the *Financial Times*, Château Latour, Penguin, Ladybird and Royal Doulton.

The Pearson portfolio has been described as the most valuable corporate art collection in the world. The present chairman Lord Blakenham, a quiet, cultured and determined man, dislikes the epithet. He regards the group's corporate collection as the consequence of a deliberate strategy to acquire and develop high quality businesses. Pearson was a brand collector before brand collecting became fashionable.

And, though I don't suppose Lord Blakenham looks at it that way, Pearson is also a pioneer of the nice strategy. The *Les Echos* incident said something about Pearson's and particularly the *FT*'s reputation in European financial publishing. In some cases it can be a pleasure or even a compliment to be acquired.

In late 1987 the managers of US educational publisher Addison-Wesley, who for years had jealously guarded their independence behind the protection of the voting control vested in their 'A' shares, decided they needed a strong partner in the increasingly competitive international marketplace.

They invited a selected group of companies they thought would be compatible to make offers. It was a private auction and the A-W managers were not committed to accepting any offer. The company was profitable and growing. It was anything but a fire sale.

Pearson won the auction with a bid of £162m. It is thought the decision had as much to do with A-W's liking for the cut of the Pearson jib as with money. 'We have similar cultures and shared attitudes,' Blakenham told me. 'We're both interested in quality and performance.'

Blakenham is rare among leaders of large companies in saying it would be inconceivable for Pearson ever to make a hostile bid. Most chief executives, even of apparently nice companies, are reluctant to be quite that categorical. They might use words such as 'improbable' or 'highly unlikely' but never 'never'.

In Pearson's case, though, the categorical denial seems no more than appropriate. Those who know the company would be astounded if it made a hostile bid in circumstances anything other than extraordinary. It is not Pearson's style. The group's reputation as an enlightened parent of quality businesses would be ruined if it turned aggressive.

But though Pearson would never be hostile it is not inviolate. Avaricious eyes are frequently cast over its mouth-watering portfolio. Rupert Murdoch, the Australian-born media tycoon who picked up Times Newspapers for a song in 1980 and then turned 'The Thunderer' into a tabloid in everything but size, bought 20% of Pearson in late 1987. He spoke of friendship and collaboration but his reputation made his protestations sound hollow.

Pearson's admirers were fearful. Murdoch also had the reputation of being a winner and Pearson, though part-owner of the Lazards merchant banking network, lacked direct experience in the rough and tumble of the market in corporate control. The bout seemed a mismatch. Saddened, Pearson's aficionados prepared themselves for the apparently inevitable act of rape.

But as we have seen, nice does not mean weak. Pearson has good friends dotted around the world. In early 1989, as Murdoch and Maxwell were picking off book publishers Collins and Macmillan of the US respectively, Pearson surprised all but readers of *Financial Weekly* by announcing a novel collaboration and share swap deal with the Dutch publisher, Elsevier.

With 20% of the shares still in the hands of the Pearson family, another 10% owned by Michel David-Weill, a director of Pearson and chairman of Lazard Partners, and 9% with Elsevier (in return Pearson got 15% of Elsevier), the Murdoch threat was neutralised. The nice company had found a way to defend itself in a rough world and it was a way not available to nasty companies. No company jealous of its independence would be foolish enough to invite Murdoch or Maxwell to become the holder of a substantial minority share stake.

An important feature of the Pearson/Elsevier share swap is that it can be, and was, justified on purely commercial grounds. Lord Blakenham had always said he did not believe companies should do things for purely defensive reasons. There is considerable scope for fruitful collaboration between the two companies in the post-1992 European and world markets. The share swap affirms a commitment to cooperate. Its defensive quality could be passed off as merely incidental.

The Body Shop International
The niceness of The Body Shop International, founded by Anita Roddick in 1976 and now one of Britain's most successful store groups, is based on a profound understanding of human nature and particularly of the business opportunities offered by society's growing environmental consciousness.

Roddick's nice strategy proscribes product testing on animals, eschews advertising, stresses minimal packaging and the use of only natural ingredients. All products are biodegradable and the shops, most of them franchises, offer a refill service for its bottles. It uses recycled paper wherever it can and as part of its mission to help the developing countries whence most of its raw materials come, Body Shop has set up local operations in Nepal, India, Bangladesh and in a Mexican refugee camp in Texas.

In this case human ethical principles have been transformed by the appetites of like-minded customers into a highly successful business strategy. So far, anyway, Roddick's prodigious

175

entrepreneurial flair has enabled her to avoid the confrontation of human ethics with the exigencies of corporate survival on which other idealistic companies have foundered.

'We are innovative in our formulations,' Roddick declared when explaining her strategy, 'passionate about environmental and social issues and we care about retailing. The image, goals and values of our company are as important as our products.' At the time of writing Body Shop was embarking on another surge of expansion. 'We're chiming in with the environmental upsurge,' Roddick explained, 'although we were environmentally conscious long before it became fashionable.'

Roddick says Body Shop, which had 400 shops worldwide by the end of 1988 and recorded a 56% increase in profits to £11.3m before tax for the twelve months to the end of February 1989, will remain true to its strategy as it grows. 'We will stick to our principles and still open up 1,000 shops and still produce new products and retail concepts that will leave the High Street reeling,' she said.

Roddick, ably abetted by husband Gordon, is evangelical about her company. 'We will have failed by 50%,' she said in May 1989 at the opening of a new Body Shop soap factory in the depressed Easterhouse district of Glasgow, 'if we don't provide a role model for other companies.' She claims Body Shop is the only UK company that educates its shareholders but predicts that within a decade 'this sort of operation will be the norm.'

The Soap Works site was chosen after an Easterhouse community leader pointed out that Body Shop's policy of helping Third World countries had caused it to ignore 'Britain's own Third World in the inner cities'. The factory plans to employ 100 people by the end of 1990 on the site of a demolished Olivetti typewriter plant that once employed 4,000. Body Shop intends to put 25% of the Soap Works' net profit into a foundation for Easterhouse community projects. Before the Soap Works had opened Body Shop's UK franchisees had raised £23,000 for a playground in the Easterhouse area.

Roddick's strategy is unfamiliar to most students of business economics, it incorporates few of the conventional ingredients for success and yet the company is by far and away the most profitable niche retailing business to have emerged in the UK over the past decade.

Earnings per share have risen more than five-fold over the past four years and, as Table 9.2 shows, the company's overall financial performance compares very well with those of Britain's leading retail groups.

Table 9.2

Company	Sales £m	Profit £m	Margin %	Staff '000s	Value+ £m	Value+/ £ of pay
Body Shop	28	6	21	0.4	10	360p
Next	862	99	12	18	295	277p
GUS	2512	354	14	31	642	245p
Marks & Spencer	4578	502	11	41	1110	216p
Burton	1590	231	15	28	537	208p
Storehouse	1171	132	11	29	339	207p

Source: 1987 annual reports.

Establishment pundits tend to be rather patronising about Body Shop's success. Because it violates so many of the orthodox principles of business, they feel more or less obliged to characterise it as a one-off – a macromutant, or hopeful monster as evolutionists would say, that just happened to get lucky.

But as we have seen, some hopeful monsters get so lucky they create a whole new species. The appearance of stockbroker James Capel's *Green Book* in the summer of 1989, containing a large number of green share recommendations (in companies expected to benefit from the explosion of environmental consciousness in Britain), suggested some City pundits were beginning to change their minds.

Hewlett-Packard
While the Pearson story shows how a nice strategy can evolve in a company with a taste for quality businesses and a tradition of adaptation to a changing environment, The Body Shop and the US computer group Hewlett-Packard demonstrate the power of being nice from the start.

H-P is 'up-front' with its mission statement. It appears on the cover of its 1988 UK report and accounts and is signed by H-P's founders, William Hewlett and David Packard – Bill and Dave as they are known within the company.

It reads as follows:

The Hewlett-Packard Company's prime business purpose is to provide the advice, technological capabilities, and ongoing support to enable its customers worldwide to improve their personal and business effectiveness.

and is accompanied by an attribution:

From the beginning, we have believed that the bedrock of our success is the talent and energy of Hewlett-Packard people. This company could not have grown to worldwide stature without the efforts of many remarkable people over the past five decades. At 50, Hewlett-Packard is a major global player in the most dynamic technological revolution ever known.

Bill and Dave have been believers in, and practitioners of, the nice strategy since they founded the company in 1939 in the garage behind Packard's home in Palo Alto, California. Their style has exemplified enlightened people management ever since.

They introduced cash profit-sharing in the 1940s, before Martin Weitzman, the arch-priest of the share economy (see Chapter Five) was born, and pioneered 'management by objective' (rather than 'directive') in which leadership is supplied not by an authoritarian hierarchy but by clear and agreed objectives that everyone must help to achieve.

Their first product was an audio oscillator used to develop the soundtrack for Walt Disney's film *Fantasia*. With sales of over $10bn a year and 87,000 employees worldwide, H-P now ranks as the world's fourth largest computer firm behind IBM, DEC and Unisys.

The 'H-P Way', its constantly articulated corporate philosophy, is based on seven objectives:

- To achieve sufficient profit to finance our company growth and to provide the resources we need to achieve our corporate objectives.
- To provide products and services of the highest quality and the greatest possible value to our customers, thereby gaining and holding their respect and loyalty.
- To participate in those fields of interest that build upon our technology and customer base, that offer opportunities for

    continuing growth, and that enable us to make a needed and profitable contribution.

- To let our growth be limited only by our profits and our ability to develop and produce innovative products that satisfy real customer needs.
- To help H-P people share in the company's success which they make possible; to provide employment security based on their performance; to recognise their individual achievements; and to help them gain a sense of satisfaction and accomplishment from their work.
- To foster initiative and creativity by allowing the individual great freedom of action in attaining well-defined objectives.
- To honour our obligations to society by being an economic, intellectual and social asset to each nation and each community in which we operate.

We will return to 'heart on sleeve' declarations of the H-P and Body Shop kinds in Chapter Eleven. 'Mission statements' articulating a philosophy as well as a business idea, that are shouted from the rooftops, are both expressions of a company's personality and strong guarantees of consistent compliance. Bill and Dave have imbued H-P with a set of principles that constrains the leaders that come after them.

Another nice aspect of H-P's personality is its predisposition to cooperate. The drive units in its big-selling laser printers are made by Canon in Japan, its portable computers are badged versions of Zenith machines and as a result of its collaboration with Microsoft large chunks of H-P software are incorporated in the latest version of Microsoft's 'Windows' software.

H-P is also cooperating with Sony in the joint development of new digital audio tape storage devices (a DAT cassette is the size of a half-inch thick business card and can store the equivalent of three sets of the Encyclopaedia Britannica), has linked with Fulcrum Technologies of Canada to develop data storage systems using CD-ROMs (Compact Disk-Read Only Memory) and has concluded a voice-messaging deal with Octel Communications of California.

A key to H-P's success has been its unusually low labour turnover, particularly in Research and Development where staff defections can be very damaging. This 'glue' is generally attributed to the high level of employee share-ownership, the low salaries of top managers and to H-P's generous profit-sharing schemes. But there is more to it than that.

H-P's enviably low staff turnover ratio is also attributable to its operating policies. Rather than run the risk of occasional large lay-offs it has declined to bid on short-run government contracts and has carefully avoided product areas where sales are volatile.

When general economic conditions have been bad, stocks have been increased and everyone, from the chief executive downwards, has worked a reduced week. This has effectively divided available jobs between all employees as a substitute for redundancies.

This consideration has helped to breed a corporate culture that was sufficiently rich in mutual trust to permit the introduction of a flexitime working arrangement. Bill and Dave were always expressing their belief that people were the essence of H-P. They used to say: 'motivation is the difference between a championship ball team and an ordinary ball team'.

One of the big questions, and it has yet to be resolved even though the two founders withdrew from their executive roles in 1978, was whether the ball players would stay motivated when Bill and Dave retired.

'Is the H-P spirit still alive?' is a question still asked with regularity by business commentators and by H-P employees themselves. The fact that the question is still asked suggests that at the very least the H-P spirit is not dead.

SUMMARY

- Value Added Partnerships (VAPs) are clusters of nice companies enjoying scale economies previously thought to be available only to large, integrated groups.

- Hollow corporations (international VAPs) like Amstrad are good extractors of value added and, contrary to popular belief, are healthy for their host economies.

- Virgin Group demonstrates both the power of the nice strategy in people businesses and its sense of obligation.

- Bertelsmann shows how a philosophy of partnership can create very large organisations that are substantially self-financing.

- The Pearson story shows how an adaptable organisation can evolve a nice strategy and use its niceness as a defence against hostile bids.

- The Body Shop International has shown how a sensitivity to its customers' ethical beliefs can produce high returns for shareholders.

- The story of Hewlett-Packard shows how thoroughgoing niceness can become a substantial competitive advantage.

CHAPTER 10

Developing a Nice Strategy

In addition to the wealth itemised in the conventional balance sheet every company possesses items of intangible wealth that together constitute what I call its 'invisible balance sheet'. This notional statement of wealth includes such things as brands and intellectual property.

In this chapter we will look at the two most important items on the invisible balance sheet: reputation and knowhow capital. Both are hard to measure and both are so general that they might more properly be regarded as 'meta-assets'. Each exemplifies one of the two basic modes of the nice strategy – external on the one hand and internal on the other.

Reputation is the meta-asset that is accumulated over time as a result of a company's conduct in its relationships with outsiders such as customers, suppliers, neighbours, government, the financial markets and the public at large.

Knowhow capital is the meta-asset that is accumulated over time as a result of a company's conduct in its relationships with its own people. Though it is convenient to treat these two meta-assets separately, they exert considerable influence over each other. A company's reputation affects its ability to recruit and keep good people – and so accumulate knowhow capital – and the behaviour of the people a company employs affects a company's reputation.

MANAGING THE REPUTATION BUBBLE
Though companies have yet to get to grips with the problem of how to value reputation, company leaders are acutely aware of the crucial role it plays. In the report on company philosophies and

182

business ethics by the Institute of Business Ethics (see Chapter One), the chairman of a major UK food group said: 'a well-founded reputation for scrupulous dealing is itself a priceless company asset'. By the same token, a reputation for unscrupulous dealing in one or both of the two ethical domains in which companies operate is a liability.

But it is not enough to recognise the value of a good reputation and to behave in ways designed to achieve one. Reputations are the creatures not of facts but of perceptions. They must be managed actively because a company's actions cannot be left to speak for themselves.

One of the most important – because most visible – determinants of a company's reputation is how it handles crises. Two case studies will illustrate the kinds of mistakes companies make in this key area of what I call 'reputation management' and will also help to show how a nice strategy acts as an automatic protector of these crucial 'reputational assets'.

Eli Lilly and Opren

Eli Lilly, the US pharmaceuticals group, launched its arthritis 'wonder-drug' Opren on the British market in May 1980, two years before its launch in the US.

Within a year disturbing new evidence of its properties began coming to light. In June 1981 Dr Ronald Hamdy, a consultant geriatrician, and Dr Kevin Woodcock of Lilly's medical staff, found Opren stayed in the bodies of old people up to four times longer than expected. Dr Hamdy recalled both he and Woodcock had been 'terribly concerned' but nothing was done.

The next warning that something was seriously amiss with Opren came in March 1982 when Dr Hugh Taggart, geriatrician at Belfast City Hospital, told Dr Brian Gennery, Lilly's UK medical director, of his suspicions that the deaths of six old people in as many months were associated with the build-up of Opren in their kidneys. He heard no more from Lilly until his paper was published in May.

Lilly said later it had been waiting until Taggart published, so Opren victims must count themselves lucky that in this case the wheels of academic publishing ground exceedingly fast. As soon as Taggart's paper appeared, and on the eve of the launch of Opren in the US (where it was called Oraflex), Lilly announced that following further trials it was changing dosage instructions.

Three months later Opren was banned in the UK and the following day Lilly withdrew the drug from worldwide sale.

Between May 1980 and the banning of Opren in August 1982 the drug had been taken by 750,000 Britons, a significant number of whom subsequently experienced serious skin problems.

Lilly's reputation among British physicians was damaged by the Opren affair in several ways. In the first place UK physicians are likely to be wary in future of Lilly drugs launched in the British market before they are launched in Lilly's home market. Secondly, they can have less faith than before in the rigour of Lilly's pre-launch trials. Thirdly, their faith in the vigilance of Lilly's own medical staff has been weakened, and fourthly, they have serious doubts about the sensitivity of Lilly's marketing department to post-launch reports of serious side-effects (whether or not such reports are justified).

Lilly's reputation among US doctors has been damaged in the same ways apart from the first. In addition, the American medical profession must have been deeply shocked that Oraflex could have been launched in the US market with such heavy promotion in full knowledge of the weight of UK evidence of serious side-effects; evidence that was to lead to the worldwide withdrawal of the drug only a few months later.

The commercial potential of new Lilly drugs has been further reduced by the public execration of Lilly's behaviour. The facts of the matter are really quite beside the point. Lilly acquired serious reputational liabilities for the following reasons:

Firstly, by insisting the drug should stay on sale until its toxicity had been positively established.

Secondly, by making no *ex gratia* payments pending investigation. (This was in contrast to the behaviour of the UK group ICI when, a decade earlier, its heart drug Eraldin was found to cause eye disorders. Without waiting for claims to come to court ICI set up its own fund to pay compensation of up to £30,000 a head.)

Thirdly, by finally making an offer to 1,300 UK claimants that was less in total than a payment to a single American. True, the English courts always make much less generous compensation awards than their US counterparts but the sheer scale of the discrepancy was bound to smack of a cynical and opportunistic attempt by Lilly to evade its moral responsibility in much the worst hit market.

The value of the reputational liabilities Lilly incurred by its handling of the Opren affair is equivalent to the net present value of future earnings lost as a result of the negative feelings inspired in doctors and their patients about Lilly and its products. The calculation is more easily described than carried out but it is hard to see how the resulting sum could be anything other than substantial.

Union Carbide and Bhopal

At around midnight on 3 December 1984 a fatally poisonous gas, methyl isocyanate, escaped from an underground storage tank at Union Carbide's facility at Bhopal, in India. By morning 1,200 people were dead and another 20,000 were so seriously ill that a further 800 died within a few days. Five years on, the official death count is 3,329 and rising.

Union Carbide responded quickly when news of the disaster first reached its corporate headquarters in Danburg, Connecticut. It called an immediate, worldwide halt to the production and shipment of methyl isocyanate and despatched a doctor and a team of technicians to India to investigate the causes of the leak. The next day Warren M. Anderson, Union Carbide's chairman, flew to Bhopal. On his arrival he and two of Union Carbide's Indian executives were arrested by the Indian authorities.

Anderson's imprisonment attracted some sympathy from the press and there was more positive comment when he announced disaster aid was being made available, that the Bhopal plant would not be reopened without Indian approval and that the company would close its methyl isocyanate plant in West Virginia. The media also reacted well to Anderson's first words on being released from prison: 'my immediate concern is to get the people affected immediate disaster relief.'

But the Bhopal court cases in India and the US dragged on and on, and when Union Carbide, which had reported profits of over $700m in the previous year, offered $470m in full and final settlement in early 1989, the company was deep in the red on its reputation account.

In reputation management terms, Union Carbide blew it. Initially it treated the reputational liability of the disaster with some skill. It moved quickly to prevent a recurrence, its chief executive flew immediately to the disaster zone (where he had the good fortune to be arrested) and the company behaved as if it was genuinely concerned, if not contrite.

Union Carbide's big mistake was to allow the lawyers to dictate the timing and size of the settlement. A nice company would have responded quickly and generously, if not with cash (Union Carbide incurred a hefty $600m loss in 1985 so would have been pushed to pay much in the short term) at least with commitments of cash.

A nice company would also have been so concerned by the threat to the value of its reputational assets posed by such a disaster that it would either have withdrawn from the manufacture of such horrifically poisonous substances altogether or, at least, would have had a comprehensive, instant response disaster management plan in place for just such an eventuality.

Michael Regester, a leading UK crisis management consultant who was Gulf Oil's European manager of public affairs at the time of the US oil group's Bantry Bay disaster in 1979, has distilled his expertise in a fascinating little book *Crisis Management: How to turn a crisis into an opportunity*. He summarised his conclusions in four checklists covering planning for crisis, planning for communications in crisis, dealing with crisis and communicating in crisis.

Altogether Regester's checklists include 52 prescriptions and exhortations. With his permission I have taken the liberty below of compressing them into seven basic principles:

- Build credibility through a succession of responsible deeds and act concerned when the worst occurs.
- Appoint and train (with the help of experts) crisis management, crisis control and risk audit teams.
- Catalogue all conceivable crises and devise for each of them written strategies and tactics for preventing them in the first place, and dealing with them in the second.
- Devise internal and external communications channels for minimising damage to the company's reputation and, when crises occur, ensuring the company is the main source.
- With the help of a 'cascade call-out list' and reserved amenities ensure the right people are in the right place with the right facilities at the right time.
- Know your audience, particularly your opponents, and engage their help, and that of independent bodies, in dealing with the crisis.
- Tell the truth, the whole truth and nothing but the truth.

Regester approaches the problem of crisis management from the company's point of view because companies are his clients. He acts as their guide and adviser in the two ethical domains, helping them to steer a safe course through the various ethical extrusions that pucker the topology of ethical domain two, and teaching them to understand and respond appropriately to the less formal resonances emanating from ethical domain one.

Regester's book also emphasises the importance of social memory in reputation management. He says the incident in 1986, when 30 tons of toxic chemicals were washed into the Rhine and thence into the North Sea after a fire at the Sandoz plant in Basle, 'focussed attention as never before on an industrial pollution problem that was there anyway, on the record of the Rhine-bank chemical firms in meeting their responsibilities, and on the will of governments to control them.'

Regester believes several relatively minor pollution accidents since the Sandoz fire would have gone unnoticed had society and its institutions, the media and politics in particular, not been sensitised to the subject of Rhine pollution.

It has a lot to do with news values. British readers may recall how in 1989 police car chases and Rottweiler dogs became 'hot' issues. In both cases the catalyst was a fatal accident which made minor headlines in the tabloid press. During the following weeks several similar, less serious incidents, were reported in the press. The quality of police driving and the viciousness of Rottweilers cannot have deteriorated so suddenly. Such incidents must have been quite common anyway – it was simply that before the catalytic accidents they had lacked news value.

The arbitrary quality of news values requires the abandonment of the old belief that it is important not to get caught sinning, and the recognition that just because sins have gone unnoticed in the past does not prevent them from returning to haunt the organisation later. A key principle of reputation management is that one can never tell which of the things a company does today will matter tomorrow.

And disasters themselves change the corporate environment. As a consequence of Bhopal the US Environmental Protection Agency launched a programme to alert communities to dangerous chemicals in their areas and involve them in contingency planning in case of similar disasters. The disaster at Chernobyl has led to two international treaties on notification and assistance in the event of nuclear accidents and all EC countries are obliged to implement the 'Seveso Directive' by identifying and controlling major industrial hazards.

187

Tom Burke and John Elkington addressed this new management issue in their book *The Green Capitalists* (reviewed by Marion Cotter in *Chief Executive*, March 1988). They say that having acquired a reputation for being 'environmentally abusive' the chemical industry has recently been making vigorous efforts to clean up its act. Dearborn Chemicals, for example, has developed low-toxicity water treatment methods to replace its zinc chromate products and the German giant BASF has reduced considerably the environmental impact of its Ludwigshafen plant on the Rhine.

BP is a particularly interesting case in point. The revelation in 1989 that it was involved in the destruction of the Amazon rain forests came when it was pushing its green image hard in a new corporate identity campaign. The ridicule and scepticism which the disclosure inspired dramatically corroborated the principle of reputation management which states that everything a company does today may matter tomorrow.

The irony was that, generally speaking, the UK oil and chemicals giant has taken its neighbourly responsibilities very seriously for many years. BP issued a policy statement, committing itself to minimising the effects of its activities on the environment, as long ago as 1980. This was followed by the deployment of its Environmental Protection Management programme to assess, monitor and report on the ecological impact of new projects. BP reckons environmental measures now account for about 10% of the cost of major projects. In 1988 BP's good neighbourliness was recognised with the award of the World Environmental Centre gold medal.

'We believe, quite simply, that you have to behave responsibly,' a BP spokesperson explained. 'If things go wrong in a field like ours the effect could be catastrophic both for the environment and the industry. We think it best to invest at the front end to ensure both are well protected.'

But such expressions of altruism should be taken with more than a pinch or two of salt. Considerable confusion reigns about the status of these apparently ethical corporate behaviour patterns and is being compounded by senior managers themselves.

For instance, when explaining Shell's policy on environmental issues, Dr Mark Scott of the oil giant's long-term planning group said: 'It boils down to wanting to be a good citizen. Businessmen, after all, are still human beings who care, so it follows naturally that as a corporation we should have a responsible attitude.' One wonders what Shell shareholders think of such indulgence of managerial altruism.

But it really has nothing to do with altruism. BP and Shell have adopted good neighbour policies not because they are managed by 'human beings who care' but because their leaders are smart enough to realise that irresponsible behaviour is inconsistent with long-term profit maximisation.

John Leivers of Redland Aggregates, the quarry group, made the same mistake when he attributed the more responsible attitude of the aggregates industry to the fact that: 'we're no longer an uncaring industry. We sometimes have more feeling for the environment than we're given credit for.'

He gave the game away when he went on to explain that: 'before, you would just throw a handful of grass over a worked-out site and wait for it to grow. Now, planning permission comes with perhaps 40 conditions attached and the demands on us from society are increasing.'

The fact of the matter is that the change in the behaviour of quarry companies probably had more to do with tighter planning controls and the insistence of local authorities on site restoration than on the emergence of a more caring attitude.

Robert Charlton, public affairs manager at Dow Chemical, was more candid when explaining Dow's withdrawal of its Plictran pesticides after they had been shown to cause foetal damage in rats. 'We've grown weary of confrontation,' he said. 'We recognise there's a more savvy response.'

This pragmatism is healthy because it is really quite dangerous to rely for a company's good behaviour on the morality of its leaders. If the reason that Shell and Redland behave responsibly is that Scott and Leivers are responsible human beings, what hope is there for the environment when they are succeeded by men and women of less moral fortitude? Companies cannot rely for their niceness on the qualities of their executives. They must be nice themselves. Niceness must be built into the system. Shell and Redland are not responsible because their executives are responsible, rather they hire responsible executives because they are themselves responsible.

Burke and Elkington sketched out a model action programme for companies wishing to formulate environmentally responsible policies. It adds up to an environmental sub-strategy of the nice strategy:

189

- Develop and publish an environmental policy stating aims and objectives. Useful references are policy statements published by companies like ICI and IBM.
- Prepare an action plan spelling out objectives and how they will be met.
- Appoint a 'champion' for environmental matters, preferably a main board director.
- Allocate adequate resources and ensure professional management of their deployment.
- Invest in environmental research and technology when developing product lines and assessing new markets.
- Monitor, audit and report regularly on the management systems put in place.
- Contribute to or sponsor environmental projects.

Burke, a former director of Friends of the Earth, ends with the following exhortations:

> Industrialists are not expected to be miracle workers – just seen to be trying. Demonstrate goodwill. Be seen to be taking the matter seriously. Don't hide from the press. Involve a senior executive who is prepared to own up if mistakes have been made. And remember that it helps to know the environmentalists involved and what their real objectives are.

It is interesting to compare the Burke and Elkington checklist with Michael Regester's. The former is the product of Burke's and Elkington's associations with environmentalist pressure groups whereas Regester's principles are the products of his experiences on the other side of the fence.

That the two sets of principles are remarkably similar suggests that in the areas of environmental protection and crisis management at any rate, evolution in the two ethical domains has been convergent.

REPUTATION AND TFT
But crisis management and environmental protection issues, though often represented by extrusions in ethical domain two, in the form of regulations and new law, are essentially ethical-domain-one matters.

To understand the importance of reputation in ethical domain two we must return to Axelrod's model. Remember that the features of the TFT strategy identified by Axelrod as distinctive were that it is nice, retaliatory, forgiving and clear. Clarity is crucial because reputation consists of two dimensions: what it is and how well it is known.

Axelrod says a player's reputation is embodied in the beliefs of others. He suggested, for example, that Britain's reputation for being provocable was considerably enhanced by its decision to retake the Falkland Islands after the Argentinian invasion.

In ethical domain two, companies are confronted by choices. If, as I have suggested, the sum of the business game is maximised when cooperation is maximised, the TFT player will tend to chose to deal with companies that have cooperative reputations. This is why nice clusters are such important agents of strategic evolution.

Companies that have reputations for cheating and bullying will be avoided by TFT players and so be denied the opportunity to engage in mutually beneficial trading relationships.

Such companies will also know that though cheating with TFT once will be profitable, it will provoke immediate retaliation. The nasty player knows that if it wishes to play again with the TFT player it will have to take the retaliation before it is forgiven. The clear TFT thus deters nasty strategies as well as encourages nice ones.

The basic principle of reputation management is that the value of reputational assets must be *actively* preserved and enhanced. A company that takes a major hit on its 'invisible' balance sheet should try vigorously to make good the damage by acquiring reputational assets to offset its new reputational liability.

There is a tendency amongst large companies engaged in hazardous activities to believe that following a disaster it is enough to take all possible steps to ensure it never happens again. The key principle of reputation management says this is a necessary but not a sufficient response. The shipping group P&O should not have just tightened operating and safety procedures following the Zeebrugge disaster. It should have actively sought ways to make good the reputational damage by, for example, associating itself publicly with popular causes not necessarily connected with the disaster.

The reputational asset is the bottom line of a balance sheet containing negative and positive items. Since it is plainly in the interests of companies to maximise the net value of their reputational assets, all cost-effective opportunities to add to them should be exploited. And cost effectiveness, in this sense, depends on the existing value of the reputational asset. If it is already negative, it is more important to add positive value than if it is zero or positive.

COMMUNICATIONS
It follows from the above that reputation management must be proactive as well as merely reactive. Companies must have a good idea of the current state of their reputational balance sheets and they must develop a repertoire of measures and policies to enhance reputational assets as well as to limit reputational liabilities.

It is not enough to take asset-enhancing steps. As we have seen reputations are created not by facts but by perceptions. A company must find effective ways of telling the world about its good deeds and all other aspects of its strategy.

As Lord Hanson says, company leaders have a responsibility to communicate on a regular basis with their shareholders. 'You have to explain yourself to the City,' he told *Financial Weekly* in January 1989, 'and you have to keep on explaining. The debate has to be a perpetual one.'

A company that decides to adopt a nice strategy because of the kind of arguments presented in this book, should explain its decision to the City and should keep on explaining.

INTELLIGENCE
A company must be able to receive as well as to transmit. If it is to adopt the right reputation-enhancing policies and target them with any precision, it must have an accurate reputational map. It must know where the sensitive areas are and it must understand the signals that emanate from them. In other words, a nice strategy requires for its successful implementation a brain and sensors as well as a voice.

Detailed analysis of press cuttings can give quite a good idea of the company's status in the minds of the people. It can put names and arguments to the groups and campaigns that are constantly pricking corporate consciences; it can give early warning of potentially important changes in news values and can identify, and help attribute approximate values to, the main reputational assets and liabilities.

Precise measurement is not possible but a rough idea is much better than nothing. And once an initial estimate has been made an index system can be used to track changes in reputational capital. Negative press clippings subtract and positive ones add. The change in any one period is the net result. And though absolute magnitudes can never be established with any accuracy, it should be possible at any one time to say if a reputational balance sheet has a positive, negative or neutral bottom line.

New books and their reception also reveal useful information for the reputation manager about changes in popular attitudes. The publication of *Rating America's Corporate Conscience* by Steven Lydenberg, Alice Tepper Marlin, Sean O'Brien Strub and the Council on Economic Priorities, was a significant business event.

The book was a good shopping guide for the ethical consumer and made statements like: 'buy Crest and Gleem toothpaste because its manufacturer, Procter & Gamble, gives much more to charity than its main competitors Colgate–Palmolive and Unilever, has more female and minority directors and officers and is not involved in South Africa'. It was widely and favourably reviewed and sold like hot cakes.

The Green Consumer Guide was published in Britain eighteen months later. The authors were John Elkington (joint author with Tom Burke of *The Green Capitalists*, see above) and Julia Hailes. There was a foreword by Anita Roddick, founder of The Body Shop. In addition to an ethical shopping guide the book contains a wealth of information about the ethical prejudices of British consumers and about their representative organisations.

Company leaders need to know about such publications because although they may not agree with such consumerist polemic they have to live with the effect it has on their marketplace.

Just as the senses, brains and communication abilities of *Homo sapiens* contributed greatly to the evolutionary success of that species, so the evolutionary success of the nice company will be greatly aided by its acquisition of sensing, information processing and communications skills. The nice strategy is, above all, an intelligent strategy. The nice company is not content to be driven by the need to gratify short-term corporate appetites. It is a seeing, listening, thinking and communicating organism.

MANAGING KNOWHOW*

These days business leaders are becoming increasingly aware of the need to maximise the value of the talent, experience and skills of

---

* The following is based on a much fuller treatment of the subject in *Managing Knowhow* by Karl Erik Sveiby and Tom Lloyd.

193

their employees. The essence of good management in people-intensive industries, and in most other industries too as the general level of skill intensity rises, is *the ability to recruit and keep good people*. If you can get that right, everything else, including a healthy bottom line, falls more or less automatically into place.

The nature of the change in the management approach required by this shift of focus from tangible capital to knowhow capital can be illustrated by the corresponding change in vocabulary:

Old	New
Revenues	Information
Machine	Human being
Capital, assets	Knowhow
Maintenance	Education
Investment	Recruitment
Disinvestment	Departure
Production	Data production
Raw material	Time

Any company or business unit that depends significantly for its ability to generate revenues on the skills and creativity of highly qualified, professional people, is strongly motivated to accumulate knowhow capital.

The possessors of knowhow capital are talented people who are not easy to manage. They are clever, opinionated, argumentative, impatient with bureaucracy, easily demoralised and, worst of all, highly valued in the outside market. You can't afford to get too tough with your 'prima donnas' otherwise they will leave and knock a hole in your invisible balance sheet.

The first task of the putative leaders of such companies is to win the respect of the professionals. Leadership is not a position conferred on you by your superiors. It is the respect earned by you from your peers. It is not a right but a reward.

The dilemma is that it is hard, though not impossible, to earn the respect of professionals if you are not a professional yourself and yet *professional knowhow does not equal managerial knowhow*. This lack of identity of professional and managerial skills has led to the evolution in some industries of pairs of leaders. In publishing, for example, the pair consists of the editor and the publisher. In films it consists of the director and the producer.

Sometimes the key professionals are so obsessed with their own professionalism that the management of the business unit in which they work seems trivial to them. The managing partners of law firms, for example, tend to lose the respect of their peers because they have had to withdraw from the sharp end – dealing with clients – and concern themselves with minor, local matters.

The good news is that professionals do not need to be managed actively, at least not in the traditional sense of active management. They manage themselves. They work hard not because they fear the consequences if they don't, but because they are strongly motivated to exercise their abilities and skills.

That is why the first secret of good knowhow management is to hire the right people. Once you have who you need to do the job the job will get done. But it will only continue to get done if the people you need stay. This is why the idea of a personnel department somewhere down the management hierarchy, into which people who do not seem much good at anything else tend to be pushed, is so absurd (see Chapter Five).

PEOPLE MANAGEMENT IN THE LARGE COMPANY
One of the attractions of working for a very large organisation is that it offers a wide variety of career paths for young and ambitious professionals. Another is the security that seems to be offered.

But these two qualities, though they help in recruitment, can actually make it harder to keep people because when they join a business unit of a large company they are also joining the group. Their immediate 'job market' is the company at large. It is relatively easy for them to 'job hop', from business unit to business unit, up the organisation's power ladder.

Another problem that can be irksome is that the usual repertoire of devices for keeping good people, like paying them more or giving them share options linked to local performance, is often strictly limited by the reward policies of the group as a whole.

But though it is hard to persuade good people that their future lies within the business unit when it is evident that the most glittering of prizes lie elsewhere, business unit leaders must do the best they can within these constraints.

Moreover, if the organisation as a whole is to improve its rate of knowhow capital accumulation – in other words, to get better at recruiting and keeping good people – business unit leaders must kick constantly against their constraints. In defending their store of knowhow capital they must be parameter pushers, constantly demanding, to the limits of what is politic, greater freedom to reward and stimulate their key people.

The tools of people management can be divided into two classes – monetary and non-monetary.

Money is not as inflexible an instrument in large companies as it is usually assumed to be. Part of its importance lies in its symbolism. Good people want to earn more not just because they want a better living standard but also because salary and profit-sharing represent an objective, readily understood measure of a person's worth. They corroborate and help to form a person's self-image.

Linking pay to profit or value added is desirable for all sorts of reasons but its effectiveness as a stimulus depends on how closely it is linked to 'local' performance. Options on shares in an organisation employing a quarter of a million people are welcome but are not stimulating because an individual cannot believe his or her own efforts can affect materially the value of the share options.

An intriguing aspect of the adaptive behaviour of large groups in the changing business world is the efforts they are making to resemble federations of small companies rather than monolithic, highly integrated organisations.

One financial example of this tendency, which should be of great interest to the leaders of business units within large groups, is the idea of 'phantom stock'.

You imagine your business unit is an independent company with its own shares, a proportion of which are under option to key people. You look at the performance of the business unit and, using stock market ratings, you work out what the value of the business unit would be in the open market. If performance improves, the value of the phantom stock rises.

Non-monetary techniques for the acquisition and preservation of knowhow capital require more artifice. Bold experimentation and a refusal to take things for granted are the guiding principles. The key professionals represent the company's core knowhow. If they want to do something a little different because that is how their own professionalism is developing it is not enough to say 'no, that's not part of the strategy'.

Something like that may have to be said in the end but first the leader should explore the possibilities of changing the business unit's strategy to accommodate the new possibility its core knowhow has thrown up. Strategy is too often a constraint. As we saw in Chapter Three a company should first decide what it is – which is determined largely by its core knowhow – and only *then* decide what to do.

Good, well-managed professionals are constantly coming up with new business ideas. Most of them are half-baked and hopelessly impractical but a few of them are pure gold. One good way of sorting the wheat from the chaff is to suggest the guy goes away and works the idea up into a formal proposal. Nine times out of ten no more will be heard of it.

Leaders must be receptive to the currents of ideas that are constantly rippling through a healthy body of knowhow capital. Nothing is more demotivating for individuals with inquiring minds than to be told to stop dreaming and get on with their work. Their frustrations will breed discontent and defection. The knowhow capital will become inert and much less competent at dealing with everyday problems.

But it is not enough to be receptive. Leaders must also be proactive if they are to keep their good people. They must have empathy with them so that they can anticipate problems and ensure that the level of motivation is sustained. Some examples will help to make the point:

- A computer company allowed one of its software engineers to work with an overseas partner company because his wife wanted to live abroad for a year.
- A publishing company gave one of its journalists leave to work freelance for other magazines in New York for a couple of years with a 'return ticket'.
- A telecommunications company allowed one of its managers to work for a competitor part-time because she saw a challenge there.
- An accountancy firm sent one of its promising associates on a two-year secondment to a manufacturing company to give him a customer's-eye view of his profession.
- A consultancy company set up an office abroad to indulge one of its senior consultants.
- Another consultancy firm recruited the managing director of a client company in exchange for one of its own consultants.

Imaginative uses of temporary assignments, secondments, job-swapping, new projects and study trips, all act as a kind of glue, encouraging people to stick around. Knowledge-intensive companies and business units should try to resemble sticky magnets. They should establish the reputation in their local employment market for being a good place to work and should make the work so much fun and so challenging that the key people seldom even think of the colour of the grass on the other side of the hill.

THE PROBLEM OF MEASUREMENT

We saw in Chapter Six how new kinds of performance measurement are needed by financial analysts if they are to avoid mistakes in valuing companies. Managers and business leaders also need new yardsticks to assess their performance.

The good thing about traditional accounting methods is that they deal with measurable things. If a company earns higher profits its strategy is corroborated. There is feedback. Success and failure are clear and unequivocal. Though intangible assets are becoming more important than tangible assets they are far less easy to measure. Traditional accounting for tangibles, though not very relevant, is at least reliable. The new accounting for intangibles, though much more relevant is, as yet anyway, not very reliable.

But intangibles are not wholly unmeasurable. If the management focus is on knowhow capital rather than the conventional bottom line it is clearly important to look at per capita performance figures. While the old methods look at return on capital, for example, the new might look at changes in the return on knowhow capital – how profits have changed in relation to the sum of many years of experience.

A better measure of knowhow capital performance than profit is value added because that shows how productive people are before taking into account their costs.

Table 10.1 shows data taken from the published accounts of Britain's largest company, British Telecom. Similar figures for Cable & Wireless, BT's only competitor, have been included for comparison purposes.

What do these figures tell us? BT has performed very well over the past four years in terms of the value added it is extracting from its employees. The value-added-per-head figure has risen by more than 50% while average pay has gone up by barely a third.

This has allowed value added per £ of pay, set to become one of the key measures of knowhow businesses over the next few years, to rise by 15%. It is easy to calculate that every 1p increase in value added per £ of pay is worth another £21m at the operating profit level.

Table 10.1

British Telecom

	1984	1985	1986	1987	1988
Employees (000s)	241	235	236	234	237
Staff costs (£m)	2715	2807	2980	3164	3492
Operating profit (£m)	1531	1856	2118	2349	2609
Depreciation (£m)	907	933	1068	1311	1525
Value added (£m)	5153	5596	6166	6824	7626
Value+/£ of pay (p)	190	199	207	216	218
Value+/head (£000s)	21	24	26	29	32
Pay/head (£000s)	11	12	13	14	15
Pay/Value+ (%)	53	50	48	46	46

Cable & Wireless

	1987	1988
Employees (000s)	26	26
Staff costs (£m)	267	250
Trading profit (£m)	268	289
Depreciation (£m)	89	100
Value added (£m)	624	638
Value+/£ of pay (p)	234	255
Value+/head (£000s)	24	24
Pay/head (£000s)	10	10
Pay/Value+ (%)	43	39

But a second point to note is that average pay is a relatively small proportion of average value added. This is quite common in knowhow businesses. In traditional manufacturing businesses staff costs often account for as much as 70% of value added whereas in pure, capital-intensive knowhow businesses, like merchant banking or securities trading, it can be as low as 10%.

The difference between value added and pay measures a person's net contribution and therefore his or her bargaining power. In a competitive labour market there is a tendency for salaries to be bid up towards the value added. For each industry there is an average percentage of value added paid out to staff. In the telecommunications industry it seems to be about 50%.

It also looks as if it is falling and this may be a signal that something will have to change. There is obviously a point at which a low ratio will discourage the value-adders.

If they see their contribution rising faster than their pay, they may begin to feel undervalued and start to look elsewhere for employment. A low pay-to-value-added ratio does wonderful things for the bottom line in the short term but if it leads to a loss of knowhow capital it will inflict severe damage on the bottom line in the long term.

The extensive overseas operations of Cable & Wireless enable it to extract considerably more value added per £ of pay than BT. But BT has overtaken Cable & Wireless in terms of value added per head. BT pays better than Cable & Wireless but it needs to in its more competitive labour market.

It seems likely that within the next few years BT will have to review its pay policies. It will need to pay more and it would also be well advised to make its remuneration policies more flexible. An organisation's competitiveness tomorrow depends on the quality of today's recruits. If pay policies do not allow enough generosity and flexibility, the company's knowhow capital will be eroded.

SUMMARY

- Reputation and knowhow capital are a company's most important intangible assets. They need to be managed actively.

- The Opren affair and the Bhopal tragedy offer examples of poor crisis management.

- Reputational liabilities can be offset by the deliberate acquisition of reputational assets.

- Good corporate manners, including neighbourliness, are key features of the nice strategy in operation.

- TFT is a good reputation for a company to have when dealing with other companies.

- The company is a listening, thinking and communicating organism.

- There are monetary and non-monetary tools for people management in both large and small companies.

- New performance measurement methods are needed by managers as well as by financial analysts.

- If a company's knowhow capital is to be preserved, pay policies need to be generous and flexible.

CHAPTER 11

Action Plan for the Nice Company

In earlier chapters I set out the philosophical foundations of the nice strategy within the framework of a general theory of corporate evolution and have investigated the features of the modern corporate environment that I believe favour the emergence of the eponymous hero of this book, namely the nice company.

In this chapter I shall list and articulate a suite of proposed policy documents and mission statements that together constitute a manual or tool-box for nice company management.

This 'document portfolio' is divided into two parts, covering the two ethical domains described in the first chapter. Each document is accompanied by a 'statement of awareness' setting out its philosophical and theoretical bases and a discussion of some of the practical implications.

For convenience in these discussions I shall, in each case, call the corporate protagonist Nicecorp.

STATEMENT OF GENERAL AWARENESS

The company is a sentient, nonmoral life-form that is evolving in response to changes in its environment. Whether by conscious contrivance or default, it adopts strategic postures towards two main groups, moral human beings and other nonmoral companies, which I call domain one and domain two respectively.

Since the company is an optimising organism, it is motivated to develop good strategies. A game-theory analysis of business economics suggests nice strategies have a lot going for them.

This general awareness can be translated into a description of a company as a nice company. Such usage will often crop up in casual conversation, just as some companies began describing themselves as 'Theory Z' companies after the publication of William Ouchi's book (see Chapter Three). The observation that a company is nice implies its management team subscribes to the general argument put forward in this book, if not to all its particulars. Describing a company as nice is comparable to, though clearly not the same as, describing it as aggressive, ruthless, acquisition-led or nasty.

The general description is a useful taxonomic shorthand. Though nice, as it is used in this book, has a technical meaning, intelligible only to the initiated, it gives the right idiomatic impression. The everyday usage of the word nice is accurate as far as it goes though it may sometimes convey an inappropriate impression of softness or weakness.

DOMAIN ONE
As we saw in Chapter One, it is important to distinguish between corporate relationships with human beings, where human ethics are germane, and corporate relationships with other companies where the corporate ethos applies. Relationships of the former class occur in what I call ethical domain one and can be further subdivided into various human constituencies.

These are actual and potential employees (the labour market), neighbours (the local community), investors (ethical and otherwise), politicians (who connect the two domains via the process of ethical extrusion) and consumers.

Employees
The nice company is aware of the existence of an invisible balance sheet that contains, amongst other things, its knowhow capital — the skills, experience and aptitudes of its employees and their familiarity with the company's business idea, its style of operation and its personality. It recognises that knowhow capital, though not yet formally acknowledged in published accounts, is a crucial component of its competitive advantage and that therefore the recruitment and retention of good people is the central management task.

This awareness can be translated into the following, publishable statement of employment policy:

Nicecorp is constantly seeking to recruit high-quality people able to enhance its effectiveness in its marketplace. It knows the skills and experience of its employees are the keys to its competitiveness and long-term profitability, so it pays above average salaries for the sector.

In addition, Nicecorp acknowledges the need to provide career paths for its employees that offer the variation and challenge they need to fulfil themselves.

And because Nicecorp acknowledges that nowadays it is knowhow capital rather than financial capital that makes the greatest contribution to business success, it operates profit-sharing and equity-spreading schemes that reflect the true nature of its partnership with its staff.

Nicecorp respects and values the ethical sensibilities of its employees. It believes employees with principles are more diligent, more reliable, more loyal and generally more valuable than those without. Nicecorp also recognises that if it is to attract and keep people of integrity it must itself behave honourably, honestly and ethically. Accordingly, it undertakes, insofar as its business idea permits, to maintain standards of conduct its employees approve of and can take pride in.

Employee policies vary according to corporate structure but the principles apply in every situation. In the case of subsidiaries of large companies, the phantom stock scheme (see Chapter Ten) is an appropriate way of expressing the partnership idea.

All companies that employ 'local' profit-sharing (linked to business unit rather than to parent profitability in the case of holding companies) and share option schemes (phantom stock option schemes in the case of subsidiaries) should publicise such arrangements in order to attract high-quality recruits.

The undertaking to behave in an ethical way (as we have seen, companies are nonmoral creatures and so can only appear to be ethical) should also be publicised. And, of course, it does not apply merely to the employee constituency.

Ethical behaviour creates a good impression, and therefore makes commercial sense, in other ethical domain one constituencies too, particularly amongst neighbours and customers.

Neighbours
Nice companies are responsible. They are acutely aware of the severe damage irresponsible behaviour can inflict on what I call their reputational assets which are key items on their invisible

balance sheets. This awareness encourages the nice company to apply the following principles to its general conduct:

- To reduce the likelihood of catastrophes and crises in its hazardous operations to well below average.
- To behave, in the event of catastrophes, in ways that minimise reputational liabilities, notwithstanding the admonitions of legal advisers.
- To adopt formally an opportunistic policy towards the accumulation of reputational assets.

These three principles can be translated into the following, publishable statements:

A. Nicecorp undertakes to do all in its power to minimise the impact of its operations on the environment. In addition, it undertakes, wherever and whenever its operations are subject to local regulations, to exceed, on the safe side, all regulatory minima and maxima by at least 10%. To facilitate independent corroboration of this commitment it invites qualified outsiders to test its compliance with its self-imposed limits whenever they wish, subject to reasonable frequency.
B. Nicecorp will do all in its power to avoid life- and health-threatening incidents and, where appropriate, it will withdraw from hazardous activities where or when the risks appear to be incompatible with the long-term maintenance of a good reputation.
C. In the event of a health- or life-threatening incident Nicecorp will act swiftly and as generously as its means allow. Its subsequent actions will be guided not by considerations of legal liability but by the perceived needs of those affected by the incident. Nicecorp would regard any justifiable accusations of callousness or insensitivity in such a situation as deeply injurious to its reputation and will therefore do all in its power to avoid such assertions.

The invitation to qualified outsiders to test compliance (the qualification test should not be unduly restrictive and should not exclude, for example, authoritative environmental pressure groups) imposes a much stronger discipline that the requirement to satisfy typically understaffed regulatory authorities.

Nicecorp is effectively saying to the world in statement A that its efforts will be devoted to ensuring that it does not breach regulations rather than merely to ensuring that it is not caught breaching them. The Swedish petrochemicals group Berol has made such an undertaking, in cooperation with its local authority in Gothenburg, and its emissions, as a consequence, are known to be considerably lower than the law requires.

Statement B will obviously require the company to adopt a fail-safe policy towards hazardous activities – that is to say, Nicecorp will not wait for a hazard to be positively identified before it withdraws from the hazardous activity. It will act as soon as there is a reasonable doubt about an activity's safety. For instance, a nice company using CFCs (Chlorofluorocarbons) in its product chemistry would have stopped using them (either by employing substitutes or by withdrawing from the activity) as soon as a significant body of scientific opinion had expressed concern about the impact of CFCs on the ozone layer.

It goes without saying that such a swift response policy to new scientific concerns about CFCs, acid rain, lead additives, dioxins and the like can, if supported by energetic public relations, earn for the company considerable reputational assets.

Statement C will be supported by an internal policy document relating to the management of reputational assets (see Chapter ten). This will stress the need for an immediate intensification of the search for opportunities to acquire reputational assets in order to make good, as quickly as possible, the reputational liabilities incurred as a result of the incident.

The constant search for opportunities to acquire reputational assets should be a routine business activity. Such opportunities often occur in the normal course of business. In 1989 the Canadian Portland Cement Association issued a paper entitled *Resource recovery: the cement kiln solution*. The report, by Michael Nisbet and Jane Hainsworth of Lafarge Canada Inc, put the case for burning refuse derived fuel (RDF) and other organic wastes and solvents in the very high flame temperatures – up to 2,300 degrees C – reached in cement kilns.

It argued that with a more liberal licensing regime, the cement-making process could make a much greater contribution to waste management. In addition to waste oils, spent solvents and RDF, other types of waste – including many hazardous wastes such as the notorious polychlorinated biphenyls (PCBs) – can be used as fuel in cement kilns and are destroyed utterly in the process.

206

'Extensive testing has demonstrated,' the report stated, 'that there were no significant changes in emissions of particulate matter, total organic compounds, dioxins, furans, hydrogen chloride, or other air contaminants when combustible wastes were burned in place of conventional fuels.'

The irony was that public opinion in Canada had by then become so sensitive to the problem of hazardous industrial waste that it was acting as a major deterrent to the burning of hazardous wastes, PCBs in particular, in cement kilns, despite evidence that this was a wholly effective disposal method. This was a good illustration of the crucial difference between facts and perceptions.

The total destruction of PCBs in cement kilns seems a much more elegant solution to the problems they pose than for Canada to ship them to the US and even to Wales for disposal. But the cement kiln solution is not yet perceived by the public in this way. When popular environmental consciousness recognises the contribution some industrial processes can make to solving the waste problems posed by others, the public perceptions of such situations will become more identified with the facts and so permit the cement kiln to fulfil the role of a 'natural enemy' of hazardous and other wastes.

It is therefore in the interests of companies not only to seek opportunities to act as natural enemies of waste and other problems posed by modern industry, but also to educate public opinion to recognise such possibilities.

It is often the case that one industry's waste is another's cheap fuel. The growing problem of industrial waste management will be greatly reduced, though not solved, when industry's considerable latent ability to groom itself is given free rein.

An example of a very different kind of opportunistic acquisition of reputational assets was provided by the response of a number of companies to Bob Geldof's 'Band Aid' charity project. It was not surprising US pharmaceuticals and toiletries giant Johnson & Johnson decided not to complain formally about Geldof's breach of copyright on its Band Aid plaster brand but it was not at all self-evident that other companies, like Geldof's record company Phonogram, vinyl maker ICI, ZTT Studios and record retailers like Woolworths, W.H. Smith, HMV, Virgin, Boots and Our Price, would voluntarily surrender profit opportunities on Band Aid's big selling *Feed the World* record. That they did was greatly to their credit and was seen as such. All the corporate heroes of the Band Aid project acquired, as a result, substantial reputational assets.

Geldof's extraordinary achievement demonstrates another aspect of corporate ethics which is that the ethical and moral sense of a company's employees constitutes a latent corporate conscience. It is hard to activate because there are no formal mechanisms for doing so, but once activated – by Geldof's tough brand of evangelism in this case – it is extremely hard to resist.

In his delightfully blunt account of his time as a modern saint (*Is that it?*), Geldof described the mood within Phonogram as the company prepared for the original Band Aid recording session on Sunday, 25 November 1984:

> I went to John Walter (Phonogram's product manager) and asked how quickly we could get the record out. I thought it would take at least two weeks. 'If we pull all the stops out, we can do it in four days,' he said. This was extraordinary. But every individual concerned was now in a professional and personal fever. This fever was their contribution. Not just money, but themselves. All the record company could think of now was this record. They would not make a penny from it. It was the same with everyone else I asked to help. There was complete commitment.

Geldof's book is very moving. I challenge anyone to read it and remain dry-eyed throughout. But it is also very interesting from the point of view of the business economist. It shows the enormous power of human altruism when combined with corporate energy. No one working for the companies which contributed to the Band Aid project could have still believed afterwards in the fundamental selfishness of capitalism. And perceptive company leaders took note too. Here was a new, hitherto unsuspected and enormously rich source of creative energy and commitment that seemed to be available to companies in return for a relatively modest, short-term suspension of the profit principle.

Investors
Since the nice strategy still ranks as unorthodox, it is incumbent upon companies employing it to explain, and keep explaining, to investors the reasons for its adoption. Something along the lines of the following publishable statement could be printed in annual reports and company brochures:

> Nicecorp employs what has come to be known as a nice strategy because it believes that only this kind of approach to business will

maximise long-term profitability. It recognises that its reputation is one of its most valuable assets and it believes a good reputation is essential if the company is to be in a position to take advantage of all business opportunities that come its way.

Nicecorp believes its policies and activities qualify its stock for inclusion in all ethically screened funds and it takes pains to ensure its vulnerability to consumer boycotts and other kinds of popular sanction is negligible. Nicecorp employs a nice strategy not because of the altruism of its staff but because it is convinced that such a strategy is in the long-term interests of shareholders.

Until the nice strategy is established it will be necessary for its pioneers to be evangelical about the idea. They should work hard at selling the arguments for the strategy to the financial and invest-ment communities with the help of evidence of superior perform-ance and examples of business won by virtue of the strategy.

The City is a dedicated follower of fads and fashions. Once it has been persuaded of the merits of the nice strategy, and by the idea that cooperation between the various members of the value chain leads to improved performance, it is likely to favour companies employing nice strategies with higher-than-average share ratings.

In June 1989 Britain's largest stockbroking firm, James Capel, published *The James Capel Green Book*. It consisted, like most stockbroker research, of share recommendations but the analysis was predicated on an unusual hypothesis. The report began:

The Dutch Government falls over a 'Green' issue. Margaret Thatcher arranges a 'Green' briefing conference for British Government ministers. Charles wants every Royal to go Green. Green issues have become big news. They have also become big money. £2bn to be spent on new sewage works by 1995 at the latest, £0.5bn on de-sulphurisation equipment for a single power station, an annual spend of a minimum £1.5bn on the waste industry that is set to rise rapidly, all show that no matter what emotional feelings the financial community may have about the Green movement, its monetary impact is becoming too large to be ignored.

Those who still think of the Green movement as the preserve of cranks and bearded weirdos have missed a fundamental shift in the attitudes of a huge proportion of the population of the developed world.

209

These people are putting their money where their mouths are, and altering their spending patterns to suit their new beliefs. They are spending their money in a way they believe will help improve the world, maybe at the worst case preventing extinction of the human race. How else can you explain the sudden death of the underarm aerosol deodorant in the USA, and the resurgence in the UK of the share of the container market held by glass?

Some companies have been smart enough to spot this trend, ride it and prosper from it. Others – Body Shop is an example – have been behaving in a Green way for many years, out of a deeply held conviction that this is the right way to be. From the investment point of view, the motive is irrelevant. Companies in tune with the Green movement are on the way up, gaining market share and often also higher margins on these rising sales. The companies that have yet to wake up to the impact of the Green movement are getting left behind.

And it works the other way too. As the report also pointed out: 'the fact that there are such things as ethical unit trusts, stewardship funds and Green Personal Equity Plans and other investment vehicles is just another example of customer demand leading to new products.' Companies that routinely pass the ethical screening tests set by the growing population of ethical investors will not only find it easier to attract ethically discriminating employees for that reason but will also enjoy a cost-of-capital advantage.

In practice, the commitment to maintain qualifying status for the ethically screened funds is likely to lead to the internal application of similar ethical screening tests to such things as capital spending decisions and personnel policies.

Politicians

As we have seen, political institutions and the laws and regulations that issue from them are manifestations of the process of ethical extrusion. Properly speaking they belong in neither of the two ethical domains, but rather act as a bridge between them. Since the political system, including government, either incorporates or has influence over most of the licencing and regulatory authorities, companies need to be aware of their political reputations.

They should seek, through their lobbying activities, to persuade politicians of their political 'safety' and 'respectability'. For example, the Conservative government would have attracted a lot less criticism when it decided to allow a technical monopoly to be created by the acquisition of Times Newspapers in 1981 if the buyer had been the nice Pearson group rather than the controversial Australian media tycoon, Rupert Murdoch.

There is not much publishable in this area apart, perhaps, from a statement in Nicecorp's annual report eschewing contributions to political parties. There is nothing wrong, in principle, in companies making political contributions because it is often the case that they will be healthier under one colour of government than under another. However, companies should also recognise that there is value in a reputation for neutrality.

Potential employees may be deterred from joining a company if it is too politically partisan and, as the screening systems of the conscience funds become more sophisticated, a company's cost of capital may also benefit from a reputation for political neutrality.

Political parties need funding but it is certainly arguable that Britain's Conservative party will do better in the long run if it shifts the focus of its fund-raising efforts from businesses to businessmen and businesswomen.

Consumers
Much of what has already been said about employees, neighbours and investors also applies to the constituency of consumers. A nice company to work for, live near or invest in will also, as likely as not, be a nice company to buy from. And, of course, many customers are also potential employees, neighbours or investors. The importance of the consumer constituency is that it focuses attention on products (goods and services) rather than on processes, strategies and general corporate behaviour.

I use the term 'consumer' here in its broadest sense to include everyone and everything that 'consumes' the company's products, i.e. corporate customers as well as the so-called 'final' consumers, human beings. It is probably here where the crucial importance of reputation is most obvious. All companies, not just nice ones, know that business success depends on the perceived value of their products, whether they be goods or services.

But the meaning of the word 'value' changes over time. It has always included such qualities as reliability, design, price, usefulness, novelty and safety but these days consumers are demanding other qualities as well, such as low environmental impact, health content (often associated with the use of so-called 'natural' ingredients), probity in business dealings, honesty in marketing and integrity in employment and production policies. Increasingly these days the provenance of products is coming to be seen by consumers as part of their value.

A survey by the research group Mintel published in June 1989 found that nearly two-thirds of British adults are prepared to pay higher prices for environmentally friendly food, toiletries and detergents. The authors estimated that by the summer of 1989 there were as many as 12m 'serious Greens' in the UK willing to pay up to 27p in the pound extra for environmentally friendly products. They concluded that we were moving away from the market-led consumerism of the 1980s to a new environmental-led consumerism.

The nice company is aware that a reputation for environmental and social responsibility, for respecting the rights and problems of minorities and for being responsive to politically sensitive issues such as South Africa and the arms trade, all add to the perceived value of its products and therefore to their competitiveness. Ozone-friendly aerosols, which 72% of adults now prefer according to the Mintel study, and lead-free petrol sell better than rival CFC-driven and leaded products for sale at the same prices.

Anita Roddick is the arch-priestess of the principle that the provenance of products helps to determine their competitiveness. The mission statement in the booklet accompanying The Body Shop International's 1987 annual report and accounts (both printed on obviously recycled paper) is a model for other companies. It reads as follows:

> We take a non-exploitative approach to the world in which we all live and work. And that approach is fundamental to our company.
>
> The products generally consist of ingredients that have been tried and tested over many years of human use: many of these are plant-based and are also used in food.
>
> The ingredients are there for a purpose – not merely to provide an exotic name for the label. They come from all over the world, and out of this we aim to extend trade with Third World countries wherever we can.
>
> We do as much as possible within the company to minimise waste. We operate a refill service for customers so that our bottles can be used again and again. Our packaging is minimal, and we

212

use recycled paper and biodegradable plastic wherever possible, and we are working on improving our environmental policy and practice even further.

The Body Shop does not exist in a vacuum. Our products are produced with regard to the natural world and with regard to the needs of real people.

The words will be different for other companies but the delivery should be no less passionate and no less loud. To be good is not enough. A nice company must declaim its virtue repeatedly from the rooftops. Anita Roddick is evangelical about The Body Shop's nice strategy. She never misses an opportunity to publicise it. Her engagingly breathless enthusiasm attracts cameras and correspondents like bees round real honey. She is outspoken, high-profile and has become such an enormously successful retailer over the past ten years that even the most hard-bitten leaders of the big chains have been obliged to regard her as a serious and potentially dangerous rival.

The Roddicks (Anita and her husband Gordon) and their company are at the leading edge of corporate evolution. The trail they are blazing will be followed by others. They are delivering a new kind of value to consumers, the demand for which is both informed (with the help of books like *The Green Consumer Guide*) and growing rapidly. Just as investors can now satisfy some of their ethical desires by putting their money into 'conscience' and 'ecology' funds, so consumers of toiletries and cosmetics can gain a sense of added environmental and social responsibility by buying Body Shop products. For Body Shop's shareholders the rewards of virtue have been very substantial indeed.

DOMAIN TWO

Morality has nothing to do with domain two interactions with other companies because companies are nonmoral beings. But as we have seen, companies abide by a code of behaviour in domain two, whether contrived or arrived at by default ('explicit' or 'implicit' in Porter's terms). Contrived codes are better because they ensure consistency and consistency implies clarity and it is important for domain two strategies and personalities to be clear.

The declaration of awareness about the basic nature of domain two interactions includes the following points:

213

- Interactions with other businesses are iterative rather than a series of one-offs.
- Business is a positive-sum game.
- The sum of the business game is maximised when cooperation is maximised.
- The TFT strategy is nice, retaliatory, forgiving and clear.

From these it is possible to derive the following statement that can be imparted to all businesses with which the company deals and can be included in all contractual paperwork:

Nicecorp recognises the inherently collaborative nature of business and acknowledges its own wellbeing is dependent on the wellbeing of its customers and suppliers. It is anxious to establish long-term commercial relationships and to this end it pursues, in all its dealings, a policy of rigorous honesty. In addition, it stands ready to do all it can to help customers and suppliers solve their own problems.

Nicecorp expects other companies with which it deals to behave in a similarly scrupulous fashion and so takes a very grave view of customers or suppliers who try to take advantage of Nicecorp policies. Nicecorp therefore reserves the right, as far as its legal obligations permit, to terminate relationships with customers and suppliers who behave dishonestly. This right will be routinely exercised.

Any company with whom Nicecorp decides, for the above reasons, to sever its relationship will be automatically 'blacklisted' and will not be reinstated as a qualifying customer or supplier until it has acknowledged its error and made a tangible conciliatory gesture.

A number of support policies, not necessarily for publication, can be derived from this statement:

- Companies with which Nicecorp deals or may deal should be classified according to the niceness or otherwise of their strategies and policies.
- Companies involved in relationships with Nicecorp will be routinely audited for niceness, and relationships with companies that have ceased to qualify since the previous audit will be terminated.

- When embarking on new relationships Nicecorp will seek out, insofar as is possible, only those companies that are employing nice strategies.
- The value-added chain(s) of which Nicecorp is part will be identified and monitored and Nicecorp will do all it can to strengthen such chains, irrespective of how far the weak links are from Nicecorp.

Clearly such policies have significant resource requirements but they should not be excessive for a company that acknowledges the need for a sophisticated intelligence system.

The assumption of responsibility for the whole of the value chain can be financed by a charging system of the kind used by McKesson Corporation in the US (see Chapter Nine). As the McKesson VAP showed, the spread of information up and down the value chain tends to improve the performance of the whole chain and so ensures that the efforts of individual members to strengthen the chain are, to a large extent, self-financing even without a charging system.

CHAPTER 12

Corporate Evolution

ECONOMICS AND EVOLUTION

Throughout this book I have emphasised the importance of death in corporate evolution. This is at odds with orthodox biological evolution, where the emphasis is on reproductive success, rather than mere survival.

The reason for this different emphasis is that in the corporate world there is no equivalent of the biological inevitability of death. Companies are theoretically immortal because they have the great advantage of being able to change their strategies. It is strategies, not companies, that die and it is strategies that reproduce. The propensity of managers to copy winning strategies makes survival equivalent to reproduction.

I have also claimed that companies are alive and constitute an intelligent, alien species – the first we humans have met (the second will probably be the intelligent computer). This is not just a metaphor. Though the idea of the company as life-form is not crucial to the case for nice strategies, it is vital to the theory of corporate evolution and for an understanding of the significance of the separateness of companies from human beings.

Moreover, there is no non-tautological answer to the question 'what is life?' that excludes the company. The Oxford English Dictionary defines life as 'the property which differentiates a living animal or plant, or a living portion of organic tissue, from dead or non-living matter'. But organic, in turn, simply means 'having organs, or an organised physical structure'. The company qualifies.

The idea of the living company helps to focus the mind on some key corporate qualities, like the will to survive, the ability to adapt

216

and the importance of a company's history, that have been neglected for far too long. The company, like all other living organisms, is a self-regulating system in a state of constant adaptation to changes in its environment, and it should be recognised as such.

In earlier chapters I have addressed what seems to me to be the central weakness of contemporary models of business and management – the lack of a theory of change.

Nowadays we have a good understanding of the structural features and qualities of industries and companies; price theory provides a sophisticated framework for the analysis of acts of exchange; the securities market, for all its imperfections, is a passably reliable system of corporate measurement and valuation; and the various tools of corporate finance, including discounted cashflow techniques, constitute a useful methodology for coping with uncertainty.

But all these models are static. They assume the immutability of their parameters. They can handle growth but not transformation. There are no recursive functions in business economics, no feedback loops to speak of, and there is precious little recognition of that commodity that systems theorists call 'noise'.

Business economics, management theory and corporate strategy are all based on a few linear functions. They can explain a lot, and so are indispensable tools in corporate planning, but they can't explain everything.

They can't answer what are, in my view, the really interesting questions, such as why and how companies in decline seek and find new and more successful strategies; why prosperous companies lose their way and fall victim to predators or indolence; how technological, social and economic change, and changes in the speed of change, transform industrial structures, and by what means the pressures of the corporate environment are felt by companies and are translated into adaptive behaviour.

I'm not the first person to look towards the Darwinian theory of evolution for answers to such questions, or at least to a framework within which answers might be found. It is a hugely rich and successful body of theory that has survived intact in most important respects since it was first proposed 130 years ago.

Darwin's version of the theory of natural selection is concerned entirely with change. As a means of *preserving* the purity of a species, natural selection was far from new when *The Origin of*

217

Species was published in 1859 but as a means of *transforming* existing species into new ones, and so as an explanation of evolution, natural selection in Darwin's hands was a revelation.

The first step in applying evolutionary theory to companies is to recognise its dualism. The idea of natural selection came before genetics and is independent of it. To acknowledge that genetics cannot apply to companies does not require the business economist to reject natural selection too.

The second step is to decide what natural selection, if it is applicable to the corporate world, can work on and here there is a difficulty. It cannot work on companies because companies are theoretically immortal. Natural selection needs death. Staying alive while mortal, which is survival, is both a necessary and a sufficient proof of selection.

So we need something else, some kind of proxy for or analogue of the company, that can die and can therefore be selected by not dying. My solution is a composite. I think natural selection in the corporate world works on strategies and on the management teams that conceive of and deploy them. Both are needed because management teams can fail, and so die, because of tactical as well as strategic mistakes. And management teams can survive, despite strategic mistakes, if they recognise them and try to correct them.

This arrangement is consistent with the parent theory. One can think of a biological mutation as a new strategic 'shell' required by circumstance to make its way in natural selection's meta-strategic space. If it can't hack it, the strategy dies. If it can hack it better than its competitors, the strategy will prosper and become more widespread.

The idea of implicit strategy has played an important role in evolutionary theory over the past decade or so. Evolutionists like William Hamilton, John Maynard Smith and Richard Dawkins have used game theory and cost-benefit analysis to show how strategies, through the process of natural selection, achieve dominance in their local biological populations.

Kinship theory, as proposed by Richard Dawkins in his book *The Selfish Gene*, casts genes in the role of evolution's *primum mobile* and suggests they are driven to maximise the number of their copies and so tend to favour behaviour that exhibits concern for the welfare of animals who carry such copies – namely their kin.

Game theory was originally merely an important methodology of kinship theory – an explanation of genetic evolution within kinship groups. Robert Axelrod, by the simple expedient of turning the game from a single-play to an iterated contest, transformed it from an explanation of a genetic mechanism into a mechanism in its own right known as reciprocity theory.

But just because Axelrod's iterated version of the prisoner's dilemma is gene-free does not mean it is applicable to business. Business may not be that kind of game, but I think it is, for the following six reasons:

- Like the iterated prisoner's dilemma, business is a positive-sum game. Wealth could not be created if it were not.
- Cheaters in business do well if the other companies they interact with play fair.
- If both companies in a business relationship cheat neither will profit much but neither will lose (except in the sense of incurring opportunity costs).
- If both companies play fair, the intrinsic positive sum of the business game will usually ensure both do reasonably well. If this were not the case there would be no business.
- Business consists of a large number of relatively long-term, iterated relationships with other companies and human beings.
- The long-term winners in the business game are not the ones who do the best deals but the ones who make the most profit.

In my view these correspondences together constitute a strong validation of the iterated prisoner's dilemma as a model for business. And we don't have to worry too much about the actual scores, because it is their relative, not their absolute magnitude that matters.

But it must be said that the first correspondence, namely that business, like the prisoner's dilemma, is a positive-sum game, is not universally acknowledged. There is an influential body of modern management thinking that asserts that business is, at best, a zero-sum game because, according to thinkers like Ted Levitt (inventor of the 'law of dominance'), business success comes to those with high market share.

If this is so, and I know of no evidence that high market share is associated with high profitability, then business obviously is a zero-sum game because one company cannot increase market share without causing others to lose it.

Indeed, the late Fred Hirsch argued in his book *Social Limits to*

Growth that this kind of beggar-my-neighbour game actually has a negative sum. He said there were really two economies – the 'material' and the 'positional' – and that a particular positional good (in this case, market leadership) 'always appears more attractive than it turns out to be after others have exercised their choice'.

In business this is because companies tend to fight too hard for the prize of market leadership. Saatchi & Saatchi is just one of the companies that have tasted the material disappointment that awaits those who achieve positional success.

Market share based strategies do well in the zero/negative-sum positional economy but not in the positive-sum material economy. And it is the material economy that matters in the end because material success is what matters to shareholders.

I cannot accept the positional view of the business world. It goes against nature. The positional economy is a horrible, self-destructive place, consumed by envy and violence. It is hard to see how anything good and creative can emerge from it, and since business plainly is creative – otherwise, how could companies and economies grow? – I am forced to the conclusion that though a positional sub-economy exists by virtue of the belief in it, it must be an aberration; an evolutionary dead end.

Axelrod's model, which emphasises the overall tournament scores rather than the number of victories, is plainly an analogue of the material economy. Its players aim to maximise profits, not market share. And Axelrod's results show that though positional players meet with some early success, they lose in the end.

But Axelrod's work also shows that time preference matters. The best gambit for the current play depends to some extent on the value each player attaches to the results of subsequent plays with the same opponent. Axelrod requires the future to cast a long shadow over the present. This too validates the model for business. The interest rate is the same as the discount for time preference so for each player the results of a play next year are worth around 90% of the results of a play this year.

The importance of time preference in this business model gives the interesting result that the best business strategy depends, to some extent, on the prevailing level of interest rates.

Axelrod's best strategy is 'tit for tat' (TFT). It shares with most of the other strategies that scored highly in Axelrod's tournaments the quality of being nice; of never being the first to defect.

220

A nice company is a cooperative company. It behaves as if it recognises the intrinsic positive-sum nature of the business game. It is competitive in a general sense in that it wishes to win the tournament – to make the most profit – but it is predisposed to be cooperative in particular situations.

I've proposed a law of business which states that the sum of the business game is maximised when cooperation is maximised. This does not mean all companies should be cooperative because such nice strategies obviously require other companies to be nice too. The law is less categorical. It says that if, somehow or other, all companies became cooperative tomorrow, more wealth would be created.

The question, and it is the sort of question that exercises the minds of evolutionists too, is: how does a population exchange an existing dominant strategy for a better one? Part of the answer is that though all dominant strategies are more stable than non-dominant strategies (if they weren't they could not become dominant), some dominant strategies are more stable than others. These super-stable strategies (technically, they have collective as well as evolutionary stability) are more successful than others at invading populations already subject to some kind of strategic domination.

The ability of a strategy successfully to invade a population dominated by a different strategy is evidence of evolutionary strength. But whether or not an invasion is successful depends as much on the qualities of the strategic population being invaded as on the qualities of the invader.

A single nasty strategy, for example, cannot successfully invade a corporate population where all existing strategies are nice. But neither can a single nice strategy, despite being better than the nasty strategy in the long run, successfully invade a population where all existing strategies are nasty.

But there *is* a class of strategy in Axelrod's game that can successfully invade already dominated populations, *if it attacks in sufficient numbers*. This is called the cluster effect. It can be shown, for example, that although there is no reasonable number of wholly nasty strategies that can successfully invade a population of 100 players using Axelrod's 'best' strategy, a cluster of 10 of these nice strategies *can* successfully invade a population of 100 nasty strategies.

This means there is a ratchet at work in strategic evolution. A

221

strategy that can invade, in quite small numbers, a population dominated by another stable strategy, cannot be reinvaded by anything other than overwhelming force. For instance, in our example it would take over 900 nasty strategies (and where on earth would they come from?) to stand any chance of invading a population of 100 nice strategies. And even if they succeeded, they would remain extremely vulnerable to reinvasion.

So once established as the dominant strategy, the super-stable strategy is safe. Its collective stability endows it with the quality of a super-strategy, strong enough to alter permanently the course of strategic evolution.

A number of results follow from all this. If Axelrod's game is a good model for business we can assume that there are such things as super-stable corporate strategies, that they can do well in relatively hostile strategic environments, that as their number grows they will do even better, and that ultimately they may well become the dominant strategy.

Axelrod attributes the prodigious success of TFT, the best of these super-strategies, to four qualities: it is *nice*, it is *retaliatory*, it is *forgiving* and it is *clear*.

A company employing TFT will be cooperative and scrupulously fair in all its dealings. It will never cheat first but will retaliate if it's cheated. It will forgive quickly if its opponent is contrite and, most important of all, its style will be easily recognised by other players. It will earn a reputation that deters aggression and elicits cooperation.

Such nice strategies have yet to dominate the modern business world but though natural selection is slow, it is inexorable. And there are already a number of strategies currently deployed by some large companies, perhaps even enough to constitute the beginnings of a cluster, that have manifestly nice qualities.

There are clear signs now that companies are being encouraged, by changes in their environment as well as by the exigencies of competition, to adopt generally nicer strategies. But we must be patient. Evolutionary theory tells us that the biological and corporate vehicles of genes and strategies impose their own constraints on strategy and on strategic innovation.

At any one time the evolutionary history of a biological species or a company imposes limits on change. The species is always a jury-rig that enters natural selection's meta-strategic space armed or burdened with the shapes, qualities, aptitudes and instincts it has inherited from the past. The company itself, with its peculiar legal status and ownership arrangements, is no more than a jury-rig, imperfectly adapted to modern conditions.

In other words, there is not now, and can never be, a perfectly evolved corporate form. Evolution has to make do with the material to hand. It cannot say that if you want to get *there*, you shouldn't start from *here*. Evolution is lumbered with the species as it is. The only change possible is change consistent with its starting point.

It is quite common these days for new strategies to be adopted on the arrival of new management teams. If the new leaders come from outside they will lack feel for the company's history, for its strengths and weaknesses, its culture and aptitudes, its psyche and its personality. In such circumstances it is all too easy to throw the baby out with the bath-water. New leaders, anxious to make their mark in the seven or so years available to them, will often wish to do too much too soon. They will be attracted by the speed of the 'quick fix' and may not take enough care to ensure the fix is compatible with the company's history.

So, when deciding what a company should do, it is essential first to establish what it is. Corporate phenomenology has precedence over corporate strategy. What a company is, determines its strategic opportunity set. If you start with strategy you can end up with something that may look brilliant on paper but which could be disastrous in practice.

I have proposed that companies employing nice strategies *never* make hostile takeover bids; that they manage their people with great care and solicitousness, sometimes at the apparent expense of their shareholders; that they are responsible neighbours, doing more than the law requires to ensure they inflict no harm on the environment; that they conduct their business dealings with scrupulous fairness and that they regard their reputation for generally behaving well, in all situations, as one of their most valuable assets.

Nowadays there are a number of new and powerful environmental features exerting pressure on the corporate population. They include the obsession with 'greenness' that has overwhelmed public opinion, the growth of the conscience funds and of other ethically- and ecologically-screened investment, and the problems companies of all kinds are encountering these days, as the knowhow intensity of business grows, in recruiting and keeping good people.

But the two most important of these new environmental pres-

223

sures are the enormous increase in the amount of information about companies that is available and in the much greater intensity with which corporate behaviour is scrutinised – by consumers, capital markets, regulators, opinion formers, journalists and by customer companies, supplier companies and competitor companies. The veils on the corporate world are being lifted. Companies are being forced to become less secretive. Corporate delinquents are running out of places to hide.

The best way for a species to adapt to a very general change in the environment of this kind is to adopt a very general strategy – a kind of meta-strategy or style that can act as a conductor or coordinator of operating strategies and of the company's general deportment. I think the best candidate for such a meta-strategy is TFT.

Its simplicity gives it very general application. It can help to define the viable opportunity set for operating strategies and it can also act as a kind of stylistic yardstick for the little decisions companies are making, day-in and day-out. In fact it is very important it *should* act in this way because the host of little, tactical things a company does, on a day-to-day basis, contribute as much, if not more, to establishing its reputation as do the really big, strategic things.

The important point is that in the business game consistency and clarity confer enormous evolutionary advantages. Consistency is needed to establish a reputation, and clarity, which is the same as simplicity, is needed if that reputation is to be recognised easily by the other players in the game.

An implicit acknowledgement of the need for such consistency is the modern interest in corporate cultures, 'mission statements' and company philosophies. There's a growing awareness these days that every company has a personality or perhaps, more topically, a 'meta-brand', the perceived qualities of which determine the way it is dealt with by the other players, both corporate and human.

I have argued that each company should try to cultivate a personality that is perceived to be honest, fair, responsible and generally well-mannered. These days a company cannot afford to gain the reputation of being too aggressive because it will make enemies and will not be as desirable a supplier, customer or collaborator.

It is far better for a company to select with care and then to cultivate a personality than to have one imputed to it. And it is wiser, these days, to select a nice rather than a nasty personality. Axelrod and Darwin have shown there is a ratchet at work in

224

evolution. Within a decade or so, the old paradigm of the nasty, ruthless company will be confined to the economic history books. Competitive advantage is to be gained from getting to the new paradigm ahead of the crowd.

Looking ahead it is interesting to speculate how companies might evolve after the nice strategy has become firmly established. It seems reasonable to suppose, for instance, that the kind of anthropomorphic process we have been considering will continue and will progressively infuse the body corporate with more and more human-like qualities.

This is, in all likelihood, how human culture evolved too; not out of an inherent goodness that somehow survived the ejection from Eden, but out of the differential survival of strategies.

If morality, ethics, compassion, altruism, unselfishness, love, loyalty and a respect for others are, for all their self-transcendent splendour, merely the behavioural and attitudinal accretions of a long and assiduous application of enlightened self-interest, then there is no reason to suppose that similar qualities and attitudes will not evolve in the corporate species.

Ethics are a behavioural short-hand – a simple coding system for standards of behaviour that have proved, over long periods of time, to produce better than average returns. Companies play that game too and are likely to develop a similar coding system.

Who knows, within a decade or two we may speak of companies that are imaginative, emotional, passionate, caring, sensitive and loving as well as merely nice.

Selected Reading

Axelrod, Robert, *The Evolution of Cooperation* (Basic Books, 1984)

Darwin, Charles, *The Origin of Species* (John Murray, 1859)

Dawkins, Richard, *The Selfish Gene* (Oxford University Press, 1976)
   The Blind Watchmaker (Longman, 1986)

Elkington, John and Julia Hailes, *The Green Consumer Guide* (Victor Gollancz, 1988)

Geldof, Bob, *Is that it?* (Sidgwick & Jackson, 1986)

Gilder, George, 'The Revitalisation of Everything: The Law of the Microcosm', *Harvard Business Review* (March–April, 1988)

Gould, Stephen Jay, *Ever Since Darwin: Reflections in Natural History* (Deutsch, 1978)
   An Urchin in the Storm (Collins Harvill, 1987)

Hirsch, Fred, *Social Limits to Growth* (RKP, 1977)

Johnston, Russell and Paul Lawrence, 'Beyond Vertical Integration – the Rise of the Value-Adding Partnership', *Harvard Business Review* (July–August, 1988)

Lloyd, Tom, *Dinosaur & Co.: Studies in corporate evolution* (RKP, 1984)
   – with Karl Erik Sveiby, *Managing Knowhow* (Bloomsbury, 1987)

Mohn, Reinhard, *Success Through Partnership* (Bantam Press, 1989)

Nielsen, Richard, 'Cooperative strategy', *Strategic Management Journal* (vol.9, pp. 475–92, 1988)

Olins, Wally, *The Corporate Personality* (Design Council, 1978)
  Corporate Identity (Thames and Hudson, 1989)
Ouchi, William, *Theory Z: How American Business Can Meet the Japanese Challenge* (Addison-Wesley, 1981)
  The M-Form Society: How American Teamwork Can Recapture the Competitive Edge (Addison-Wesley, 1984)
Peters, Tom, *Thriving on Chaos* (Macmillan, 1987)
Popper, Karl, *Objective Knowledge* (Oxford University Press, 1972)
Porter, Michael, *Competitive Strategy* (The Free Press, 1980)
  Competitive Advantage (The Free Press, 1985)
  'From competitive advantage to corporate strategy', *Harvard Business Review* (May–June, 1987)
  The Competitive Advantage of Nations (Macmillan, 1990)
Rawls, John, *A Theory of Justice* (Harvard University Press, 1972)
Regester, Michael, *Crisis Management* (Hutchinson, 1987)
Thompson, Sir Peter, *Sharing the Success* (Collins, 1990)
Weitzman, Martin, *The Share Economy* (Harvard University Press, 1984)

Index

Page numbers in italics refer to diagrams and tables